MISSION TO INDIA
by Sally Robertson & Bill Robertson

Order this book online at www.trafford.com
or email orders@trafford.com

Most Trafford titles are also available at major online book retailers.

© Copyright 2009 Mary E. (Sally) Robertson & William Bickerton Clyde Robertson.
   Edited by Bill Robertson.

All rights reserved. No part of this publication may be reproduced, stored in a retrieval system, or transmitted, in any form or by any means, electronic, mechanical, photocopying, recording, or otherwise, without the written prior permission of the author.

Printed in Victoria, BC, Canada.

ISBN: 978-1-4269-1269-6 (sc)

Our mission is to efficiently provide the world's finest, most comprehensive book publishing service, enabling every author to experience success. To find out how to publish your book, your way, and have it available worldwide, visit us online at www.trafford.com

Trafford rev. 11/6/2009

North America & international
toll-free: 1 888 232 4444 (USA & Canada)
phone: 250 383 6864 ♦ fax: 812 355 4082

Dedication

This book is dedicated to my daughters, Barbara, Christine and Marjory, my son, Gregory, and my grandsons, James, Robert and Alexander.

CONTENTS

Foreword .... *vii*

CHAPTER 1:   Frontline Emergency 1

CHAPTER 2:   Roots of Service 5

CHAPTER 3;   Off To India 39

CHAPTER 4:   South India 51

CHAPTER 5:   North India 111

CHAPTER 6:   Change of Direction 179

Notes & References 205

FOREWORD

The material in this book has been taken from the memoirs of William (Bill) Bickerton Clyde Robertson, my husband, who in the mid-nineteen fifties went to India as a medical missionary for the Church of Scotland. He joined the post Second World War impetus of internationalism and humanitarianism which saw many individuals reaching out to a global community to aid the healing and restructuring after years of conflict. It was a time of immense change.

The narrative provides background information on why a young Scottish doctor would contemplate a medical missionary career. The material shows that service was prevalent within his clan and family, particularly as members of the British Empire, but a wider perspective was also evident in his religious upbringing, schooling, Boy Scouts and medical training. In addition, growing up British in the midst of an international war left an indelible imprint on those who just missed being called up for combat and, who were affected by the ex-military push for education once the war was over. As with most people, decisions made at critical points in ones life tend to produce both immediate and long term outcomes, some positive and some negative.

Bill arrived in India not long after it had regained its independence after one hundred and fifty years of British rule. British Missionaries were still tolerated as they continued to provide educational and health services in an evolving country. He also arrived in India at a time when the missionary role was shifting and being gradually transferred to educated Indians. Such change will be evident in the narrative as he describes his journey through south and north India.

My role has been to reshuffle his memoir material, insert a few geographical notes, edit certain components to better fit a book format and insert photographs taken by Bill during his time in India. The narrative is provided by Bill as this was his journey and can only be described in his own words.

Over the past decades, missionaries have received mixed reviews. Those who share the values of such individuals have tended to portray them as heroic figures who risked their lives for what they believed. Others have portrayed them as the visionaries of modern history. Yet, to many historians of the late twentieth century the missionary was not so much an idealist as an ideologue, someone who pursued single-minded goals in collusion with such forces as colonialism, imperialism, modernization, or globalization. However, this negative opinion has begun to shift since the 1990s as by 2000 over two thirds of the worlds Christians lived in Asia, Africa and South America. Missionaries are now being viewed as cross-cultural transmitters of the faith and have begun to regain their former respected position. Irrespective of ones viewpoint, many truly dedicated individuals came from these ranks, and many thousands of individuals in many countries owe their health care and education to their commitment. This story is about one such individual.

Sally Robertson

Chapter 1

FRONTLINE EMERGENCY

The night, alive with the sounds of India, was warm and humid as I sat down to a late, meager meal after a long grueling day at the Kalimpong missionary hospital, nestled in the foothills of the Himalayan mountains. Being the sole surgeon of a small health team attending to the needs of both the local population and many Tibetan refugees pouring over the mountains into India, there was little time to savour the magnificent beauty of my new environment. I had barely started eating when a runner arrived requesting that I return immediately to the hospital to treat a Tibetan man with a severe hand laceration who had somehow managed to climb the steep road to the hospital seeking help.

Returning behind the runner, I climbed the familiar hilly path to the hospital in the pitch black, a small lantern guiding my footsteps. I entered the outpatient department (i.e. emergency room) and found a tall heavy set Tibetan lying silently on the treatment table, the nurse having just removed a bloody rag from his wounded hand. As I was examining his hand with my back to the outpatient door, suddenly, with the speed and silence of a jungle tiger, someone slipped into the room and in an instant stabbed the patient in under my elbow, up beneath his ribs and into his heart. As swiftly as he had arrived, the assailant exited the room before I could turn round. Out of the corner of my eye I caught a brief glimpse of the attacker, another tall Tibetan, his foot long dagger dripping with blood as he ran into the night. There was nothing I could do for the patient had died instantly from the attack. The Chopi, a weapon carried by every Tibetan Khamba warrior, had been swift and accurate. I telephoned the Bengal State Police and went to sit on the hospital veranda waiting for their arrival. While my medical training in Scotland had prepared me for many surgical emergencies, such war zone demands presented their own unique challenges.

As I sat there I thought of the many twists and turns of my career which led to my present circumstances. My dream of becoming a medical missionary with the Church of Scotland had become a reality. I had now been in India for about three years, first serving in Ranipet in southern India and now here in the north. The Church of Scotland had been in the mission field in India since 1824, first in Bombay, then Calcutta and later in the Punjab, Poona, Darjeeling and Madras. Kalimpong was located in the Darjeeling District of West Bengal. The mission began in 1870. Kalimpong, as it's name indicates, had been the summer resident of the kings of Bhutan and in the late 1950s, Bhutan's only legation to the outside world. The Queen mother, the Rani Dorji, made her permanent residence there and was one of the main contributor's to the hospital. Kalimpong had also attracted a number of western residents interested in Tibetan Buddhism. It was a multicultural community. In addition, Kalimpong was the key centre of the wool trade with Tibet. Being perched in the Himalayan foothills, its coolness was in stark contrast to the sweltering plains of India below. I had been reassigned from south India to fill in for an older medical missionary who had to return to Scotland due to illness. In my brief time in India I had learned much about India and the missionary world.

Prior to the mid-19th century, missionary doctors and nurses were not always welcome members of the mission family. Initially, missionaries were encouraged to learn the rudiments of first aid for their own survival. The medical missionary role evolved slowly. By 1850 there were only twelve to fifteen medical missionaries, the best known being Dr. Albert Schweitzer in West Africa. By 1900 there were approximately 650 medical missionaries, 128 of whom were British. Between 1850 and 1950 more than 1,500 British medical missionaries had served in numerous developing countries. There had been many distinguished medical pioneers who had preceded me in serving the health needs of people in foreign lands. While the medical role evolved to become a vital part of the overall mission, rivalries continued between the preaching and medical groups. But even these rivalries were being eclipsed as the respect for and glamour of earlier missionary life were fading. By the late 1950s, India, freed from British rule, was embarking on its national journey and the country was training its own people to take over the health services. I had chosen a missionary career at a time of immense change.

As the British departed in 1949, India created its own constitution bringing some two hundred and seventy five principalities together into a number of states. The constitution created a parliamentary system similar to that of the United Kingdom, but with nearly four thousand representatives, elected by a society that in the 1940s was eighty percent illiterate. India was also the first country to recognize the People's Republic of China which came to power in 1949, with Tibet becoming a major issue between these two large nations. Circumstances changed dramatically in 1950 when China invaded Tibet eliminating it's independent nation status. By the summer of 1956 a full-scale guerrilla warfare had broken out in Tibet, and by 1959, nine years after the Chinese takeover, a nationwide uprising was followed by the escape to India of some one hundred thousand refugees, including Tibet's political and spiritual leader, the Dalai Lama. Upon his arrival in India, after passing through Kalimpong, the Dalai Lama re-established the Tibetan Government in exile in the safety of the far off western Himalayans.

Chinese army intelligence reports later admitted that the People's Liberation Army killed eighty-seven thousand members of the Tibetan resistance in Lhasa and surrounding areas between March and October 1959 alone [1]. The facts were that in a population of over a million, over half would be massacred or imprisoned, and the Tibetan youth transported to China for Communist indoctrination. Thousands of refugees were fleeing to the borders of India, Nepal, Bhutan and Sikkim. The Kalimpong missionary hospital became the key destination of many of these wounded and sick Tibetan fighters and refugees. The incident with the Tibetan was one of many which made up my routine hospital duties. Just as I was completing this thought, the police Jeep roared to a halt outside the hospital, half a dozen Bengali armed police briskly stepping towards me.

I quickly reported the details of the incident to the officer in charge who seemed somewhat undeterred, as he indicated the dead man had been a Communist spy from Tibet sending back information on Tibetan fighters who had sought temporary refuge and treatment in Kalimpong. His collaboration had led to the torture and killing of many of the fighter's relatives still living in Tibet. There was no detailed discussion, simply a brief report from me and no action expected by the police. It brought home the realization that the hospital was practically in the midst of a war zone. It was a credit to the wisdom and moderation of India's leaders that by moving thousands of troops up into Sikkim to the border with Tibet, they gave the Chinese Communists pause to think about the consequences of invading their country and prevented outright war in that critical period between 1959 to 1962.

As I retraced my steps back to my residence, I again reflected on my decision to come to India. Many factors went into this decision and the outcome had presented, as one might expect, both positives and negatives. As the years passed, it was difficult to explain to those in the western world, enamored over material gain, why I would give up a professional career in Scotland to work for the poor and destitute in another country. The following narrative is my attempt at this explanation.

Chapter 2

ROOTS OF SERVICE

Out of the mists of Scotland strode many an individual on a global mission. The question is whether this is due to genetics, environment, destiny, or fate. Perhaps it is a combination of all four. For me, my quest to be a medical missionary likely came from three sources; my heritage, Scouting and the Second World War. The first, my heritage, instilled in me deep historical and religious roots for such a decision.

The true history of Scotland has been shrouded under a politically correct version fostered for centuries by those in power. Since the 1990s, a different rendition is emerging. According to HRH Prince Michael of Albany, the senior legal descendant of the Stuart Kings of Britain, all kings of Scots can trace their succession from the biblical Kings of Judah, from the Princes of Greater Scythia, and from the Pharaohs of ancient Egypt.[1] He also points out that Scotland's royal heritage, the oldest in Europe, was hewn on the Stone of Destiny, the venerated relic of the Beth-el Covenant in the Old Testament. This stone, known as 'Jacob's Pillow', in 586 B.C.E., was carried to Ireland from Judah during the reign of the High King Eochaid of Tara, accompanied by the prophet Jeremiah. There it became the sacred 'fealty stone' of the Irish Kings, and later the Kings of Scotland.[2] It is said that it was Jeremiah who established the Druidic learning centers.

This historic information is of importance to the Robertsons of Struan, my clan, as the Robertsons were considered the oldest family in Scotland and the sole remaining branch of the Royal House which occupied the throne of Scotland during the eleventh and twelfth centuries. The Robertsons, are also known as 'Clan Donnachaidh'. There appears to be some evidence that the Clan Donnachaidh existed for many centuries in Scotland. The Roman historian, Ptolemy, noted in the second century, that one of the five great clans of the Kaledonioi in prehistoric Perthshire, was the Clan Donnachaidh[3]. Later records indicate that the clan descended through Crinan of Dunkeld, who belonged to the kindred of St. Columba, being himself a descendent of Niall, High King of Ireland.

In the Middle Ages, Duncan I, King of the Scots, was a member of the Clan Donnachaidh, which resulted in the clan being called the Royal Clan. In 1745 the Robertsons (i.e. the Clan Donnachaidh) supporting Bonnie Prince Charlie at the Battle of Culloden, suffered great losses and had their lands forfeited by the Crown. Many Robertsons eventually migrated to cities in Scotland and England and to North America. My clan had not only deep historical ties to Scotland but also ancient links to the Old Testament. By the twentieth century, at the time of my birth, my family were very much part of the British Empire.

I was born on May 18, 1929 in Kilbowie, Dunbartonshire, Scotland and christened as William Bickerton Clyde Robertson, later to be called 'Bill'. I spent my early years on the periphery of Glasgow, first in Kilbowie and later in Kirkintilloch.

Dunbartonshire, a small county in the west of Scotland, forms what was anciently known as the Lennox. It is bounded on the west by Loch Long and Argyllshire; on the north by Perthshire; on the east by Stirlingshire and Lanark; and by the river Clyde on the south. It is described as having beautiful and varied scenery, mountains and with many fruitful valleys, watered by numerous streams. Kilbowie, the small village in which I was born, stood on the ridge overlooking Clydebank, the site of the once great ship-building centre of the British Empire.

My parents lived for almost nine years on a short, dead-end street, in one of a row of small, dull, red-brick houses, standing on one side of the street, looking out over the Clyde to the south. The panoramic view must have been inspiring, maybe the one redeeming feature of the place. The house was also within a half-hour's drive from downtown Glasgow, situated to the south-east. W.B.Robertson & Co Ltd., the family business, had a main store in King Street and another five small stores selling ladies underwear and corsetry in Glasgow and its environs. I would only spend a year and a half in Kilbowie before the family moved.

When my grandfather Gray died in 1931, he left his home in Kirkintilloch, eight miles north-east of Glasgow to my mother. The house was called 'Rosebery' by Grandpa Gray, a British custom of giving names to their house of residence. Lord Rosebery was the Secretary of State for Scotland after the First World War and was much admired by my grandfather.

Rosebery, where I would spend my youth, was a well-built, two-storey house standing in its own property of approximately a third to a half acre. The style was typical of such houses built in the mid-nineteenth century, being a large cottage with a pseudo-pillared entrance and several steps up to the front door. From the front door there was a small hallway beyond which was a corridor reaching to the back of the house where a short flight of stairs led down to a large kitchen with a pantry and maid's bedroom leading off to the back. On either side of the hall were two large rooms at the front (the Dining Room and the Sitting room) and two bedrooms and a bathroom further to the rear of the house. A steep flight of stairs led upstairs to two large bedrooms with camp ceilings and gable windows.

The house, dating from the nineteenth century, was situated on the edge of town on Industry Street, an unimaginative name since there was, to my knowledge, never any industry on it. The front gate looked up Loch Road and the west end of the front wall marked the beginning of Waterside Road, which led, about a mile and a quarter on, to Merkland Cottage where Grandpa Gray had been born in 1855. The front garden had a sizeable lawn, with deep borders of trees and shrubs on the south, east and west sides and a large rose garden with espalier-trained plum trees along a seven foot wall. A curved driveway of fine loose pebbles swept around the rhodos from the front gate to the concrete area surrounding the front door steps.

The house itself stood on a slope to the rear. Dad's car was safely housed in the garage which had originally been for a light carriage of some kind in the pre-motor-car days when the house was built. Beyond the garage to the west was a flat area leading to a wash-house and the adjoining stable which later became a work-shed. Outside the stable there was a dung heap, no doubt previously contributed to by the horse. Every spring, Dad had a load of fresh manure delivered for the garden. A rather unkempt snow-berry hedge and a huge Horse Chestnut tree and two tall Lime trees, separated the flat area at the back from a steep slope which flattened out at the foot of the hill to form part of the bank of the River Luggie which flowed westward. I would later discover a deep, thirty to forty foot well which had been dug centuries before by monks. The whole escarpment had formed the eastern extremity of St. Mary's Roman Catholic church Glebe in the past, the church becoming Presbyterian after the Reformation.

The name Kirkintilloch was originally Caer-pen-tulach, which in the Brethonic/Welsh of the local inhabitants of that time meant "The fort at the end of the hill". Even today Caer means castle in Welsh, pen means a hill and presumably, tulach meant, 'at the end of'. Beginning its life as a Brythonic village sheltering beneath one of the Roman Castles along the length of Agricola's earthen Wall, over a thousand years later in the 12th century it was accorded the honour of being a Royal Burgh. After that distinction it seems to have ambled along for the next 800 years in undistinguished but sturdy contentment, proudly and faithfully for a total of 1,800 years conforming to its motto, "Ca canny, but ca awa", ("Go carefully, but keep going"). In the 1930s, the population of Kirkintilloch was about ten thousand, and there were about ten Presbyterian churches. In my father's time devout Presbyterians went to church twice on Sunday. There was no cooking on the Sabbath and afternoons were spent reciting chapters from the Bible. By the time of my arrival this tradition was changing but I would regularly attend a local Presbyterian Church with my parents and my older sister, which was to be the total complement of my immediate family.

My father, John Bickerton Clyde Robertson, born in 1889 in Milngavie, was forty when I was born. He was the oldest child of six siblings, two dying in infancy. Lydia, the elder of two girls, was placed in the family business at eleven, and stayed there as a 'shop girl' in the main store for the rest of her life. His younger brother, William, destined to take over the family business, was killed at Gallipoli, in the First World War. His sister Jessie, the younger girl, married a wealthy British Hong Kong business man and spent most her adult life in Asia.

Dad entered Glasgow University Law School at the age of nineteen. He was in his final year of studies, when he was called up for the First World War. He would later use this legal training to successfully defend several military men in their Court Martials but he would not return to the legal field after the war.

After being called up as a Glasgow University Cadet, my father was sent into the Cameronians Regiment and, as a private, went off to war against the Kaiser's invading armies. He was one of the few survivors of the first great and bloody battle at Mons in Belgium, for which he received a Mons Star. He was also an expert marksman and had additional duties as a sniper. Soon thereafter he entered officer training and was commissioned as a Second Lieutenant in the Highland Light Infantry Regiment and in charge of its Machine-Gun Battery. Later his regiment was sent to the Middle East to face the Turks at Gallipoli. However, by the time he arrived, his regiment was redirected away from Gallipoli to fight the Turks in the Sinai Desert in southern Palestine. By the end of the war, at thirty-three, he had reached the level of a substantive Captain in the Regular Army and no doubt looked forward to a long and successful military career. However, Dad's blossoming military career came to an abrupt end when his father, because William had been killed in the war, ordered him to return to Scotland and, for an assured salary, run the family businesses, which would provide remuneration for his parents, and his two sisters, Lydia and Jessie. This offer came with the understanding that it was time for John to settle down, the family deciding he should wed, Jennie Gray.

Under the leadership of my grandfather, William Bickerton Robertson, the family businesses had flourished in the late nineteenth century, with its burgeoning middle class families benefiting from the peak years of the British Empire economy. In the after years of the First World War it was suffering from the economic down-turn of the post-war economy and Grandpa at sixty-seven was wanting to retire and concentrate on painting in watercolor and oils, which in fact had occupied much of his 'working' time for years. With his other son having being killed in the war, he expected my father to abide by his wishes and take over the business. Thus, when I arrived my father was managing six ladies underwear and corsetry stores in the Glasgow area.

Physically, Dad was above average height for his generation at five feet ten and a half inches. His lack of athletic interest was reflected in his mainly sedentary life, although in his youth he played tennis and in the army was involved in boxing.

In my adult years looking back, I would see my father as basically a sensitive, kindly man, who due to his up-bringing and the negative aspects of his marriage, did not always feel safe in expressing his feelings to his children. Intellectually he had a well-educated, sophisticated and widely knowledgeable intelligence. His judgment of character was invariably accurate and he knew from the outset whether or not a person could be trusted. He was a first-class military officer and undoubtedly would have risen to the highest levels if his father had not shattered his career.

Spiritually, he was quite reticent, which was probably a reaction from having religion more or less stuffed down his throat as a youth. Although he never volunteered an opinion, I am sure that he believed in an Almighty Creator of the Universe, but found that the narrow dogmas of established religions were unacceptable. This made church attendance with his wife and children, largely a boring duty, only illumined when he was stimulated, usually incensed, by any inaccurate politically tinged opinion expressed by a clergyman. I remember his trenchant comments on the left-wing, pacifist views preached by a certain Rev. John Hamilton. Although we never discussed religion, I know that he treasured the book, "The Meditations of Marcus Aurelius", a Roman emperor who was a Stoic.

My mother, Janet (Jennie) Morton Glass Gray, first met my father when she was about sixteen while working as a typist in a Glasgow lawyer's office, an acquaintance which was nurtured during her four year stint in London when she worked for the War Office during the First World War. The two families, the Robertsons and Grays, knew each other even though they lived in different communities. The connection was likely through the businesses of the two senior patriarchs.

My mother was born in 1896, was 33 when I was born, and was the youngest daughter of Andrew Gray, a tailor, with his own business in Motherwell, a large industrial town and burgh in North Lanarkshire, south east of Glasgow. Twenty-six by 1922, she was an attractive brunette with blue eyes but according to the standards of her day, getting somewhat past the marriageable age. The families thought bringing the two young people together would settle a number of issues.

The Grays came to Scotland from the town of Gray in Burgundy, France, as weavers in the twelfth century on invitation of King David I of Scotland. These weavers added a key element in the infra-structure of mediaeval Scotland and the excellent cloth which they wove came to be called by the Anglian speaking low-landers, 'Hodden-Gray' because it held well together. The Burgundian weavers were all called Gray because they came from the region of the town of Gray, which to this day stands on the banks of the River Saone about ten miles north-east of the city of Dijon. They may also have been Cathars.

Historically the word Cathar refers to the people who believed in a medieval Christian religion that sprang up on the continent around the middle of the 10th century and disappeared four hundred years later. This long period shows that Catharism was not some minor event, it was a major occurrence in religious history. Historians have found traces of the Cathar religion in Bulgaria and Asia Minor, in Greece and Northern Italy, in Catalonia and even in the Rhineland as well as in Burgundy, Flanders, Aquitaine and Bosnia. It was in Occitania (Occitania covered all southern France), that Catharism took on the mantle of a socially acceptable religion. Here, Catharism experienced its golden age backed by the great feudal families and the commitment of several generations of faithful. Its competition with the Church of Rome provoked the Vatican hierarchy. In 1233 Pope Gregory IX set up the Inquisition, demanding that the entire Occitania population appear before it. For the first time in the history of western Christendom, an entire population was suspected of heresy. Legions, on orders from the Pope and the King of France, set up a crusade against the Cathars massacring hundreds of thousands and confiscating their lands. The end result was that a pre-democratic entity, which had developed its own culture and religion was no more, the hostile act recorded as the first European genocide. Irrespective of these tragic historical factors, by the twentieth century the Grays were Presbyterians. Thus, in 1922, the Robertsons and the Grays were united when my parents married. My sister, Marjory, was born five and a half years before my arrival. After marriage my mother remained at home, never returning to her secretarial career.

Mother's family consisted of two groupings of three children due to her father's second marriage after his first wife died in childbirth. She had three step-sisters. Marie, the oldest, had an extensive career in nursing and died in the flu epidemic following the WWI. Anne, went to university and qualified as a school teacher. After several years of teaching she married an engineer, had three children, spending some time in London and later returning to Scotland. Agnes, called Nessie, also qualified as a school teacher, went to the Gold Coast (Ghana) as a missionary, where she served for over thirty years.

In the second grouping of three, Mother had two siblings. Her older brother, David, became a lawyer and immediately volunteered for service in First World War, and was mentioned in dispatches for acts of bravery. After the war he joined the Colonial Service and was a District Commissioner in Tanganyika and Uganda. He married a Dutch aristocrat, had two sons, his wife and sons being held under house arrest in Holland for the duration of Second World War. Reentering the army in 1939, David saw action in several theaters completing his service as a General and Military Commander of Austria. Mother's sister Margaret, a petite woman who was called 'Pearl', trained as a children's nurse and married a British rubber planter. She lived in India for many years, was loved by the plantation workers and their families, knew Jawaharlal Nehru, and was a friend of the president of the Theosophist's Society. Of the three siblings, only mother remained in Scotland.

A late marriage and early death of her beloved mother would leave my mother with child raising problems, my sister the main recipient of her anger. From my earliest recollection my parents quarreled a lot and did not appear very happy with their arranged lives. When my father left for the Second World War, I, at eleven years of age, would be left with many household responsibilities and an awareness of my mother's mounting frustrations. Perhaps my interest in medicine and administration came from these early years of trying to find some compromise in a disruptive home.

Thus, on both sides of my family, going back more than one generation, I had members pursuing international careers, having lived and/or worked in various parts of the British Empire and other foreign countries. So, my thought of an overseas career was in keeping with this viewpoint and it was understood and accepted in my family.

My sister, Marjory Anne Alexander, was born in November of 1923. Being almost five and a half years older than me we would walk different paths over the years. She grew up to become a very attractive, tall, blue-eyed brunette. She trained as a Radiographer (x-ray technician) and worked at the Glasgow Royal Infirmary and later in a military dispersal hospital in Scotland during WWII. After the war she worked in a Deptford hospital outside London where she met her husband, Conrad Vidot, a medical doctor who served in the Royal Air Force in different parts of England, Southern Rhodesia, and Aden. After Conrad retired from the Air Force, the family emigrated to Australia where he became the Chief Medical Officer of Veterans Affairs. They would bring up their family of three sons, Peter, Nicholas and Anthony in Sydney, Australia.

Attending school in Scotland in the 1930s and 1940s presented a range of challenges, the most obvious one being the pending and then actual European war practically on our doorstep.

After my fifth birthday I attended a local school. The Townhead School was a rough, tough, punitive, almost barbaric environment in which corporal punishment (e.g. a multi-stranded heavy leather strap) was used on the hands and wrists of young children, often drawing blood. Looking back I realize that such abuse achieved little, damaged young souls, and instilled the idea of corporal punishment into another generation. During this phase my parents, as most during this time, gave teachers complete authority, and never visited the school or met with the teachers. I spent five years in this awful environment which left me not only with bad memories but a deep sympathy and understanding of the poor and an immense dislike of injustice. It likely was one of the basic incentives in propelling me towards a medical missionary career to heal the sick and ease the misery of the poor and down-trodden in the world. During these years I did enjoy the Cub Scouts, music and the peace of the garden at Rosebery.

1933 was the year of the rise of the Nazi Party under Adolf Hitler in Germany. My father as a staunch supporter of Winston Churchill, regularly gave impromptu 'lectures' at the dinner table on the dangers of the complacency of the British people in the face of this growing disease of national socialism. Every word of Dad's ominous predictions, in the end came true; the Anschluss, invasion of the Sudatenland, leading to the take over of all Czechoslovakia, German Rearmament, the invasion of Poland leading to the Second World War in 1939, the Holocaust and the war between Hitler and Stalin. I found his judgment excellent.

When the Second World War broke out, my father, then fifty, became involved in Air Raid Precautions and worked as the Superintendent for Eastern Dunbartonshire. Fired by his old military experience, he then reenlisted, this time in the Air Force, first as a Station Defense Officer. Later he attended Cranwell Military College, was promoted to Squadron Leader in Flying Training Command and was placed in charge of Anti-Gas Warfare for all RAF Stations in the United Kingdom.

In 1938, I began weekly violin lessons under Miss Carruthers, who played in the Glasgow Symphony Orchestra. I made reasonable progress over two years, until 1940, when at the age of eleven, Miss Carruthers said that I could become a first-class violinist, if I practiced at least two hours every day for the rest of my life. Since this was not feasible I stopped, a decision which I would later regret.

With the outbreak of war in 1939, Dad decided that I should go to a better school. His first choice was Allan Glen's School in Glasgow, an excellent school for boys which provided classes for the Pre-Qualifying and Qualifying years followed by five or six Higher Grades leading to University studies. However, when the military informed him that Glasgow might be a prime wartime target, after several months, my father had me relocated to the Pre-Qualifying class at Lenzie Academy, closer to Kirkintilloch, where I would remain until 1943. Lenzie Academy was still a vast improvement over Townhead, and I responded by making good progress. I also began to play rugby, and participated in middle- distance running.

At this stage of my life, Boy Scouting became increasingly important. I enjoyed the Friday evening meetings of the 1st Lenzie/12th Glasgow Troop where I was taught more in a few hours a week than all my schooling about the wider possibilities of life. My involvement with scouting would continue into my early twenties.

During the war, I volunteered, as a keen young scout from the Glasgow area to help in the running of some week-end camps at the Glasgow Scout Camp Grounds at Auchengillan (Gaelic for the place/village of the young men), northwest of the city. For me, at my humble level, this involved setting-up tents and digging latrines, helping prepare meals, cleaning up and generally doing all the 'dog's body' chores from a Friday evening to a Sunday afternoon. These were special camps organized by Jack Stewart, a Commissioner for Scouts in Glasgow, Chief Scout of Scotland, Deputy Chief Scout of the World and a key member of the World Scout Council. The purpose of these camps was to provide a meeting place between older scouts from occupied Europe who had been involved in Underground activities against the Nazis and had to escape to avoid certain death in a German concentration camp. They came mainly from Norway, Denmark, Holland and Belgium. I don't remember any from France. Jack invited them to meet with Scottish scouts and tell their stories, usually in broken English of the highly dangerous activity of sabotage against the German war machine; of how they escaped capture and eventually got to Britain by submarine or by hair-raising travels through to the south of France (i.e. Vichy France), on to neutral Spain and, by sea, to Britain. I was just a boy of fourteen sitting quietly at the back listening with rapt attention and admiration for their great courage. Knowing something of how the Nazis ruled the European continent from 1939 to 1945, we Scots' boys had some inkling of how brave these scouts from occupied Europe were, only four or five years older than us.

After the war, the world learned that the forces of the European Underground were in two groups, the Boy Scout Movement and the Communists, both of which were banned by Hitler. Many teenage scouts and older leaders were captured by the Gestapo, tortured and eventually executed in concentration camps. The boys we met at Auchengillan were true patriots and heroes by any standard and I felt privileged to have known them. After the war they became much respected heroes back in their own countries and were major leaders in the reconstruction of their badly abused societies.

It was some years later after the war that I learned Jack had been appointed one of the key leaders of the Shadow Underground in Britain, with a secret underground headquarters somewhere between Edinburgh and Glasgow. In anticipation of the somber, but realistic possibility that Hitler might successfully invade and conquer Britain, arrangements were made to plan, organize and as necessary recruit members for such an Underground, just as had been done in Occupied Europe. Jack Stewart was, I believe, scouting out potential recruits for the Underground, at these Auchengillan camps. Although never put to the test, I am quietly proud that he thought me worthy of such a role. Jack, as a member of the World Scout Council had worked under the chairmanship of Colonel Campbell who, during the war remained behind enemy lines as the 'mole' who headed up the Underground in Nazi Occupied Europe. It was natural then that Jack would be asked to work with Colonel Campbell after the war.

Fortunately Hitler was unable to invade Britain, although my father assured me that Hitler tried unsuccessfully to do so, his invasion fleet being totally destroyed before it reached shore. Some time after the war I also learned that Jack was on Hitler's list of Brits who were to be immediately found and executed after the invasion. Thankfully this never came to pass. Jack was like a second father to me, especially in these critical years when my father was away in the Royal Air Force.

By 1943, my father felt the Allies were going to win the war and Glasgow would not likely be bombed, so he arranged for me to go back to the fee-paying, Allan Glen's School and complete the final four years of my Higher Grade education. I don't remember him discussing it with me. Nevertheless, I was quite glad to be attending *Glen's* as we called it.

Allan Glen, a Glasgow business man, was well ahead of his time. He saw back in the mid 19th century, Great Britain was in dire need of properly trained scientists and engineers. At that time education largely concentrated on the Humanities, both at school and university. He therefore established Glen's as a Science School. Within a few years The Glasgow Technical College was established, most of the students coming from Glen's. The technical college would later change its name first to the Royal Technical College and later to Strathclyde University.

Glen's prepared boys, approximately twelve hundred of them in eight grades, with one hundred and fifty boys per grade, for careers in science, including Engineering, Chemistry, Physics, Mathematics and Medicine. Only about one percent became medical doctors – a rather select group. In addition to the sciences, the curriculum also included the humanities, languages and art for those who found these more conducive. One other key-note of Glen's was its classless, interracial, interdenominational approach. In my classes at Glen's were Jews,

Orthodox Greeks, Hindus, and Christians of all denominations. In those years we learned the basic tenets of our similarity and how to get along together. Glen's was in fact a unique school in Scotland and in fact in the whole of the United Kingdom.

For the next four years, I began each school day, dressed in a uniform of navy blazer with the Glen's badge on the breast pocket, gray pants, shirt, tie and cap, containing the same Glen's badge. I sat on the top deck of a Glasgow bus, a trip that usually took about twenty-five minutes. The school consisted of a number of large gray stone buildings off Cathedral Street.

I enjoyed and benefited immensely from my years at Glen's. Most of the teachers were well above average, several were outstanding. In addition to my studies, I was also involved in playing rugby and in my fifth and sixth years played for the 1stXV team. I also continued as a Patrol Leader of the Owl Patrol (Scouts) and a Junior Bible Class teacher at St.David's Memorial Church, the church my grandfather Gray attended and the one that supported my Aunt Nessie in her missionary work. During this time I ventured into boxing under the excellent coaching of Mr. Charles Carswell, in Blythswood Square, Glasgow. Charles was the first non-Japanese to win the World Ju-Jitsu Championship in Tokyo in 1902. He was a marvellous instructor and I became a first class boxer with, as he noted, a deadly left hook. He wanted me to go on into amateur boxing at the university but I was already fully occupied with other activities. All this physical activity in addition to my studies and other interests, kept me very busy, perhaps a deliberate, conscious preparation for my anticipated enlistment in the armed forces, which in the dark days of the war most teenage boys expected was their inevitable fate.

At Glen's, as one might expect in a Science School, they organized all athletic sports in groups according to a mathematical calculation including ones age, height and weight, which was an excellent way of teaching us how to compete. We competed in metric measurements away ahead of the situation in the country as a whole. The main events were 100 metres sprint, 110 metres Hurdles, 400 metres, 800 metres, the High Jump, the Long Jump, the Discus, Javelin and Shot Put. I loved them all. In the annual school sports championships in 1946 and 1947 I won the School Senior Athletic Championships.

As I and my classmates approached our sixteenth birthdays, and nearing our last year at school, we had several dramatic pep talks at Allan Glen's, from war heroes recently returned from active military service in Europe. One I particularly remember was an RAF fighter pilot who had been shot down over enemy territory, captured, imprisoned and tortured by the Gestapo. The story he told of his torture, highly dangerous and hair-raising escape and how he had managed to find his way out of Germany, through France and Spain to Portugal and then by sea back to Britain, riveted our attention for over an hour. So it was in that somewhat unsettling atmosphere of war that we pursued our studies and activities with a sense of purpose and firm resolve.

Looking ahead to my final year at school (I thought) with the School Leaving Certificate Examinations coming in June 1946, I aimed to pass with enough credits to enter Glasgow University Medical School later, after the war. I fully anticipated being called up to the armed forces as soon as I left school. I was drawn between being a pilot in the Royal Air Force, probably in bombers, or following the traditions of the family and going into the infantry, preferably in the Black Watch or the Gordon Highlanders, which were the Scottish Highland Regiments in which the Robertsons traditionally served. With any luck I could go on to the commandos, or be like my cousin Anno MacLaren who served in the secret Panther Brigade in Europe. These were Commandos who penetrated and operated behind enemy lines, in advance of the Allied forces.

However, such enthusiasm for defending our country was somewhat thwarted when the war with the Germans came to an end in 1945. Although a wonderfully exhilarating time for Britain and the Allies, for me, just after my sixteenth birthday, there was a brief feeling of let down, of deflation. After all, this was the war in which I expected to participate. Yet, continuing action in Asia meant we still might be called up to fight the Japanese.

That spring I led the 12th Glasgow Scout Troop team to victory in the West of Scotland Scout Ambulance Competition. By the fall I entered the 5th grade (12th grade in North America) and began working in earnest for my Senior Leaving Certificate Examinations which I passed in June 1946.

Was there anything else? Well yes, there were girls. In those far-off, pre-Woodstock days, boys from respectable church-going families, had almost platonic relationships with girls. Sexual intercourse was not on our agendas. Apart from the immorality of it, we knew the dire and far-reaching consequences of sexually transmitted disease. This was long before the catastrophic appearance of AIDS, Hepatitis V, Genital Herpes and Chlamydia. No doubt we thought about sex, but confined our activities to occasionally meeting girls at dances, walking them home and giving them a good-night kiss.

ALTHOUGH I luckily did not have to serve in 'Jack's Underground', after the war he asked me as a Scout leader to lead twenty-five British Scouts to the first Post-War International Scout Camp in Holland (or more correctly, The Nederlands) in 1946; fifty British Scouts to the International Scout Jamboree at Grenaa in Denmark in 1951, and thirty British Scouts to a National Scout Camp in Voss, Norway in 1953.

Perhaps the most exciting incident occurred at the first Post-War International Scout Camp in Holland. One evening the general peace and harmony of the camp was suddenly shattered by the arrival of five or six siren-sounding Dutch Police cars in the camp, with armed police running hard to surround one of the Administrative tents. They soon emerged as a posse, surrounding a handcuffed man who had been masquerading as a Scout Officer. He was bundled into a police car and driven off to jail. We heard later that he had been hanged as a key Dutch collaborator with the Gestapo causing the death of many of his fellow citizens.

I had barely returned from Holland when Jack invited me to join his team in organizing the first International Scout Jamborette at Blair Atholl in Perthshire in the summers of 1946, 1948 and 1952. All of these were wonderful experiences on an international level. Blair Atholl was a glorious site for a camp, situated, as it is in the heart of the grandeur and beauty of the Hills of Central Perthshire. Incidentally, Perthshire is where the Clan Robertson has its seat and its own Church, where the chiefs of the clan have been buried, since the eighth century. I shall cherish these memories.

I, as a member of Jack's team prepared and organized the camp-site for the two weeks of the actual camp. The plan involved a dozen separate camp-sites arranged roughly in a wide circular area within the beautiful grounds which the Duke of Atholl had generously made available to Jack. In each camp there was one tent of Scottish Boy Scouts acting as hosts to three other tents which housed Scouts from all over Europe and a few from Canada and the United States. During the first week each group of Scouts from one particular country, did everything together in projects, wide games, sports, camp-fires, hikes and climbs. Then in the second week the boys were asked to mix voluntarily, so that one tent could hold, for example, a Scot, a Dane, A Frenchman, a Dutchman, an American, and an Austrian. For the second week each tent worked as one team carrying out everything from cooking to crafts, to competitions of many kinds. It took a lot of organizing, but

Jack Stewart's genius made it all work and the Blair Atholl Jamborettes were an immediate success and became very popular throughout the world. This idea of a truly integrated international Scout camp was totally new in the 1940s. Eventually Jack was awarded an Order of the British Empire (O.B.E), by the authorities in London, but, I believe, it should have been a Knighthood. Jack was a man ahead of his time. The young men who attended these biennial camps at Blair Atholl became true ambassadors of friendship in the post-war rebuilding of Europe and the world. I made good friends of Scots, English, Norwegian, Danish, Dutch, French and German young men, to mention only a few. I kept in touch with most of them for some years, but after I 'disappeared' into India and they scattered to other countries such correspondence faded.

During these years I was also the recipient of the King's Scout badge, which was presented to me by Princess Elizabeth and the Duke of Edinburgh at Windsor Castle.

In 1947, at the age of 58, my father resigned his military commission with the rank of Acting Wing Commander. He once again returned to running the family business. On a part-time basis during the fifties and sixties, he would return to his first love by serving as the Commanding Officer of the Air Training Corp for the West of Scotland.

Between the wars he had studied and became a Fellow of the Society of Antiquaries of Scotland, becoming a qualified archaeologist, with F.S.A. (Scot) after his name. As a Fellow of the Society of Antiquaries of Scotland he also had a significant part in helping Ludovic Mann in major archaeological digs at the Roman forts near Glasgow on what had been part of Antonine's Wall, connecting Agricola's forts. Paleolithic history however, was his main joy and I inherited his love of history.

During the post-war years he enjoyed making trips to archaeological sites in England, the Orkneys, notably the Dwarfies Stane and in France, visiting the caves at Lascaux and the Dordoigne.

Early in June of 1947, having passed the examinations for the Scottish Senior Leaving Certificate, I proceeded to apply to Glasgow University Medical School.

Jack Stewart gave me a reference which, I am sure, helped my application, as I was subsequently accepted. However, due to the huge number of demobilized servicemen who were applying to enter Medicine, I was asked to wait a year. Many applicants just out of school were given the option of returning to school for a further year, or signing up as military conscripts for two years. I chose to go back to school. Thus, I entered the 6th grade (13th in North America), still a Prefect, still in the 1st XV Rugby team and still very much involved in my usual church, Scout and other activities. I took extra classes in Dynamics, Geometric Analysis, History, English and I think Art.

The American bombing of Hiroshima and Nagasaki ended the war against the Japanese, and cancelled any possibility of us young Scots being called up for war duty; we would miss the war by months.

In October of 1948, the interlude of relative calm stopped abruptly when my medical studies began. We entered a changed university world from the prewar leisurely pace of passing examinations. The hard realities of medical studies in post-war Britain created new challenges for students. Free access to university for war veterans meant competition for every learning position was intense. To control the burgeoning size of the classes, the university introduced new and stringent administrative policies. Nevertheless, classes still doubled in size to over two hundred and fifty. Lecture halls were grossly overcrowded. Laboratories in Anatomy, Physiology, Botany, Zoology, Physics and Chemistry were choc-a-bloc. It was total mayhem. Medical training is proverbially grueling, but, as they say, this was unprecedented. Pass marks were raised and only one attempt at a re-sit was allowed, after which a student was thrown out of the course. In most instances students were not informed of these changes, they would learn about the new restrictions the hard way. Administrative changes were occurring 'on the fly'.

By the end of the first term, in December, I was in deep trouble in my studies. There were no kind professors to offer advice, they just unceremoniously dumped masses of information on us and it was "the devil take the hindmost", with a vengeance. My mistake was to think I could continue with all my extra-mural activities (i.e. rugby, Scouting, church work) and still keep up with my medical studies. At best, a student could survive if he studied every week-day until one am and did nothing but study all and every week-end. I was giving only part-time attention to my studies.

The pace of study continued into the New Year, but I refused to change my priorities as they all seemed so praise-worthy and noble. By the summer I had failed to meet the new passing grade in one third of my subjects and was expelled from the University and told to await call-up to the Armed Forces, as a conscript. I made myself the victim of 'misplaced duty'. This hard lesson would send me off for two years in the Royal Air Force ranks losing two years in my quest to be a medical doctor. This was a very hard lesson.

IN January 1949, I left Kirkintilloch, by train for R.A.F. Padgate in Lancashire, England, for my military service. I had chosen the Royal Air Force (RAF) partly because Dad had served in it during Second World War, and partly because it might provide me with the best opportunities for some kind of training relative to my medical goal, which I had every intention of getting back to. I signed up as an Aircraftsman, was allocated to Flight # 3 and billeted with thirty-five other recruits in Hut # 294. Our Drill Sergeant was Sgt. Baxter, inevitably called 'Baxter the Bastard'.

Sgt. Baxter was a very efficient Drill Instructor and his guttural but unusually precise Glasgow accent was soon to be "making it cleeer" to the one hundred and ten members of our Flight, mainly from Scotland, as to all the niceties of military drill. He had, as all good drill sergeants have, a slightly sardonic humour, such as when one of the 'little dears' in our Flight had not made sure that his hair was no longer than the standard eighth of an inch, he would stand behind such a recalcitrant, with the toe of his boot touching the heel of the long-haired ones boot, then suddenly shout in his ear, "Am a hurrtin yeu ? A pregnant silence followed, during which we all waited in humorous anticipation for a possible 'interesting' reply from the hapless recruit, who was undoubtedly a nice boy, recently wrenched from the tender care of his Mummy in some comfortable suburb of the realm. Almost immediately the silence was shattered by Sgt. Baxter's outraged rejoiner, "Because A'm Staundin on yer bluidy hair – Get it cut !". Whereupon the recruit was ordered to proceed, 'at the double', to the Station Barber who was ever ready to fashion a cut of such billiard-ball smoothness that the sergeant might even be able to see in it, his own reflection. This environment was a far cry from my earlier world.

My first Sunday was enlightening. I soon discovered the vast majority of Brits in 1949 never darkened the door of any church. Sunday mornings were for the inevitable long lie after the excesses of the previous night. As a dutiful Presbyterian I got dressed and made my way to the Other Denominations (OD) church, housed in a Nissan Hut in one corner of the camp, to attend 10 am service. Only one other recruit from our flight ever went to church and he was an Irish Roman

Catholic from a mining village in Scotland. Of course he went to a different hut. The OD Chaplain was a Welsh Presbyterian who appeared pleasantly surprised with the turn-out of about ten worshippers, who were mainly Scots with, I think, two Welshmen.

Back at the hut (billet) just after 11 am, a few disheveled bodies were stirring, muttering curses at being disturbed "in the middle of the bloody night". Another hoarse voice asked if I had brought the 'News'. For one unguarded moment I thought his query was of a religious nature, but soon realized he was wanting, like the majority of my fellow recruits, to feast his mind on the scandals and juicy stories which filled the "News of the World", Britain's Sunday tabloid at that time.

After lunch there were chores to be done, like cleaning the billet, polishing ones' 'brasses", blancoing ones' belt and kit, ironing ones' uniform and polishing ones boots so that the sergeant could see his face in them. All this took most of the rest of the afternoon and evening, if one wanted to be properly turned out for Parade next day. The penalty for being in a shambolic state was 'Fatigues', which included a variety of time-consuming and dirty jobs cleaning administrative buildings, cleaning the dozens of large 'tins' in the cook-house or digging holes on Camp property, deemed vital to the general order of things. For major misdemeanors the punishment was to appear every night at 9 pm at the Guard Room, at the Main Gate, in full-kit, perfectly in order, to be inspected by the dreaded Military Police (The Red Caps). The slightest flaw was rewarded by an extension of the punishment for more inspections. I fortunately never did have to go to the Guard Room or do Fatigues. That is with one exception, when a wee fellow from Glasgow wanted to go on a 48 hour Pass to a relative's funeral, but had been put on Fatigues for the Saturday night. I felt sorry for him and did his fatigue duty for him. This involved hours of polishing office floors followed by a long session cleaning vats in the 'Tin Room'. In the latter I met a poor, slightly simple soul, who was probably in hindsight slightly mentally retarded, who for his troubles spent most of his service 'in the Tin Room'.

Ten days after our arrival we were transferred to a different billet; No.2 Wing of C Squadron in Flight No11, in Hut No.82, under the supervision of Corporal Webb. Cpl. Webb who turned out to be a really nice guy, was a tall and well-built, pleasant Welshman and more importantly for me, a rugby player. He and I hit it off immediately. He quickly made me the Head recruit of Hut No.11 and most evenings left us to ourselves while he went off to court his girl friend. Later we discovered that he was in the process of getting engaged to be married, which he did several weeks later. This of course left me 'in charge' of the Hut in the evenings when the thirty-five men were supposed to be preparing their kit and the Hut for inspection the next morning. My experience in the Boy Scouts helped me to both organize, encourage and help as required, so that we were in tip-top shape for each mornings inspection by the Flight Sergeant and other Non-Commissioned Officers (NCOs). This was a bit of a challenge given that most of the men were not accustomed to being very organized. With some of the men I had to see that others, including myself, helped them to get all their kit and uniform clean and in order, so that they would pass muster at inspection. In this world there are definitely those who are just naturally untidy and more or less disorganized, but even they can be trained into passable soldiers.

The rest of January passed quickly, as we spent long hours on the parade ground learning the intricacies of military marching and rifle drill. Not really too complicated, but nevertheless requiring complete concentration to achieve the required perfection. I loved the drill, including the over-done comments of the drill Non-Commissioned Officers. Theirs is a language all of its own, which, though many would deny, manages to teach "an 'orrible bunch of recruits", from all kinds of backgrounds, to march like soldiers, in a relatively few weeks. I had then and still do, have a quiet admiration for how they do it.

Eventually, Cpl. Webb put together a Padgate rugby team composed of thirteen Welshmen and two Scots. I was one of the Scots. With a team composed of all those tough Welsh rugby players, plus the two of us Scots who had already been playing for major league teams, we enjoyed a few wonderful romps. The first of these was against the 43rd Anti-Aircraft Battery team, whom we beat easily by fifty points to nil. It was a joy to play with those quick passing Welshmen.

Cpl. Boyle replaced Cpl. Webb who left on leave to get married. Cpl. Boyle did not like me at first, as I had more or less been running things. Cpl. Boyle was from a British slum and was intent on making an impression. He was on his own little power trip. He was small in stature, but fancied himself as a strong man and did not take to me as a rugby player, as rugby in England at that time was largely the game of the upper class. One evening his enmity for me came to a head. We were all in the billet cleaning our rifles and brasses when he came striding in from his room, demanding "Books, Books!" I said that I had left all mine at home, which was a comment he did not take a shine to. What I discovered was that he meant comic books, like the "Beano", "Dandy", "Hotspur" which were read by boys between five and fourteen years of age.

These were all that he liked to read, in fact all that he could read, as he depended mainly on the cartoons which they included. He did not find many such comics in our billet of Scots, most of whom had long since graduated to the tabloid newspapers, or better. With no reading material available, he foraged around looking for something or someone to pick on, which he soon did, as there are always a few easy victims to be found in a training unit. After exhausting that source of amusement he came up to me as I was tidying the two billet tables. These are heavy wooden boards about 3ft across by 7ft long and ¾ inch thick and each weighing about 70 lbs. which had to be put away in the middle of the hut, propped up by their two heavy metal supports. He stopped me and advancing on one of the boards proceeded to grasp it in the middle of its length with the fingers of both hands and then lifted it to chest height off the floor, saying tauntingly to me, "I bet you couldn't do that Robertson". I had to accept the challenge and was able to achieve the lift. Discomfited, he then pulled the two boards together and tried to repeat the lift which now weighed in at 140 lbs., but just failed, the boards slipping out of his grasp. I was relieved, thinking that would be enough for him, but oh no, he repeated his challenge. This time on the two boards. I knew that I was regularly lifting the 250 lbs barbell in the Station Gym. One can get a sure grip around a steel bar, but two boards together at over one and a half inches thick is a different kettle of fish. With the whole billet watching this contest, I had to give it a try. Fortunately, I succeeded with feigned effortless ease, probably due to my longer fingers and greater height, plus my weight-training which he would not know about. I expected that my success would only make him more antagonistic towards me, but to my surprise he seemed genuinely impressed. Henceforth, throughout the basic training his attitude changed and he never tried to cross me again. This was a lesson for me in the currency of the tough guys of the streets. It still puzzles me.

On the final day the two Flights of the Wing, totaling two thousand men, paraded past the Wing Commander and his entourage on the Saluting Base. They then performed various drills en masse, before finally marching forward towards the Saluting base "By the Centre". The parade went very well, then happily and to my surprise, I was awarded, by the Wing Commander, the prize as the top recruit in the wing! Later, I was also voted the best and most popular recruit in our Flight by the officers and men, another pleasant surprise. Quite a day!

Our basic training over, we were all posted to our various stations (Military bases), to undertake whatever trade or specialty we had put down on our application sheet. I could have applied to go for Officers' training, but that would have meant signing up for at least three years as a 'Regular' and I was determined to return to my medical studies. Accordingly, I selected training as a Nursing Orderly, which turned out to be about the same level as a Canadian Licensed Practical Nurse. This I hoped would give me an idea of what a nurse's life was like and keep me in touch with the medical world. I have always been glad I had that training as it helped me to understand the work and responsibilities of a nurse and to form a respect for their role in the health care system, which most doctors never do, to the detriment of the overall care of the patients.

For this training I was first posted to RAF Moreton-in-Marsh in the north-east corner of Gloucestershire, at the northern end of the Cotswold Hills. The base was about a mile out of the little town of the same name. Its main street was Fosse Way, a famous Roman road of Brittania, and the White Hart Hotel which was a place in which King Charles I slept in 1644, thus giving a certain antiquity to the quiet township of less than 1,400 people. To the north lay Stratford-on-Avon, to the west Cheltenham and to the south-east Oxford, all about twenty to thirty miles distant. Recently historians have discovered that the Court of King Arthur I, who ruled over Brythonic/Welsh Britain after the Romans left early in the 5th Century, was situated at what is now Hinkley, about fifty miles north of Moreton-in-Marsh. As no doubt King Arthur knew, this lovely, quiet and picturesque part of England's green and pleasant land, is in fact at the heart of England.

I could relate many memories of my time and training there, but will mention only one incident in which a certain Glasgow-Irish fellow trainee Bob Fitzpatrick lured me to a pub, I think the one King Charles I visited, and dared me to see who could drink the most pints of the local cider. I ultimately beat him by downing a 12th pint, which he could not match. I was sick for days after that and have never taken a drop of cider since. Just thinking about it almost makes me ill.

After completing my Nursing training, I was posted to RAF Halton, the central hospital of the Royal Air Force. This huge hospital had the full range of medical services, including Medical, Surgical, (General, Orthopedics, Otolaryngology, Ophthalmology, Maxillo-facial, Plastic and the central Burns Unit), Obstetrics and Gynaecology, Dermatology, Psychiatry, Tropical and Infectious Disease and Tuberculosis units, plus all the Surgical Operating Suites and Outpatients Units as required by this large variety of services. RAF Halton was a mile or two from the old village of Wendover which lay on the north slopes of the Chiltern Hills in the pleasant countryside of Buckinghamshire, less than fifty miles north-west of the centre of London. It was a lovely site for a hospital and within easy reach of

London with all its facilities. Along with a few of my colleagues from Moreton-in-Marsh we were immediately put to work in the various wards.

We were allotted for spells to each of the wards for experience and further training. I remember learning to change the linen and remake the beds in an open ward of thirty-five patients in record time, attending to all the basic nursing needs of the patients, in the chronic orthopedic wards especially helping crippled patients moving around the bed or into wheel chairs. As fit young men we were well suited to this heavy work. We also had spells in the Operating suites and probably the most taxing experience was working in the Burn Unit. There we had to do dressings and take patients with over two-thirds of their body surface destroyed by third degree burns, to the Saline Tank. Two of us had to lift the poor patient in a sheet off the stretcher and immerse him in the 3-4ft tank and then try to gently remove the large areas of green, fungating dead skin. The smell was appalling and lingered with us the whole time we worked there. We never complained for our minor discomfort was nothing compared to the excruciating pain felt by the patients as they submitted to this necessary removal of dead tissue to enable extensive skin grafting. In later years, as a physician I always made sure that such a patient was sedated to the maximum possible. This was a good example of how this nursing training prepared me for a medical career, giving me an insight into the needs of patients on a 24-hour basis. I think that all medical doctors should have to spend at least several months working on long shifts caring for the kind of patients they will be treating throughout their careers.

I should mention that we worked under the supervision of RAF Nursing Sisters, who were a special order of officer nurses in the RAF. They were mainly Registered Nurses with a year or two of experience, in their early to mid-twenties. In retrospect, I realize that we were some of the first males ever to work under the supervision of women. I remember deciding that, if they were nice, fair-minded women, it was better working for them than for a man, but the majority were not so nice and visibly enjoyed having a bunch of men to boss about. Women, I decided, if not of the best quality could be more ruthless and vindictive than men; a conviction which changed little with the years.

After some months in the central, more acute services, I was moved to the large TB (Tuberculosis) Unit, which was full to capacity with young servicemen afflicted with that terrible, in those days, often fatal disease. This was a few years before the discovery and use of Streptomycin and Izoniazid for Tuberculosis. I worked Night Duty for these months. It was hard work as we were under-staffed. This experience gave me a deep insight into the treatment of patients who would not survive and helped me to develop that deep compassion for the plight of those who are suffering and dying through no fault of their own; a compassion which I would later need so much working among the sick of India's poor.

I soon learned that I was eligible for further training as an Operating Room Technician, working in the large suites of operating rooms, in which were treated, RAF servicemen and women from all over the British Empire. During the Second World War, which had only ended a few short years before, the hospital had been especially busy treating the many RAF pilots and air-crew, badly wounded in the air battles, especially the Battle of Britain. Most of the senior staff had worked there during that momentous time, from 1939 to 1941, when Britain fought alone for its very survival. The hospital was full of memories.

Subsequently, I was accepted into a training course which involved an intensive training period of on-the-job learning and experience, in a largely practical and technical activity which was and still is the best way to learn. In due course I passed written, oral and practical examinations set and carried out by the Group Captain surgeon in charge of all the operating suites. He was one of the top surgeons during World War II who treated the grave and extensive wounds of the Battle of Britain RAF and RCAF pilots. I thus qualified as an Operating Room Technician (ORT). This knowledge and experience stood me in good stead in India and later throughout my medical career in understanding the problems and requirements of operating and critical care units.

In time, I was posted to RAF Uxbridge and worked as the sole ORT in a smaller operating suite. The senior Sister in charge was a man-hater, but the junior one was a sweet young girl a few years older than me who was as happy as a queen, as she worked out the remaining months of her service before leaving to get married. I remember that she sang almost all the time, especially the current hit song, "Met a girl in calico…". This job involved more responsibility and longer hours. I enjoyed the experience and the challenge. In off-duty hours I kept fit doing athletics and began serious study, in the evenings, for my medical course Re-Sits.

During this time I had brief secondments to RAF Wroughton Hospital near Stonehenge and visits to the main Royal Naval Hospital at Chatham. I also had personal trips to visit Auntie Nan and Anno in London, and to Dick Hewer, another medical student and son of Dr. Langton Hewer, and the rather odd experience of attending a 'closed' Plymouth Brethren service in a bare Nissan hut, with a dozen Rolls-Royces, Bentleys and Daimlers in the car park outside. An interesting insight into the world of exclusive Christian Fundamentalism.

At the approach of my demobilization from service I was called for an interview with an Air-Vice Marshall who offered me the choice of a permanent commission either as a pilot (i.e. air-crew) for at least six years, or as an Administrative Officer for four years. To his amazement I declined, saying that I very much wanted to complete my medical studies. He gave me no time to reflect on his offer. I have sometimes wondered what my life might have been like if I had accepted.

In 1950, once demobilized, conscripts were placed on military Reserve with the requirement of annual weeks of military duty for an unspecified period of time. But such service was not on my mind as I immediately shifted my focus to the medical Re-sits.

BEFORE being allowed to take the Re-sit examinations, students pursuing a medical career had to go for an interview with the Assistant Dean of the Faculty of Medicine, who was at that time an unlikeable fellow called Westwater. It so happened that Gordon Barr, (who had been in the Army) and I attended on the same day. At my interview it became apparent that Westwater was determined to stop returning students like Gordon and myself from resuming their medical studies. This was no doubt due to the continuing glut of ex-servicemen who were overwhelming the faculty resources. He proceeded to abuse me with vituperative assaults by insulting my background and assuring me of my complete unfitness to continue medical studies. I waited until he had exhausted his obnoxious peroration, then asked him if he had the authority to prevent me from re-applying to sit the examinations, which I understood was my right under the regulations. When he admitted that he had not that right, I excused myself and took my leave from his pitiable presence, briefly warning Gordon what to expect and then made my way directly to the administrative office and signed up for the Re-sits.

The worst kind of bureaucrats are those who misuse their authority by abusing 'the people' in order to please their masters and protect their positions. It is unfortunate to have to report that many such types populate the many bureaucracies around the world. Several years later Gordon and I qualified as doctors, but refrained from further contact with Mr. Westwater. Gordon went on to a challenging medical career in the West Indies.

Just after being demobilized, I met with Jack Stewart, Chief Scout of Scotland, and sought his advice and encouragement.

I successfully passed my Re-sits, turned to get ready for the next four years of medical studies, and pick up the threads of the rest of my activities in Kirkintilloch and Glasgow.

October 1950 saw me absorbed more and more in my medical studies, keeping fit and attending church regularly with occasional contacts with Jack Stewart and friends like Bob Fitzpatrick, my friend from the RAF. I was enjoying my studies and can remember most of the professors and colleagues. One outstanding and, I choose to believe God-given fact, was that by good fortune, I joined a special class in which there were three Honors B.Sc. Physiology students, including Mary Wishart, the daughter of the Dean of the Faculty of Medicine. Mary needed a class, as did her B.Sc. colleagues, Ian Connell and Frank Moran. So a small class was formed consisting of Mary and her fellows, plus those who had passed their Re-sits including Gordon Barr, Robin McDougal, Hugh Sutherland, Janie Taylor, Sheila Cooper and another two or three whose names I cannot recall, plus me. Thus I escaped the rat-race of the huge 250 student classes and proceeded with a select small group which received the very best teaching possible.

By 1951, I was into deep study and enjoying Anatomy both in theory and practice under the guiding, skillful eyes of Dr. Scothorne, a humorous Yorkshireman recently arrived in town, much to our benefit and enjoyment. Physiology and Biochemistry and Histology more than fully occupied the rest of our study time, but I preferred anatomy.

On some evenings, with the help of a Scout friend, Dr. Bruce Allan, I attended the 'Gatehouse' at the Glasgow Royal Infirmary. That was the very busy Emergency Department, where ambulances and walk-ins appeared every other minute, seeking treatment for anything from a fanciful pain to a serious fracture, from a hangover to a major Stroke, or an aborting fetus to a deadly intestinal obstruction. There was more treatment needed there in one night from 8 pm until the small hours of the morning than you'd see in a whole town during a normal day. I watched and slowly began, where it was not prejudicial to the patient's care, to help with suturing, dressing and assisting all manner of sick people. It was there that I began to learn just what it was going to be like to be a physician. It takes time, a lot of energy and if you have compassion, it gives you a wonderful sense of doing something really worthwhile in this big, materialistic world we live in.

IN my twenties, Dad began again to seek my company on visits to places of interest. Back in the years before the war I had gone with him dry fly loch fishing on fairly frequent occasions, mainly to row the boat. I was not greatly attracted to fishing, but I enjoyed the challenge and exercise of rowing the rather slow cumbersome loch fishing boats. Now, over ten years later, we occasionally continued these fishing excursions. He also went to church at St.David's Memorial (Presbyterian) Church with me once or twice. He wasn't a great churchgoer. In fact, I think he had difficulties with the details of Christianity as it conflicted with what he knew, as an archaeologist.

Throughout my life I regularly attended church services. St.David's was the church to which my family had belonged in Kirkintilloch. The Rev. John Heron was the minister, and although a rather heavy preacher, both in time and content, at that time I probably needed this type of service. I sang tenor in the choir and was a member, and latterly Chairman, of the Youth Fellowship. In 1952 I attended both the morning 11 am and evening 6.30 pm services on Sunday. Before church services I conducted the Junior Bible Class at 9.30 am and after evening service I chaired the Young People's Fellowship at 8 pm. So my Sundays were almost totally immersed in church duties. The afternoons were occupied with medical studies. I would retain links to this church from 1931 to the end of my missionary work in 1962.

The Church of Scotland is the national church of Scotland. It is Presbyterian in denomination as it has been since its establishment in the sixteenth century under the leadership of John Knox. I am therefore a Reformed Christian.

My religious life and understanding were deepening. This was reflected in my attendance, on March 17 at a Mission Rally for youth at Auchendennan centre, outside Glasgow, at which I remember talking at some length with a Dr.Gray, a medical missionary working in the Belgian Congo (now Zaire). His insight into medical mission work was inspiring and probably marked a turning point in my life. It certainly was the time at which I began to think seriously of the possibility of becoming a medical missionary in the Third World, as it was then called. Later that year I attended a huge Missionary Rally in St.Andrew's Hall, Glasgow at which a number of Church of Scotland missionaries from all over the Third World gave interesting and first-hand accounts of the need and nature of their work. The world war being over, the pressing needs of the poor and sick of the Third World could no longer be ignored. Although I kept my thoughts to myself, I was from that time directing my efforts towards helping the sick and suffering of poor countries who badly needed skilled professional people from Western countries. I was also aware of my respect and admiration for my Aunt Nessie who retired from her missionary service about that time.

Back at Rosebery, Kirkintilloch I was fully occupied in studies, but also found time to do most of the household chores, as chopping wood, washing and drying dishes, helping clean various rooms, doing odd jobs of repair and, when necessary, cooking meals. In the garden which I continued to look after following Dad's absence in the war, there was lots of grass-cutting, weeding, pruning and general maintenance work to be done. Dad had a hothouse built in the Rose Garden and spent his gardening time totally and happily absorbed in growing tomatoes.

Sometime in 1951, I made an entry in my diary that I was attracted to a young girl of seventeen in the church choir named Frances Anderson. As a tall, young, brunette she stood out in the rather older choir. I soon learned that she had arrived from Montreal, Canada, being placed with her Scottish relatives and living a few houses down from Rosebery. I would later learn her father had died of lung cancer and her mother becoming deeply depressed, was subjected to a pre-frontal lobotomy (also known as leucotomy). This despicable procedure caused her to lose all her maternal instinct for her daughter. She took Frances to England and tried to leave her with relatives. Finally she went to Scotland where a grand-aunt took Frances in.

Our relationship would grow in the next four years. In retrospect it is obvious that I was a very naïve young man and, in addition, I was unfortunately totally devoid of much parental advice in such matters. I think my parents were shy of giving me advice about relationships and marriage since their's had not been a very happy one. They both indicated they did not especially like Frances, but such a mild comment, was, I fear, not sufficient to deter me. Although, perhaps, subconsciously there were signals. In 1953, I made a puzzling note in my diary about a serious difference of opinion between us. It should have been a warning, but I was too sure of myself to change direction.

In my twenties, I was concentrating on my medical studies and the extra-mural activities and entered a relationship which, with hindsight, would become the biggest mistake of my life. Perhaps my life was too full of activities and other people for me to truly appreciate the ramification of this emotional decision.

I had friends in many parts of my life. Jack Stewart and I had frequent lunch-hour meetings to discuss Scouting and my progress as a medical student. At medical school I got along well with my colleagues. Periodically, I met with Bob Fitzpatrick whom I had known in the RAF and we took in a movie or had coffee and a chat. I had friends in the Rover Scouts, and went sailing with a young doctor and a medical student, both older than myself, whom I met in scouting. I had many Rugby colleagues, but my special friend was Alastair Murdoch. We teamed up during the Rugby team's travels around Scotland. He would be the best man at my wedding.

Scouting continued to be an important part of my life. I was Treasurer of the 1st Lenzie (12th Glasgow) Rover Scout Crew. We went on several challenging Night Hikes into the Fintry Hills. Occasionally we helped the Scout Troop by training and testing boys for various badges and George Rich and I organized a troop camp at Gartshore, which is about five miles east of Kirkintilloch.

On the national scene, as one of Jack Stewart's special team of helpers, I worked in the preparation and organization of the 4th Blair Atholl International Scout Jamboree. The team organized the Wide games, did chores and provided First Aid for the minor injuries and ailments typical of such camping. I was introduced to the current Chief Scout of Great Britain and the Empire, Lord Rowallan, a Scottish aristocrat from Ayrshire. He was an ex-army officer, standing about 6ft 8ins and very friendly with a rich, very deep voice. My last scouting duty would be in 1953 when I was asked to lead a group of about fifteen Scouts on a three-week trip to Norway.

In the summer break from my medical studies in 1951, I prepared to go off to Forestry work in the Argyll National Forest Park, based in Glenfinart off Loch Long, just a mile north of Ardentinny. This was in order to make a little money and to work in the fresh air. We climbed straight up the hillside for about two thousand feet to the upper edge of the forest near the tree-line, led by our 'ganger' John Smith who we called 'John'. He was already sixty-three years old and had been in the forest all his working life, except for several years in First World War. The work consisted of brashing and snedding as the need dictated. We used large aluminum scythes which enabled us to cut a swath from above down between seven and eight feet. This was a truly athletic pursuit, especially since the bracken grew to between seven and eight feet and was about three-quarter of an inch at the base where we cut it. We formed a line up and down the steep slope and then worked our way horizontally across the hillside. When you got used to it, which we quickly had to, a team of six or so men could cover a whole hillside in a day.

Reserve RAF duty found me on one occasion at West Kirby, in South Lancashire and later at RAF Cosford, near Wolverhampton in England where I met several medical students and other fellows who were similarly doing their Reserve Duty while studying at university. I eventually received an official notice that I would no longer be held on the Reserve strength, which brought to an end my association with the armed forces. In reflection, I was quite happy being a soldier even for a short time and fortunate not to have been in the war.

In the fall of 1952, I returned to my medical studies re-immersed myself in the study of Pathology ('Path'), Materia Medica and Bacteriology ('Bugs') I realized that I was thoroughly enjoying every minute of it; always a good omen of future career contentment. Long hours happily poring over large text-books was rewarded in June when I passed all my professional examinations without difficulty. Completing my medical examinations meant that the next step was the clinical training portion. In passing my examinations I would comment that anyone can pass medical school exams if they study hard enough. Of course that does not guarantee their success as a physician translating all that information into a career of caring for sick and suffering humanity.

Next we began our introduction into the mysteries of Clinical Medicine and Clinical Surgery in the first half of the year, which made all of us quietly brimming with medical enthusiasm.

I again attended the Glasgow Royal Infirmary's Gatehouse (Emergency Department) on some evenings where I gained much valuable and stimulating experience helping in the treatment of the many sick from the east end of the city.

In the summer, I learned how to administer an anaesthetic and assisted at a number of surgical operations carried out by Mr. Bonar one of the best surgeons in 'The Royal'. In Britain, surgeons are honored with the title of Mister. Mr. Bonar's surgical practice and technique were of the very highest standard, both surgically and ethically and, I lived to be eternally grateful to him when doing lone surgery in the Himalayas in the years ahead.

Entering the penultimate year of study in October, really intensive work began in Clinical Medicine and Surgery in all their varied aspects. Our surgical professor was 'Pop' Burton, a delightful and often amusing teacher, who imparted all the basic theory in a memorable way.

Dr. Snodgrass or 'Snoddy' as we affectionately called him, was our professor in Medicine. His unit was in the Glasgow Western Infirmary and his teaching was impeccable, imparted in an unforgettable and eloquent style, which over the months and years imbued all of his students with a deep love and respect for the practice of Medicine and for being a doctor. I recall one light moment. We students were all standing around the bed of an elderly gentleman who had agreed to our attendance and examination for the purposes of a tutorial on diagnosis. Snoddy asked Alistair Connell, one of the Honours Physiology graduates in our class, the cream of the crop so to speak, for his differential diagnostic review and decision. Alistair, as expected, painstakingly took the history from the old fellow, made a careful examination and then gave an excellent resume of what he had found, ending confidently with his definitive diagnosis, which turned out to be a complex, obscure and certainly rare disease. Snoddy smiled and turning looked out of the nearby window for a moment, then asked Alistair, "Mr. Connell (we always use surnames in the United Kingdom.), do you see that bird out there sitting on the ledge ?" Alistair peered out somewhat puzzled and replied, "Yes Sir". Snoddy continued "What kind of bird would you say that it was Mr. Connell ?" Alistair becoming slightly uneasy and confused replied hesitatingly, "A sparrow sir". Snoddy smiled seraphically and said, "Yes indeed Mr. Connell, well done ! Please always remember in diagnosis that common things commonly occur !" He then briefly explained that the patient's history and findings pointed to the all too common diagnosis of Pneumonia.

We also had classes in Infectious Diseases (Fevers), including Tuberculosis (there were 10,000 TB beds in the Glasgow area), Poliomyelitis (one of my school friends died in an Iron Lung at Belvidere Hospital after contracting the disease on a visit to France), all manner of bacterial and viral fevers (their number was considerable); childhood fevers, as Mumps, Measles, Chicken Pox, Diphtheria, Scarlet

Fever (for which I was hospitalized at the age of six in Duntocher Fever Hospital for three rather educative weeks) and a host of others, excluding Tropical Diseases which I learned years later first–hand in India. We also studied Dermatology in this year, or as we called it 'Skins' for short.

During these years, Mother, who had seemingly recovered unscathed from her 'Multiple Sclerosis' episode, suffered periodic short illnesses and remained unhappy with life and her marriage. Between 1951 and 1952, mother became an enthusiastic attendee at a Pentcostal Crusade, led by a Rev. Tee. All I recall of this Crusade was that Mum donated our piano to Rev. Tee for its duration. After the successful conclusion of the Crusade, Rev. Tee and his team left town, taking our piano with them. I encouraged Mum to accept the loss, as all in a good cause which she readily agreed.

By the early fifties Dad started selling off the more distant and/or less profitable stores. Profitable I believe is a two-sided word or better still refers to a project or business which can lead to benefits both for the owner and the staff, as well as the customers. Dad in his democratic way treated his staff of shop assistants generously, did not overcharge the customers and in the end sold the stores at almost bargain basement prices.

My medical studies continued with more Clinical Medicine and General Surgery including studies and exams in Ophthalmology, Otolaryngology, more Infectious Diseases such as Syphilis and Gonorrhea, and Respirology, Dermatology, Mental diseases, Obstetrics and Gynecology, Anaesthetics, Operative surgery, Medical and Surgical, Outpatient Practice, Clerking and Dressing and finally Public Health and Medical Jurisprudence.

The fourth year passed rapidly with much interesting study, ending in Class Exams which I passed without difficulty, receiving Distinctions and the Class Prize in both Public Health and Medical Jurisprudence. Although these were not what I considered my favorite subjects at that time, in the years ahead they would be of great importance.

My Final Year commenced. Nine months until the final Examinations. Every day and almost every hour was filled with Clinical Medicine, Surgery, Obstetrics and Gynaecology, and Pediatrics. The time between October and December 31st passed in a flash, ending my studies of 1953.

In Scotland, at that time, final year medical students were allowed to fill short locum appointments under supervision, which allowed the full-time doctors to take short holidays. The one week Surgical locum was good experience and involved the typical range of duties and responsibilities carried out by young newly-qualified doctors, for at least a year after graduation .

The week's locum over, immediately my final year studies recommenced. One-third of my final year had passed. The next six months period was the hardest grind of study up to the Class Exams in May and then the Finals at the end of June. I worked consistently hard as did most of my fellow students. The months passed. Much more was learned of Medicine, Surgery, Pediatrics, Obstetrics and Gynaecology. I enjoyed all of it.

My diary was packed with the details of each day's study requirements. In due course I passed all my examinations (having already passed with Distinction, Public Health and Medical Jurisprudence in 1953) and graduated as a medical doctor on June 29, 1954.

The next day I Joined the British Medical Association and the Medical and Dental Defence Union; signed my Provisional Registration as a doctor; got my ticket for the Graduation Ceremony and paid the Graduation fee. Dad was away fishing in Sutherland in the north of Scotland. I never knew if he realized that my graduation was imminent. I also told Deacon's court at the Church that I had qualified as a doctor. I visited Dr. J.B. Rennie's office at Stobhill and confirmed the arrangements for my first residency and then at the church, helped to clean and paint the Vestry.

The following Sunday, Rev.John Heron preached on the text from Jeremiah chapter 1 verse 6," Say not, I am a child, for thou shalt go to all that I shall send thee" . After the service I told Mr. Heron that I was thinking of offering myself for service as a medical missionary. Somehow I don't think he was surprised. During this time I recall having a very distinct dream. I was standing on top of a high mountain, seeing in the distance wonderful snow capped peaks which I would one day ascend. In between the mountains I saw lower mountains ranges and hills with valleys between, some of which were deep, dark, dense tropical jungles full of danger and trial. There were rivers and swamps and lurking dangers. I knew I had to descend from my viewing place and address myself to the sea of challenges which awaited me. Yet, no matter what happened I would never lose the sense of certainty that my destination was the limitless peaks ahead and that I would be with God. This was the calling which I was about to pursue.

On the Monday I telephoned the Headquarters of the Church of Scotland in Edinburgh to arrange an interview with Rev John Hamilton, whom I knew, as he had been the minister of St.David's Memorial Church prior to Rev. Heron and who was now a senior officer. He arranged for me to meet Rev.Ian Paterson of the Staff of the Overseas Mission Department the next day. The interview was long (3 hours) and thorough and would be the basis for further talks and eventually my firm offer of service commencing September 1955.

On 10th July I attended Randolph Hall, Glasgow University, signed the Graduands Album, attended a short Service in the lovely University Chapel, reassembled in Randolph Hall and was capped and graduated at noon. I had achieved my first goal!

THE years from the 1930s to the 1950s were years of growth, uncertainties, and challenges. From an early age, nurtured by my family, the church and Scouting, I was focused on service to humanity, with my interest in caring for the sick and less fortunate. I had relatives who had entered the health field, and others who had already seen duty overseas. I admired their efforts and felt I also could follow in their footsteps, forging my own path. I did not have a specific country in mind, feeling I would be guided. With my medical degree in my hand, I would pursue the next step in my plan. As I waited to hear from the Church of Scotland, I proceeded with my first year of medical residency. The next year would be packed with change, further study and preparing for my overseas assignment.

Chapter 3

OFF TO INDIA

The missionary world was well established at the time I thought of entering its ranks. It had existed for over a hundred and fifty years. The Church of Scotland had a well structured selection process under the stewardship of the Overseas Mission Department. Its membership mainly consisted of Presbyterian clergy, and lay church members. However, by the 1950s, with the shift in the global influence of the British Empire, much change had occurred and was ongoing, which affected the lives of missionaries in the field. Two changes would have a direct bearing on my missionary life.

One change, which was not entirely clear to me on departure, was to what extent qualified indigenous people were being appointed into former missionary positions. Another change was a decision that Presbyterian missionaries could be married before leaving Scotland. Prior to 1950, most missionaries of Reformed Churches, such as the Presbyterian, were not allowed to go overseas married, missionaries were mainly unmarried, and often remained so for their entire careers. A few married other missionaries, while others waited until they retired to Scotland. While I was entirely happy with the first change once I was in the field, the second would present more challenges, as there were pros and cons to both married and unmarried missionary choices. For me in these early days, I thought that I would have a better picture of what lay ahead if I was able to talk to as many missionaries as possible. Unfortunately, some of these individuals were ending their careers and reflecting on the past, not the future.

I had several talks with Rev. John Heron, our minister, about my interest in missionary work. He and his wife had done chaplaincy work in Northern India and although he had been happy, Mrs. Heron would not go back, as, I would learn, their first baby was snatched from their verandah by a tiger. They were very supportive and I believe John Heron was one of God's agents in guiding me into that life.

Later, I met, in Glasgow, with Dr. Dougall, General Secretary of the Overseas Mission Department of the Church of Scotland, to discuss my offer of service. At the time he was the only member of the Overseas Department who had missionary experience, having retired after forty years in China. He was a man of great experience, character and charisma. He, if anyone, confirmed my decision to go as a missionary. With such a man at the helm, I thought, the church's missionary work would be well steered. Unfortunately soon after I left for India, Dr. Dougall died suddenly of a heart attack and was replaced by a clergyman with no overseas experience, which probably had a decided effect on the way things went in the field. At the time of my meeting, Dr. Dougall asked me if I was planning to get married before I went out. I said it was probable. He seemed to favor new missionaries not being married before they went overseas, a view which was difficult to understand at the time. If I had my life to live again I would not have gotten married before departing for India. However, this was not my thinking in the fifties, as I felt it best to have a partner before venturing out to a foreign land.

I managed to attend the After Evanston Conference in Edinburgh, organized by the World Council of Churches. This reflected the tremendous interest and enthusiasm in the fifties, the Post-War world, for the world's churches to help the Third World, in addressing the millions of sick, starving and uneducated poor needing support.

This mission by the churches was one of the greatest philanthropic and compassionate undertakings of the eighteenth, nineteenth and twentieth century, a service to humanity which received limited respect. A sad commentary on our society. On a similar vein, I also volunteered to be a Counsellor at the Billy Graham Crusade in Glasgow. This was an interesting and inspiring experience.

On December 8th I was interviewed by the Overseas Mission Committee in Edinburgh at 121 George Street in response to my offer of service. I was subsequently accepted and assigned a location in South India. I did not specify a country, contrary to many missionaries who stipulate where they want to work. This acceptance enabled me to start preparing in earnest for the great challenge which awaited me.

I felt 'called' to the Mission Field. God touched me and I had to respond. Nobody should volunteer to go as a missionary unless they feel "called", otherwise they rarely stick it out. Of all the people who volunteered to go as missionaries in the twentieth century about a third of them returned home within one year. This was particularly true of those men who went out married. Most of the returning missionaries came back because their wives could not accept the conditions of life in a Third World on a minimum salary. My salary, including a peak family allowance for three children would be 700 pounds ($1,500 Canadian) a year.

I was now a fully-fledged and registered physician and ready, or at least getting ready to go overseas as a missionary. Looking back, I doubt if I truly understood the huge and life-long implications of my decision to offer my services as a medical missionary to a Third World country. Being young, I also did not fully understand what I was expecting of a wife as a partner in this decision.

My relationship with Frances grew quietly with meetings at choir, walks, family get-togethers. It was progressing in the usually middle-class, church oriented community way with me still ignoring the differences and problems which arose periodically. Irrespective, of any misgivings, I proposed marriage to her in 1955. Despite having achieved my goal of becoming a doctor and successfully working through my hospital residencies; despite having researched the realities of medical missionary work in the Third World and of being assured in my mind that this was what I felt called to do, I had an intuitive feeling that something was wrong. There remained a lingering doubt about the wisdom of marrying this young woman from Canada and taking her a further six thousand miles from her original home in North America. Yet, I resisted such negative thoughts. Why, one would ask? The reasons are both obvious and complex. The urge of a young, virile man to consummate a marriage, to secure a mate and, hopefully, a friend to accompany him to a distant, foreign land, full of strange cultures and customs. Perhaps it was compassion over how bad life had treated her. I kept assuring myself that I could handle all the problems through love and understanding. The die was cast and despite my mother's, one-time only, advice to 'think again', I proceeded, arrogantly sure of myself that I was following God's plan.

The marriage ceremony was held on August 20, 1955 in St.David's Memorial Church, Kirkintilloch. But this was much more than a marriage. It was also the marriage of two young people who had offered themselves to go out to help others in a land of poverty, hunger, ignorance and disease, as missionaries of the Church of Scotland. We were going as missionaries whose salary would be covered by that congregation. We were going as 'their own' missionaries. It was even more special in that my Aunt Nessie Gray had recently retired as the missionary sent and supported by the same congregation during more than thirty years of service in the Gold Coast (Ghana). It was a very solemn and special occasion and I was absolutely sure, that God was guiding us on our destined path. Photographs of the occasion appeared in the local Press. We then went to Glasgow for a Reception at the Burlington Hotel. Alastair Murdoch my rugby and school friend was the Best Man. Following a brief honeymoon in the Highlands, where, by coincidence, we met a family of Sutherlands who were staying in Badachro. The man was the son of the famous pioneer of leprosy work in India, Dr Sutherland of Chingleput, and a medical missionary of the Church of Scotland. He had been born there and was very familiar with all of South India. When I told him that we were being sent to Kanchipuram he told us much about that major Hindu temple centre. It was a brief honeymoon as we would be starting our missionary lives as students at the St.Colm's College in Edinburgh on September 15, weeks away, as one of the first married new missionaries of the Church of Scotland.

We arrived at St.Colm's Missionary College on the evening before the start of our missionary studies. Because I was a medical missionary, I was urgently needed in South India, so I and the other doctors were given a very concentrated three-month course in all the essentials. It was understood I would continue my theological studies in India. Frances was not obliged to attend all courses, just the ones she preferred.

As expected, study, prayer and meditation filled our days. Missionaries were expected to be conversant on a variety of topics. The courses were; Old and New Testament studies, Evangelical methods, Comparative Religion, Tamil Language studies (for me), book-keeping, car maintenance, personnel management, social studies, self psychoanalysis, keeping fit in the tropics, meditation and forms of prayer, world affairs, Christian Education (including how to run a Sunday School) and problems of Inter-Church Cooperation. While we were expected to be in bed by 10:30pm, some of us worked well into the wee hours studying or preparing talks on specific topics. In addition, we visited many churches around Edinburgh, including those of other denominations. We listened to the sermons of several dozen preachers over the months.

We had visits from numbers of overseas missionaries and visitors from Third World churches, including Rev. Subramanium, Miss Brock and Dr. Baxter all of whom were or had worked at Kanchipuram, the city to which I was being sent as a medical missionary. We also met many retired missionaries from India. In this, as I look back, we were very honoured, since we two were the only missionaries being sent to South India among the fifty being trained that year.

There was time for relaxation including the creative activity of short plays and sketches. Frances was busy organizing the student extra-mural activities, including Scottish Country Dancing. She also took her share in leading prayer and gave several excellent little talks on specific religious topics.

We took part in Silent Retreats in which, as in all such activities, there are continuous periods of silent prayer for specific people or needy places, which continued from morning until night. A very interesting, peaceful and spiritually fulfilling experience. In addition, we met and studied with young trainee missionaries from other countries, as well as Church of Scotland Deaconesses; Presbyterian 'Sisters' who worked in collaboration with ministers in large congregations throughout Scotland.

We made many friends, who we unfortunately lost touch with once we went to India. I remember especially the College Principal, Miss Jean Fraser, a world famous and forward thinking theologian. A very fine and inspiring lady.

In summary, the three months went all too quickly. Like many concentrated periods of study, one establishes close ties with fellow classmates. In this case, we were all focused on helping mankind and wanted to make a difference in the world. We had accepted the call to service. Mostly it was a joyous time hindered by one episode of a falling out between Frances and myself; another signal. Now fully committed, turning back was unthinkable. We left the College on December 14 and travelled to Rosebery where we would stay to make final preparations before leaving for India eight days hence.

THE days before our departure were hectic. December 15 and 16 were days of packing trunks with us working until 4am on the 16th. With little sleep, that morning I travelled by lorry with the trunks to St.Enoch's Railway Station Left Luggage in Glasgow. We would be travelling by train from Glasgow to London where we would catch another train to transport us to the docks and our ship to India. I returned home for a quiet time with my parents and a church dedication.

The Service of Dedication was held at St.David's Memorial Church in Kirkintilloch, on Sunday, December 18. There were many important church dignitaries in attendance, including Dr. Stewart the Principal of New College in Edinburgh, Rev John Hamilton, Head of the Overseas Mission Department of the Church of Scotland, Rev. Subramanium of the Church of South India, Dr.Baxter retired medical missionary from Kanchipuram, Representatives of the Overseas Committee from Glasgow and members of the Presbytery of Glasgow and, of course, Rev Heron. It was a truly memorable event. The occasion was followed with a lunch at Rosebery with the Baxters as guests and an evening tea at the Herons.

The following day, we attended a very fine social which the congregation of St. David's had kindly arranged as a send-off for us and where I delivered a brief thank you speech. This too was well attended with many dignitaries.

On the 21st, I finalized several administrative matters, such as our Wills, met a few old school friends, and we relaxed at a movie with several family members. The next day was full of the usual last minute arrangements.

Thursday December 22, 1955, I mailed some last minute Christmas cards, telephoned Jack Stewart and we left Rosebery by car with my parents for Central Station, Glasgow, where family and friends waved us goodbye. As the train for London steamed out of the station at 10.30pm. I did not expect to see Scotland again for many years. Little did I know it would only be six years. The great adventure had begun!

We arrived in London on the morning of December 23, having a pleasant meeting with more relatives before boarding the liner S.S.Strathmore of the P & O Shipping line. The ship had a gross tonnage of over 35,000 tons, a large liner in the mid range size, with first and second class accommodation. We were in second class, which was quite comfortable. Also on board were Miss Jess Anderson, a fellow Church of Scotland missionary from the Orkneys who was returning from furlough to start her last five years of service as a nurse at the Leprosy hospital at Chingleput, about twenty miles from our destination. She was a very fine, reliable and good-natured lady, and as strong as an ox. Of Norse origin, Orcadians, often travelled the world in ships and were great pioneers. In addition there was Dr. Constance. She was an Indian Christian medical specialist on the staff of the great mission hospital of North India at Lhudiana in the Punjab. She was a delightful person with a lovely sense of humour. We usually teamed up with them for meals and other activities.

The ship steamed out of Tilbury Docks in London, at 3.12 pm, in fine sunny weather, bound for Bombay, with an official stop scheduled at Port Said in Egypt. Customs had been easy, we didn't have much of great monetary value. We had lunch, then unpacked. Bon Voyage telegrams were delivered to our cabin as well as flowers and candy from the Smith's. In the evening after dinner we talked with

Jess and Dr. Constance before retiring. Before us lay a fifteen day sea voyage before we would reach India. Travelling in December we could expect some difficult seas.

THE next day dawned dull, windy with rough seas in the English Channel. Frances became sea-sick and would remain so for the next week. As we moved into the Bay of Biscay, famous, we discovered, for its winter storms, heavy seas developed. As the day wore on the seas became mountainous. The huge ship climbed up waves twice its length, the bow split through the crest of the wave, then with a sickening shudder, crashed down into the trough of the next giant wave. I had never experienced anything like it, even when I crossed the North Sea in stormy weather. Truly, as I stood at the stern of the ship, holding strongly to the back rails, looking down I could see the bow of the ship plunging down into the trough, and looking up I saw the crest of the next wave. It was exhilarating, but at the same time a little frightening to see and feel the power of the ocean.

The Captain informed the passengers that the ship was listing thirty-one degrees to the both sides with every wave, a rare occurrence even in the Bay of Biscay. I was not sea-sick and was able to eat all my meals. But many were too sick to leave their cabins. That night I had to stay awake, lying on the deck of our little cabin, leaning my back against my berth and supporting Frances on her berth with both feet, otherwise, she would have rolled onto the floor.

Christmas Day, Frances, being sea-sick stayed in our cabin. By morning I was starving. So, binding Frances securely into her berth with a bed sheet, I proceeded to the Dining Saloon. The seas continued very heavy, resulting in the ship having to slow down occasionally to maneuver the waves. It was still rolling crazily making it difficult for anyone to walk about. Finally, I reached the Dining Saloon, a room equipped to serve at least a hundred guests, but only Jess and I were present. We were served our complete Christmas dinner, by a team of admiring Goanese stewards. The soup was the most difficult, but they made it easy by providing a contraption to hold the plate steady, but one still had to lap up the soup quickly. Then there was turkey and all the trimmings. We missionaries ate everything offered to us as I suspected it would be some time before I ate such fine European food again.

While the storm eventually abated, the ship continued to roll. By evening we passed Cape Finisterre at the north-west tip of Spain and sailed through the night down the coast of Portugal. Finally, we were able to get some sleep and Frances slowly began to recover.

We awoke the next day to fine weather and wonderfully calm seas. We watched the coast of Portugal, and later southern Spain slip by and by evening we had reached Gibraltar, brilliantly alight in the gathering darkness. Four of us played scrabble, and watched a movie in the Dining Saloon. It was a lovely day.

After breakfast on Tuesday the 27th, I continued studying Tamil while Frances did some embroidery as we both sat comfortably on deck chairs. The weather remained bright with a mild breeze. Later I played a game of deck tennis with another passenger. About 5pm we passed Tangier on the starboard side. That evening we met a Mrs. Solomon, a white-haired Indian Christian lady who was returning to India from England. She sought our help in putting on a Nativity Play for the children. We agreed.

The weather became unsettled again the next day which returned Frances to our cabin with another bout of sea-sickness. I worked with some other passengers to practice the Nativity Play, ten children having been recruited for the show. With deck games, writing, canasta and movies, and caring for Frances there was lots to do.

By Thursday we were sailing through the Mediterranean Sea. Frances, slowly recovering, remained in bed while I studied and read, occasionally playing deck tennis with another passenger. With stormy weather from the English Channel through the Bay of Biscay and into the Mediterranean, Frances had been mainly confined to bed for the first week of our journey. By Friday, Frances, feeling better, accompanied me to the First Class section of the ship for choir practice, organized by another passenger. Later I wrote letters for mailing at our stop in Port Said, Egypt scheduled for the next day.

Arriving at Port Said at 6am, we left by taxi for a brief tour of the town. It was an enjoyable trip, passing Coptic churches, Mosques, streets, canals and many shops. Back on board by 10 am we proceeded through the Suez Canal in brilliant sunshine. This was the demarcation point from a European climate to the heat of the Middle East and the anticipated tropical heat when we reached India. The strong sun glare forced us to put on sunglasses. I continued studying Tamil, did deck sports, played scrabble and later we all went to a New Year's Dance.

On New Year's Day 1956, we had another choir practice prior to Church service and prepared to present the postponed Christmas Nativity play (i.e. due to so many being sea-sick) which we had helped organize. With a few minor glitches all went well. After dinner I had a long chat with Drs. Constance and Baythan, both Indians, on the Church in a changing world. We agreed on many points.

It was late that evening, as I lay on my tight little ship bunk that I fully realized my life might never be the same again. I had made the decisive move. The ship had left the European waters of the Mediterranean Sea and now was quietly steaming south, down the Red Sea, with Africa on the starboard bow, and Asia on the port bow. The temperature that day was around 27°C (80°F) and except for exceptionally cool nights, I was going to live in temperatures of 25°C (78°F) to 45°C (104°F) until I passed that way again some years later. As I fell asleep, the different world of Asia, specifically India, had already begun to enfold me in its subtle embrace.

The next morning I took 'ship' prayers for the first time and continued my Tamil studies after breakfast. The crew and all passengers had now changed into tropical clothing. In the afternoon I studied Tropical Hygiene, realizing that it was imminently important to have its many mysteries at my finger tips. The rest of the day was spent in the usual deck games, scrabble and canasta. There would be little time in India for such recreation. Most of the time Frances spent sunning herself or reading in a deck chair, with occasional bouts of ironing clothes in our cabin. In my youthful, confident enthusiasm I kept ignoring her evident pattern of non-involvement.

By January 4th we had arrived in Aden. I noted this day as 'the highlight of the voyage' in my diary. Everyone was up for 6.30am to view 'the Barren Rocks of Aden'. At that time they were indeed totally bare, pale brownish and jagged, as far as the eye could see, not a vestige of any living plant or tree. The Arabian Desert in all its arid loneliness is a memorable sight. Many Scottish troops had served on garrison duty in Aden over the years, protecting this key port on the sea voyage from the oil states in the Persian Gulf and the bag-pipe tune composed by one of them called "The Barren Rocks of Aden", well reflects its lonesome aura. With a brief stopover I took the opportunity to visit the Sheikh Othman Hospital and meet Dr. Affara, a message from the church office in Edinburg having reached him about our arrival.

The ship was met at 8.30 am by a launch which ferried passengers to and fro to the port of Aden. Frances and I were met by Dr. Affara and Gloria McGowan of our Church of Scotland Mission Hospital at Sheikh Othman some miles out of the city. They were very kind to drive us first to the Express Postal Service at Steamer Point where we mailed letters to family back home, then to the shopping area where, I was able to buy a 32mm Zeiss Ikon camera with a built-in light meter and hood, plus two rolls of color film, very light crimp nylon socks, and sandals of the type much needed in the tropics, all for under twenty-five pounds (i.e. about $55 Canadian). Even in those bygone days all these things would have cost us three or four times as much in Britain. Then Dr. Affara and Gloria took us via a short stop at the Government Hospital to meet another Scot, Dr. Gemmell, who looked after the health of the British troops and business people and any other 'white' people, to Crater and the vast oil storage tanks. We then travelled on to the Mission Hospital at Sheikh Othman. The mission hospital and little school offered the only health and education services to the Arab Moslem population of that very poor, bleak and frankly miserable little town.

Dr. Affara kindly took me on a medical round of every patient in the hospital. It was a good introduction to medicine in Asia, at that time. We talked to patients suffering from many diseases including; tuberculosis of the spine, lungs and abdomen, leprosy, schistosomiasis, filiariasis, malaria, cancer and general surgical cases.

We also visited the obstetric unit. It is difficult for me as a doctor to accurately describe the bare simplicity and poverty of most mission hospitals of that era. Yet, its limited facilities and supplies did not mean it was unable to provide good care. I was left with a deep sense of the dedication of Dr. Affara and his colleagues, working in a very difficult climate and in a largely unsympathetic Moslem society.

On our return, he took us via the aerodrome where I visited the RAF airbase. Later at the wharf we thanked him for his kindness, wishing him well in his chosen work. We then boarded the launch back to the ship.

Back on the ship we played more deck tennis and later canasta. Later that evening we witnessed a kind of miracle. After the short shower of rain earlier in the day, by evening the Barren Rocks of Aden were clothed in a mantle of gentle green. Apparently this only happened once in many years. I took it as a truly positive omen.

As we were getting closer to India, we were informed that Bombay customs would require a detailed inventory of our belongings upon our arrival in three days. This was an unforeseen and difficult task, which if the shipping authority had warned us of could have been done prior to our voyage, but it had to be done from memory since all our belongings were packed in crates in the ship's hold.

By Friday, January 6th, we were still working on the inventory and customs declaration forms. When time permitted I wrote to my parents and attended an afternoon tea provided by a wealthy Indian Christian lady in the first class Saloon.

It was very pleasant and salubrious with a wonderful view of the sea and just as if we had called for them, large shoals of Flying Fish provided us with a magnificent show. Later that evening there was a Fancy Dress Parade and Dance, entitled "East is East and West is West and both shall meet". Interestingly enough it was all the missionaries and Indian Christians who organized the event.

The next day we steamed across the Arabian Sea towards Bombay. We were still busy finalizing the customs documents and packing and rearranging our trunks and suitcases. I wrote a letter of thanks to Dr. Affara and later we sat in the warm, sunny and refreshing breeze on deck until supper. Afterwards we played our last game of canasta. We were all ready for our landing in India the following day. The somewhat unreal atmosphere of a sea voyage was about to end.

Sunday, January 8th was hot and humid. We received a message from a South Indian business man whom we had met on board the ship. It was written in Tamil and meant "Welcome to India". It was a very nice gesture.

About 4 pm, the ship steamed slowly into Bombay Harbour and that was when I had my first and lasting impression of India. Bombay was then the biggest city in India at about ten million people. As the ship crawled into the dock, the scene was of a hodge-podge of huge, dirty yellowish, multi-storey buildings, against a deep azure cloudless sky and mirrored in the dark, mustardy green filth of the harbour water. The gentle breeze blew into our nostrils the unforgettable stench of human ordure, mixed from time to time with the exotic, sensual perfume of jasmine. That first impression of Bharat, (the Correct name for 'India') was a metaphor for that land of stark contrasts. A land in which indescribable beauty mixes randomly with scenes of utter squalor, where exquisitely expressed philosophical truth survives embedded in ancient and pervasive corruption and where people live easily with dualities. In short, India for me is a bitter-sweet place; the very contact embedding itself under ones skin, forever.

We docked at 5pm. Very slowly the passengers filed off the ship into a sea of Indian porters, all offering in Mahrati or broken English, to help with our luggage. It was chaos, especially to the uninitiated. I looked around hoping someone was there to meet us, but there was no one. We had travelled thousands of miles to a foreign country, and the reality of no one to greet us would herald the challenges which lay ahead.

Chapter 4

SOUTH INDIA

Bombay, located south of the tropic of Cancer and north of the equator, is often referred to as the 'Gateway of India'. It is regarded as the financial center of India as well as a major national commercial, transportation, entertainment and manufacturing hub. Having one of the world's largest harbors: a broad, sheltered bay between the city and the mainland, it was regarded as India's premier and busiest port. It's name, from the Portuguese *Bom Bahia*, meaning 'Fair Bay', reflects its prestigious harbour status. Indians call it *Mumbai*. Originally Bombay consisted of seven islands which were eventually linked together into a contiguous stretch of land known as Bombay Island. The city, which lies on the west coast of India, is framed to the east on the mainland by the towering Western Ghats mountain range.

Bombay became the capital of Bombay state (later the state of Maharashtra) when India received its independence in 1947. In the fifties its population was about ten million. It had a rich history. In the third century B.C.E., it was under the Maurya Empire, ruled by the Buddist emperor, Asoka. The Hindu rulers of the Silhara Dynasty later governed it until 1343, when the kingdom of Gujarat annexed the islands. By 1534 the Portugese appropriated the islands and ceded these to the British as dowry when Charles II married Catherine de Braganza, sister to the Portugese king. In 1668 the East India Company took over the area, making Bombay an important trading port. With the opening of the Suez Canal in 1869 Bombay prospered as one of the largest seaports on the Arabian Sea.

Finding ourselves in this bustling, international port after weeks at sea with no one to greet us was an abrupt awakening to our new environment. In retrospect, it was the first moment I had doubts about the Church of Scotland Overseas Mission Department's management of its Indian operations. Here were two missionaries, trained and ready, sent at great expense halfway around the globe and apparently no telegram or letter had been sent to the six missionaries in Bombay forewarning them of our arrival.

By the time we had gone through the laborious process of Indian Customs it was past six o'clock and pitch black. Sunset comes quickly in South India. When we found our way to the Railway Station we discovered, contrary to what we had been told by Head Office, no tickets had been purchased for us. We would have to return to the booking office at 9am the next day. We immediately returned to Customs to confirm that our luggage would be able to remain there for the night. Alone in a huge, hectic Indian city at night with nowhere to go, no Indian currency and little British money, we were stranded with no idea where any of the Presbyterian missionaries lived. We had been assured by Edinburgh that we would be met with the expected transportation, accommodation and meals. It was a mess!

Eventually, using my Scouting skills, I found a public telephone. I had, as yet, no Indian currency, but hoped to find the name of one of our missionaries. That proved fruitless as all our Bombay people worked in mission schools or colleges with Mahrati names which meant nothing to me. As a last desperate move I looked up anything that was remotely Christian, may be a church with an English name. With luck I discovered under 'colleges', an Anglican College, noted the address, and looked for a taxi. Fortunately the taxi driver understood enough English and we took off.

The taxi wove its way through heavy traffic eventually stopping outside a large, darkened three storey building on a back street. With no Indian currency (rupees), I nodded confidently indicating (and silently praying), that the people in this residence would pay for our ride. The driver waited unhappily while I rang the bell.

At first no one responded, so I gave it a long hopeful ring. Finally, a window opened on the second floor and a rather strident English female voice asked us who we were at this time of night. It was now 9.30 pm. I quickly tried to explain our situation and asked if she could help us. Her head disappeared and she reappeared at the door, welcoming us coolly, and invited us to come in but I had to explain our taxi dilemma. She told the taxi driver something in Mahrati which seem to pacify him for the moment. We then went upstairs to what were obviously living quarters. There she handed me some rupees to pay the driver, which I did. We now had a roof over our heads. Then I explained, in more detail, what had happened. The lady was stunned that nobody from the Presbyterian Mission had met us.

She introduced herself as Mrs. Kellock, wife of the Anglican Bishop of Bombay and marveled that we had managed to arrive at their church office and living quarters. She noted with happy logic, that it was too late for us to contact any Scottish missionaries. We would spend the night with them. At which point her husband emerged from his study and introduced himself, gently observing that we had certainly had a difficult baptism to India. Mrs. Kellock said that we should have something to eat before we went to bed and that the mission car would take us into the Central Station the next morning. She was most gracious in the best tradition of a Bishop's wife. By this time we were starving, not having eaten since a light lunch aboard ship. We gratefully consumed the light offering provided.

So began our first night in India. I remember briefly looking out the guest bedroom window, over a bay, lined with high rise apartments, with the constant hum of traffic not far off and the faint murmur of the sea breaking on the beach. Frances was already fast asleep in her mosquito-netted bed. Finally, I maneuvered into my bed, for the first time in my life under a mosquito net. With the sound of the waves gently breaking on the distant shore I too was soon fast asleep. It was a rather odd ending to a difficult first day in a new country.

The next morning we rose early and drove to downtown Bombay in the Kellock's chauffeured car. It was customary in India to have car drivers to guard the car while one was doing business, to prevent the removal of parts or theft of the vehicle.

We were met at the Central Station by a Mr. Duncan of our Scottish Mission, whom Mrs. Kellock knew. In the endless noisy bustle of a large Indian railway station, Mr. Duncan helped us find the correct ticket office for the Madras Express. Then he led us through the streets first to Cook's Tour Agency, then to the Crawford Market to buy a cheap container and some fruit, cheese and sardines which, he advised us, would be needed on the overnight trip, rather than trusting our knowledge of the Indian food offered by the various vendors en route. I also went to a telegraph office to send messages to Rev. Roy Manson in Kanchipuram and Rev. Ellis Shaw in Chingleput, that we would be on the 2.41 pm Madras Express that day. In 1956 the quickest and most reliable way to contact people was by telegram, a useful remnant of the British Raj. Then it was back to the Anglican Bishop's house, where Mrs. Kellock served us lunch and later waved us goodbye. A charming lady whom we never saw again.

Mr. Duncan appeared once again at the train station to bid us bon voyage on our sixteen hour overnight journey south and east towards the great city of Madras, where it was said, St. Thomas preached the Word and was crucified in about 50 C.E. on what is still called St. Thomas Mount.

A longish train trip in India was interesting and full of activity. Our introduction to train travel in that multi-lingual, multi-ethnic and multi-religious land was always full of interesting and challenging activities.

A Flight Lieutenant in the Indian Air Force who spoke English engaged us in lively conversation for the first part of the journey to Poona, which has a big military barracks, left by the British. By 1956 India had eight years of independence, so everywhere there were still signs of the British presence. People were quite friendly and full of new found self-confidence and hope for a bright future. They seemed to know that we were no threat. I guess what we were must have been very obvious, since the only white people left were either a few businessmen or Christian missionaries come to boost their inadequate health and education systems. Most Indians, the majority of whom are Hindus, find it hard to understand why missionaries come to help them, but once they have satisfied themselves that we intend no harm or disruption, are friendly and welcoming.

We went First Class, particularly as there was the danger of thieves and because we had so much luggage. In fact since most of our trips were long and we had much luggage, and later children, we usually went First Class.

Indian trains are always crowded. Millions of people travel daily by train. First Class had upholstery seats for about four to six people. At night, beds were pulled down from the side for those wanting to rest. We ate the food purchased at Bombay, adding coffee and plantains at the various stations. As the train approached a station, I had to be ready with the correct amount of rupees to quickly exit onto the platform going straight to the vendor and return to the train before the crowd got too thick. With many train trips, the cries of the vendors would become indelibly etched onto my memory; "Capee-capeeah! Capee-capeeah! (Tamil for coffee), 'chai' (tea), 'roti (bread) and a biscuit'" Varaipuram! Varaipuram! (Plantains = the small sweet, bananas of India). Coffee and plantains were two of our favorites, both tasty and safe.

Weather and security are the two key factors in Indian train carriage design. The windows have three layers; the first two layers (glass and mesh) having the convenience of being able to be pulled up from below. The third layer of metal bars was immovable. The inner glass layer is used only in the torrential rain of the monsoon season, as when closed it soon results in suffocating heat. The next layer of very sturdy wire netting is to keep out the hands of possible thieves and monkeys when the train stops en route. Monkeys inhabit all Indian railway stations, mainly seeking food from travelers. Monkeys represent living incarnations of the Hindu god Hanuman the monkey God, who is a powerful member of the Hindu pantheon of gods. It is regarded as good luck for Hindus to give food to monkeys. We didn't, but one had to be always vigilant as their small clawed fingers could rapidly steal anything small through an open window at a station. The outermost layer was a row of fixed, stout iron bars to keep out human thieves who could climb along the outside of the moving train and, without bars, easily enter and steal or hold up travelers.

A long train journey in India could be described as lengthy periods of rumbling train wheel noises, interrupted happily, by the musical and welcome cries of the station vendors. No train official sang out the name of each station. Even if they did it would have been inaudible in the general commotion and the noise of hundreds of people. So, one had to keep a sharp look-out for the dimly lit station names, to avoid missing ones intended stop. So, as the train steamed out of Bombay, I began to carefully note the Indian signs as our trip progressed; Poona, Kolhaour, Belgaum, Hubli, Chitradurga, Bangalore and finally, our destination, Arkonam. We were heading south then east to the state of Tamil Nadu.

Tamil Nadu is one of India's twenty-eight states. It lies on the south-eastern part of the Indian peninsula. A largely low lying fertile region it is bordered by hills on the north and west, and the sea on the east and south. It is the fifth largest contributor to India's GDP, the most urbanized state, covers an area of 130,058 square kilometres (50,216 sq mi), and is the eleventh largest state in India. The climate of the state ranges from dry sub-humid to semi-arid. All this lay before us as our train ride continued.

Another feature of Indian train travel is talking with fellow travelers. There is not the austere, stand-offish coldness of British, particularly English travelers, or even the quiet but usually independent friendliness of a Canadian train. Once you start talking with an Indian who can speak English or if you can speak his language, things get very personal from the outset. The following might be a typical conversation.

"You are Englishman, yes?" "No I am Scotsman". Ah, my late professor at Madras University was a Scotchman. He was very good man".

"Are you married?" "Yes, this is my wife".

" How many children have you ?" "None as yet". Aah you will soon have many children. It is good". Later when I had three daughters, the response would be. " Aiyo (Alas) all girls, you will be bankrupt by three weddings. It is very bad luck to have only girls".

" What is your job ?". "How much money do you make ?".

"Why do you come to India?". "You are Christian no ?". " I am Christian yes". "Are your parents alive ?". And so it goes.

The hours would quickly pass and suddenly the train would come to a stop. The person with whom you have shared all the details of your life says goodbye and alights with a wave of his hand. You will never see him again, not ever. Such is India with millions of people. At once so personal and yet so impersonal. Such travel experiences become an unforgettable part of life in India and form part of the culture which gently creeps into ones soul.

The train eventually crawled into Arkonam Junction at 6.40 pm. It was pitch black. In the dimly lit station we could just make out the name. We stumbled out into the darkness of the platform along with dozens of others, all going in different directions.

Our thoughts were mixed as we slowly walked towards the bright exit light. Then I had to detour to the luggage van at the end of the train. Just at that moment Rev. Roy Manson, his wife Noreen and a Mr. Manuel appeared out of the gloom greeting us with warm welcomes. We had finally arrived!

Roy, a Presbyterian minister about my age, had been in India for about a year. He was the district pastor in Kancheepuram, with administrative and clerical responsibilities for several church communities each with an Indian minister. He was a really nice guy, maybe the best Church of Scotland missionary I met during my years in India. After he and I got our belongings safely off the luggage carriage, he directed us to the Mission Land-Rover.

Roy drove us first to Kancheepuram, where, as I understood it, I was to be posted and where he worked. After dropping off Noreen, he showed us briefly around the huge temple city of South India. Then we had to hurry off to Chingleput, about twenty miles away, where Rev. Ellis Shaw, the Senior Missionary of the Church of Scotland in Tamil Nadu, was stationed. It was after eight o'clock in the evening when we tumbled out of the Land-Rover. After Roy completed the introductions, he left. We went into the Shaw's large bungalow and, after freshening up, sat down to our first Indian meal, with Ellis Shaw, his wife Mary and their two children.

It was after midnight when we got to bed, each in our own rather small, mosquito-covered iron bed, in the Shaw's spare room. Frances quickly fell asleep. Dog-tired, I was fascinated by the noises of a South Indian night in the relative peace and quiet of the country. The Shaws lived on the outskirts of the taluk town of Chingleput, from which location Rev.Shaw was able to administer the churches 'missioned' by the Scots Presbyterians. The mission had existed from the early years of the 19th century.

Rev Shaw was a tall, medium built, middle-aged man with graying hair who had been in Chingleput, India for over twenty years. He was well experienced in the complexities of mission work in the area, was responsible for the assignment of the new missionaries and spoke fluent Tamil, a skill I admired.

Lying quietly inside my mosquito net, I became aware of the buzzing of many hungry mosquitoes, maneuvering around my net, hoping that I was foolish enough to allow some part of my full-blooded European flesh to touch the net, giving them the opportunity of stabbing me through the holes in the netting. Squirming into the middle of the little bed I felt safe. This enabled me to hear other interesting sounds, such as the heavy buzzing of large moths which intermittently flew against the netting. This puzzled me as I thought that moths, as creatures of the night, would be well able to avoid such collisions. The reason for their confusion soon became apparent when I heard rapidly repeated swishing sounds like the beating of wings. It was just that. The wings belonged to bats. Like every other small creature of the night, they could easily fly between the window bars; there being no glass in un-air-conditioned tropical windows, only bars to keep out thieves. Every few minutes a bat caught one of the large moths, then flew down under my bed to land on its rusty springs. There it crunched through the moth's tasty body, the sound of which reverberated up through my pillow to my ear. At which point I banged the mattress with one foot causing the bat to fly away. One other major and memorable sound of the tropical night in a mission bungalow which I remember well, was the frequent padding sound, as of many little feet, which circled my bed in a continuous drumming. It was the sound of a number of large field rats, obviously enjoying their nightly romps, foraging for anything they could find. Lulled by this tropical symphony of nature's orchestra, I was soon asleep, floating safely in my warm cocoon.

LIKE sunset, the day dawns quickly in South India. You can virtually see the huge ball of the sun rising into the sky, a wonderful time, when everything comes alive. We arose early, ate a breakfast including 'cunji' (a Tamil kind of basic, nourishing porridge). Then we were off in a rather beaten-up mission car, a UK Standard, for a tour of the region.

We first went to the Bazaar (an old Mogul word for the shopping area) in Chingleput, in all its hubbub of vendors cries, friendly conversations, barking dogs, lowing Brahmani bulls, together with a thousand smells, most exotic to my inexperienced senses. While these impressions would soon become commonplace to me, they would never be forgotten. We walked around the old Fort, where Ellis talked to a local sadhu (Hindu holy man) whom he obviously knew. Later we walked along a country road past some small typical roadside Hindu temples for one of the panoply of Hindu gods, tended by a lonely priest, ready to receive the offerings of passing worshippers. Sometimes an Indian Christian evangelist would stand near such a temple offering Christian tracts about Jesus. Indians are mainly tolerant and interested in reading or hearing about 'another' god. There was a huge business in Christian tracts, New Testaments and Bibles, first because of this interest and second because they can be printed at minimal cost in numerous local languages as well as in English. Can you imagine a Hindu priest offering Hindu tracts outside a Christian church in Europe or North America? I expect there would be a frightful outcry.

Next we went to a Christian Indian village with its little church and primary school, everything neat, clean and relatively tidy. Then to a typical Hindu village, with some larger houses belonging to Brahmin families. In India, the Brahmins are the highest and priestly caste, the best educated, wealthy and politically powerful and one way or another, they rule the country. Gandhi, and then Nehru, officially abolished 'caste', but it will take centuries to break down the barriers between the different groups; priests (Brahmins), soldiers (Kshatria), traders (Vaishna), and farmers (Sudras), not to mention the Scheduled Tribes (lower aboriginal tribes overrun by Aryian Hindus centuries ago), and the lowest caste, the Sweepers, considered 'outcastes' until Gandhi. Prior to that, outcastes had no status or rights and were virtually slaves or at least serfs to the caste people above them. Following Gandhi's lead, they were later called Harijans, meaning 'the people of God'. In an ironic way, which I believe is God's plan for India, the majority of converts to Christianity belonged to the outcaste group. The missionaries gave them a chance for education and self respect. The first Minister of Finance of the newly independent India in 1948 was an outcaste Christian. He was a mathematical genius although his forebears for many centuries were illiterate cleaners (sweepers) of human and other excreta. He was also the only top politician whom everyone could trust to handle the wealth of the State.

At the little Christian primary school we met a class of small girls and boys, all mainly Harijans, who would eventually become an important part of India's educated class. Maybe that will be the greatest legacy of the nineteenth and twentieth centuries' Western Missionary movement; honest, educated people. But they have a big job ahead of them, as they are a small percentage of the one billion Indian population. Many of the best schools and hospitals in India were operated by Christians under the various Christian denominations. Happily for me, Indian Christians had a laudable tendency to ignore the sectarian differences imported by the Western Christian denominations.

Before leaving Scotland, it was my understanding that I would be working in the small Christian hospital in Kanchipuram, the great Hindu temple city of South India. Its giant twenty storey temple towers, (Goporams), dating from the early centuries. The Tamil people had existed in the area from about 500 B.C.E.. Centuries later, under their powerful Palluva kings they ruled most of South India for over five hundred years and sent Hindu missionaries and conquering soldiers to what is now south-east Asia. This explains the Indian-looking temple architecture of countries like Thailand, Vietnam, Laos, Malaysia and Indonesia.

On this initial tour of the Kanchipuram's hospital, Rev. Shaw introduced me to a Dr. Azariah, the son of one of the new Bishops of the Church of South India and his wife. As was the practice, Frances took off with Mrs. Azariah while I went with Dr. Azariah and Rev. Shaw to tour the hospital.

As we walked around the hospital wards it suddenly dawned on me that Dr. Azariah, the superintendent of the hospital, was in my position. I knew there wasn't room or need for two doctors in this small hospital. If my first shock was that nobody welcomed us in Bombay (Mombai), the second shock was that the mission didn't need me at all. The frontline seemed out of step with the Edinburgh office. While in Scotland, Head Quarter staff insisted that I was urgently needed at this hospital, the reality, however, appeared to indicate otherwise. Trying to grasp the enormity of the situation, I felt cautious tact and diplomacy were needed, and said nothing hoping that somehow the situation would be clarified. No explanation was forthcoming from Dr. Azariah or Rev. Shaw. Having been transported thousands of miles to another country, I was left with no explanation as to what had happened to my position nor what other options might be available for me.

That night, as I lay in my bed in Roy Manson's bungalow in Kanchipuram, I struggled with the situation and my predicament. At twenty-six years of age I was not a naïve child and understood that, not to my complete surprise, politics likely had some role in my two 'surprises'. I had much to learn about the world of the Indian Christian Church. I was encountering familiar political maneuverings which I thought were back in Western churches and institutions. Irrespective of my feelings and uncertainties, I believed God had sent me to India for a purpose and that He would guide me.

The next day we were off to Madras, the great sprawling capital of what the British called Madras State, but was now called Tamil Nadu. In the east end of the city we arrived at the Christina Rainy Hospital for Women. It had been founded by Scots Presbyterian women medical missionaries in the mid eighteen hundreds to provide vital obstetric and gynecological services for the poor women of the Madras slums. A truly worthy and needed service of Christian compassion. As I toured the hospital, Frances, as before, spent time with other missionaries or hospital staff.

The Superintendent of the Rainy Hospital was a female doctor from Dundee, Scotland, Dr. Anderson, assisted by Dr. Mary Findlay, who with her mother, had been ejected a few years before from China by the communist government. The Matron was a pleasant Indian lady, Sister Margaret Simpra. The title 'sister' used for nurses was retained from the time of the British. It was not a religious title.

The Rainy Hospital was doing a wonderful job of treating needy women, but as we toured the wards, it was obvious the facility needed considerable repair and upgrading. I looked prospectively at the large adjoining vacant land owned by the Mission and imagined new extensions which might be built. Later I would find out that Rev. Shaw had some idea that I would work at the Rainy Hospital, expanding its services, but Dr. Anderson would have nothing to do with a male physician on the premises.

That night we stayed at the hospital in Dr. Anderson's bungalow. About 5am, I heard a soft shuffling of bare feet and was aware of a shadowy figure laying a large cup of something on my little bed table. As he, for it was an old man, whispered "Chota Hazri sahib". I knew that the Rainy hospital was still locked into a British Imperial time warp when sahibs were gently awakened by an early morning cup of tea. The term was inherited from the mogul rulers of India and more or less meant 'a little morning snack'. I was not used to this and did not like it, although many British Army and ex-members of the British Civil Service continued to prefer 'their morning cuppa char'. This was my only encounter with this rather outdated practice.

The grand inaugural tour of the area then continued with an interesting visit to the site of the ancient capital city of the Palava Empire at Mahabalipuram. The Palavas were a great Tamil nation which reached its peak in the first three centuries of the modern era. That was the time when these Hindu Dravidian people invaded and colonized much of what is now the East Indies. Tamil is still spoken in many parts of Malayasia. The great city stood on the shores of the Indian Ocean, but in time it was submerged by the rising sea and most of it is now under about fifty to two hundred feet of water, perhaps due to a previous 'Global Warming'. On what had been a hill overlooking the city, they had built a temple and a huge carved elephant out of stone which still stands as a wonderful work of art and a popular tourist attraction.

Later we visited the old, but ever active, Leper hospital at Chingleput, founded by the great Scottish Presbyterian medical missionary, Dr. Cochrane, whose son we met on our honeymoon in the Scottish Highlands. A leprosy hospital, as I came to know in my own experience, is a place of special compassion and hope, mingled with an overwhelming atmosphere of sadness and resignation. In the fifties there were over three million lepers in India. Fear of the disease caused lepers to disguise their infection until it had taken a strong hold on their bodies making it more difficult to cure. This fear was because once the disease was identified, the individual faced the inevitable outcome of being abandoned by their family and community.

The final part in our welcoming orientation, as organized by Rev. Shaw, was attendance at the St. Columba's School Sports Day in Chingleput. A part of the Sports was an 'old' boys competition for young men of seventeen to twenty-five. Rev. Shaw had, unbeknown to me, enrolled me in the half mile and some other events, including the Shot Put. This was not a nice thing to do to someone twenty-seven, who had been out of athletic training for some years, in a temperature of over ninety degrees, with no athletic shoes on uneven ground. Shaw had me cornered. Nevertheless, I came second in the half mile to an eighteen year old farm boy, won the Shot Put and, I think, came second in the Slow Cycle Race. Such trickery was hard to understand from a clergyman of his stature. On that uneven ground in my bare feet I could have sustained a serious injury. I would later learn that Rev. Shaw was known for his political and self interested actions, something which I was encountering in this initial meeting. Since we would not be assuming our missionary work for six months, I kept such thoughts to myself. Our immediate task would be in language studies at the South Indian Missionary Language School in Bangalore, in Mysore State. This round of orientation and time with Rev. Shaw would be brief, but the unanswered situation of my job would hang like an albatross over me while I was studying.

AFTER another long train journey, we arrived at the language school on January 14th. We were given quarters in a small room with a bed, two small chairs and a little study table, using our two steamer trunks as extra tables.

The Language School was located in the old British section of Bangalore, tucked into the Church of South India, United Theological Seminary campus, where pastors were being trained for churches throughout India, the Middle East and South-East Asia. In total, there would be over a hundred theological students on campus. The language school had First and Second year classes in the four main languages of South India; Tamil, Telegu, Kanarese and Malayalum. Our focus would be in Tamil.

This college was the only Christian Divinity School in South-East Asia. Divinity students came from all over India, Nepal, Burma, Sri Lanka, Pakistan, Iran and other parts of the Middle East. The language of instruction was English. The first Indian to be Principal of the College was Dr. Russell Chandran, a scholarly, gifted theologian. With his charming and attractive wife they made a charismatic couple, eminently appropriate to lead the college into the era of Indian leadership. Among his faculty were Bishop Hollis, an Englishman, the retired first Moderator of the Church of South India, Rev. Dr. Harrison an eminent American theologian and Rev. Hancock, a theologian from Northern Ireland.

Our Language School and quarters were off to one side of the seminary compound, near the perimeter wall, looking out onto the back of the Bangalore Racing Club's horse stables. The sight of rows of horses' swishing tails alerted me to possible disease and an immediate need for window netting for our dormitory room, not easy in a setting of open windows.

There were eight of us in the First Year Tamil class. Our Tamil teachers or munshis, as they are called in India, were Rev. Jeevanasen (we called him affectionately, 'Jeevas') and Mr. Dawson. Jeevas, an ordained minister of the Church of South India, a theologian and philosopher, was a very nice man with a fluent knowledge of English and Tamil. He was an excellent teacher of a rather difficult language. Mr. Dawson, who had anglified his name from its Indian name of Dasan which, as he told us meant 'slave of God', was an intelligent man, but very sensitive about his lowly birth, and anxious to impress us with his impoverished state, which we couldn't personally do anything about as we were virtually as poor as him.

As I recall, my Tamil class colleagues were, Helga, a Danish Lutheran nurse, Rev. Peter Doble and his wife Gwynyth, Methodists from Wales; Daphne (?) and Anne Judson, teacher and nurse missionary, Anglicans from England; Gunwer Johansen, a Lutheran nurse from Sweden; and Frances and myself, Scots Presbyterians. A varied group for sure, but all intent on offering our skills and hard work to help the people of India, regardless of their religion. I also met others in the other language programs, such as Billy and Cathy Mularchie, Baptists from Ulster, an English couple, both medical doctors, Gladys Klassen, a nurse from Saskatchewan, Canada, an American Congregational couple with their baby Homer, three American fundamentalists, Barbara Wetterquist, daughter of the Bishop of Lund, Sweden, and a few others who were near the end of their training.

The language students attended various divinity classes at the college, for me this would be a continuation of my studies at St.Colm's Missionary College in Scotland. Divinity studies had to be fitted in to the Tamil lesson schedule. It was a pleasure to study and talk with this group of young clergy from many places of the world.

In the Language School, in addition to providing medical advice, I was also on the Hostel Committee, which discussed the problems/complaints of students about the accommodation, food, Tamil classes, other issues which arise in such circumstances and, of course, health problems.

Our group studied in one of the small basic class-rooms, next to the hostel in which we lived. Classes ran weekdays every morning and afternoon. We also studied in the evenings and week-ends. Tamil is considered the second most difficult language in the world after Chinese. It has one hundred and sixty-nine letters and a number of sounds which do not exist in any European language. It is a complex tongue dating back for thousands of years. The Tamil Lexicon comprises over five thousand words, more than most other languages. It is certainly more complex than the five hundred words of Basic English. One example may help to explain its complexity. The Lord's Prayer in English has over ninety syllables and can be spoken fluently in about twenty-five seconds. In Tamil it has twice the number of syllables and was routinely spoken in less than twenty seconds. It is a language of greater complexity and usually spoken quickly. As expected, in addition to our language studies, in a religious environment prayer and church services were included.

Morning Prayers took place in the hostel dining room and we shared the leading of these prayers. As we came from a wide variety of denominational backgrounds it provided an excellent and interesting broadening of our worship experience. Colleagues from American and Canadian Fundamentalist, Anglican, Baptist, Congregational, Presbyterian, Welsh and English Methodist, Danish and Swedish Lutheran and a few other religious backgrounds, provided a rich miscellany of Christian prayer forms. The most memorable prayers were those fervently offered to God by the two Ulster Baptists, Billy Mularchy and his wife. They had been sent out from one Baptist congregation in Belfast, who considered themselves to be the only true Baptists and in fact the only true Christians in the world. Billy had come straight from being a butcher's message boy and he and his wife were ready and willing to 'deliver the goods' to all of India. Their prayers were an incantation to the Almighty, to provide us all with an endless supply of 'The Precious Blood of Jesus'. This of course was a theologically acceptable petition, but the endless repetition, in a very strong, loud Belfast accent of 'Oh for the Precious Blood' was a bit wearisome, especially as our breakfast was getting cold. Finally, Miss Money-Kyrle, the House-Mother of the School, was heard to plead, "Oh Billy, have we not all had more than enough of the Precious Blood?" All of us, including Billy were speechless. To Miss Money-Kyrle's credit, after that we got less of Billy's 'Oh, for the Precious Blood'. Sunday service, however, offered more challenges.

Every Sunday we wended our way on foot across Bangalore to one of a variety of churches, both to worship and to improve our knowledge of Tamil. I remember little Rev. Raja Manikam in St.John's, Church of South India church. He was a devout and charming little man. Other churches included St.Mark's, a Wesleyan Church, and a Lutheran one. Of course, when we got too cross-eyed trying to keep up with theological complexities in Tamil, there was also the United Theological College Chapel service in English. In time I managed to follow both sermons and worship in Tamil.

You might wonder with all our other activities how we found any leisure time. Without radio or television there was time for many activities. The only radio was the dawn to dusk Indian film Git (songs) blaring out from loudspeakers in the Bazaar. This music provided a constant background of sound in every Indian town and village.

We had time to shop, to visit the huge, newly constructed Kanarese (Mysore) State Legislature where we were present at the visit of Emperor Haile Selassie of Ethiopia. We also went to the Ramadan Muslim festival and the Hindu Dasara Annual Parade. We sung parts of the Messiah with the United Theological College students. Gwyneth, our little Welsh colleague, had a magnificent soprano voice and made our singing presentation a great success. We also visited the Kodando Raos. Dr. Rao was the head of the Theosophists Society of India (a philosophical society which tries to bridge the beliefs in God of Hindus, Christians and other religions) who with his American wife were a charming and hospitable couple. They were introduced to us by their friends, Aunt Pearl and Uncle Tommy, who also came up from Pullangode to visit us. Dr. Rao was concerned that I, as a missionary, should not proselyte in words. I reassured him that I would not do so. Practical, needed medical service would be my mission. There were also the inevitable letters home to family and church.

For someone in a far off land, in the mid-twentieth century, letter-writing was essential. I wrote regularly to my mother and father. They were, I fear, rather hurried dull compositions. Letters were also required to our sponsoring congregation, St.David's Memorial, Kirkintilloch. These I managed to have printed by a local printer. India had a wealth of small printers, who charged very low fees. There were also official letters to the mission Head Quarters in Edinburgh. There were also occasional letters to other missionaries in India. Telephones were often unreliable and too expensive on our meager stipend. The other cheapest and most reliable form of communication was the telegraph.

But my time at the Language School turned out to be much more than Tamil and divinity studies, two of these additional activities follow.

WITHIN the first few days two facts became abundantly clear. First, the location and physical condition of the Language School seemed to me, from a public health point of view, to be asking for trouble. The back of the two-storey dormitory wing was separated by a five foot wooden fence from the horse stables of the Bangalore Horse Racing Club, thirty to forty feet away. At any time of the day or night, except on racing days, the view from our dormitory bedroom window was a long row of horses' bottoms, each surrounded by a dark cloud of horse flies, the horses' tails vainly trying to swish away the persistent flies. Below each horse's rear end was a pile of horse droppings, a fertile pabulum for breeding flies, which were also swarming around the Language School.

Second, was the realities and problems of personal hygiene in India; a land with a chronic shortage of water and deficient or non-existent sewage systems. In 1956 only missionaries stationed in big cities, and better-off Indian professional and rich people in the main cities had the 'benefit' of flush toilets. Small towns had 'dry' toilets and the countryside had 'sit-upons' for Europeans and 'squatters'. In the towns and country where most missionaries lived and worked, dry latrines were the rule, much like camp latrines. Basically, you sat on a frame with the 'fall-out' going into an enamel pan. The enamel pans were removed discretely in the early morning by a servant called 'a Sweeper' (Harijans), an outcaste. In my time in India the age of reservoirs, clean, potable water supply and flush toilets had not arrived.

This brings me back to my second initial comment on the Language School in Bangalore. As the medical doctor among other missionaries, (the two English doctors kept much to themselves, looking after their infant baby), I became aware of the results of poor public health facilities, as one after another of us came down with dysentery. A check-up showed that this was occurring irrespective of the fact that we were drinking only boiled water and Miss Money-Kyrle, kept assuring us that the kitchen was clean and the kitchen staff were' healthy'. As newcomers to the tropics we were told that 'everyone had tummy upsets for the first few months' due to the differences in the water and the spicy nature of Indian food. So we soldiered on. Several of the more trusting believed that it was God's will and this was part of missionary life. The tough ones survived, though left chronically ill, while others were invalided home. The waste in terms of loss of skilled personnel, and the cost of transportation to and from the mission field was enormous. However, this was 1956, Penicillin and other antibiotics had been discovered and medical science understood the life history of most tropical diseases and the steps needed to prevent such illness.

As a physician of the antibiotic era I was skeptical of the 'you'll all get sick' line of thinking and wondered why Frances and I fell victims to bacillary dysentery, which I successfully treated with sulphonamides, despite the assurances that our food and water were 'clean'. Something was not quite right. As a doctor I had to investigate.

Early one morning about 5 am, as dawn was nearing, I decided to have a look around the Language School. Snooping around to the rear of the building I abruptly halted in my tracks, just in time to avoid being seen by a row of squatting figures, just visible in the dim pre-dawn light. Crouching motionless behind a scraggy shrub I could just make out the forms of about a dozen Indian servants, male and female, at about twenty-five yards distant, facing towards the school, but with their exposed buttocks facing the wall and having their morning stool. This was the same wall over which were arrayed the row of Bangalore Racing Club horses rear ends.

Medical diagnosis is rather akin to detective work and at that moment I had come upon my first clue. Horses droppings breed many flies, which in this situation made daily visits to the servants 'offerings', within easy reach of our school kitchen.

If even one of those servants was excreting the bacilli of Bacillary Dysentery, the cysts of the amebae of Amebic Dysentery, or the eggs of Round or Hook worms, those clouds of flies could easily deliver them to the kitchen food. In addition, Indian people wipe their bottoms with their bare left hand (one reason it is very rude to touch anyone in India with your left hand, which in called 'sinister'). They do carry a small can of water to rinse the hand, but it is quite inadequate to eradicate these different kinds of organisms. I realized at once that bacilli, cysts and/or eggs could be easily carried to our food.

Later that day I presented my findings to Miss Money-Kyrle that the servants might be potential carriers of infection to our food and, in addition, the thousands of flies could also be carriers. I spared her the details of how I had come to form this opinion. She was not convinced. In her loud, stentorian, fog-horn delivery, she replied "All the servants have been 'tested' and are 'clean' and the kitchen has double-screen doors which prevent the entry of flies, if there were any", which she said she hadn't seen.

It must be said that Miss Money-Kyrle was a loyal and well-intentioned Anglican lady of wealthy English county stock, educated at an exclusive girls school, who was 'doing her bit' for the church in volunteering for several years as the house mother of this inter-denominational language school. She was a heavy-set, middle aged woman, with a deep, upper-class English voice who wanted no trouble during her tenure and made it abundantly clear that she regarded my advice, as the opinion of just another 'nuisance of a Scotsman'. The centuries old upper class English (Norman) approach to problems which they don't understand, certainly applied in this case as she concluded our discussions with "Why can't you just leave things alone, when nothing can be done about it? After all this is India!". At that point I realized that if things were to improve I would need to employ greater skill and tact.

Since she refused to have the servants stools tested, my first effort was to prove the prevalence of the flies. I found time to construct a 2x 1ft, double-chambered fly trap as designed by the British Army Medical Corps. Once installed within sight of our bedroom window and near the kitchen, it collected thousands of flies a day. After two days it was choked up with flies and I asked Miss Money-Kyrle to come and have a look. At first she refused, but since I had raised the topic at the lunch table with everyone present, in the end, she relented. With several other students in tow she went to view the fly trap. She was shocked and repelled by the unpleasant sight, but now had to admit that there were thousands of flies near our kitchen. My first point had been made. But what about her contention that the double-screened doors would prevent the entry of any flies?

The servants knew all students were occupied during meal preparation time, so felt safe in negating the usefulness of the annoying double-screen doors. One day, I found an excuse for leaving class early, so as not to arouse any suspicions among the staff, and Miss Money-Kyrle, who was often reading in her room and able to see any movements around the front of the building. I crawled around to the back and observed the double-screened doors from some distance. What I saw clinched my suspicions. The kitchen help was laying out on the bare hard earth, our portions of salad (lettuce etc.) and other food with many flies alighting on the food. In addition, in order to more easily carry the food out and in to the inadequately small kitchen, she had propped both screen doors open. The flies were everywhere. I was now able to prove to Miss Money-Kyrle that the screen doors were being improperly used. Nevertheless, she remained unwilling to have the servants stools tested again as she didn't want to incur unnecessary expense which would only upset the campus accountant. The Accountant, Mr. Moulton, was a rather irascible red-haired Englishman whose unenviable job was to try and keep expenses down to levels which the supporting missionary organizations back in England were able to meet. 'England' for Mr. Moulton was a generic word used to cover the USA, Scotland, Northern Ireland, Denmark, Sweden, Canada, Australia, as well as England.

In the face of such obfuscation my next move was to summon the power of the masses, so to speak. One evening after our evening meal, half a dozen students were complaining of diarrhea and asked my opinion. I explained the situation and my findings. Most of them agreed that the servants had to be tested and that the screen doors had to be properly used. But several still held to the view 'it is God's will'. While I have faith in the Almighty I have always believed in the age-old adage that 'God helps them that help themselves'. Unfortunately, I still did not have 100% support which I needed to get Miss Money-Kyrle to act.

It was several weeks later that an American girl, a missionary from, I think, the Assembly of God church, who was not the type to be too polite if she felt upset, contracted a really bad bout of dysentery. One week-end she had visited a hospital of her own mission and been tested. They found a bad infection of Amebic Dysentery and she was in danger of being invalided back to the USA. She was madder than hell. As often happens in this complacent world it took this girl's anger and outrage to provide the necessary impetus to make Miss Money-Kyrle have the servants stools tested.

When she asked me for assistance, I made the necessary arrangements for the tests. The cook and one servant both had Amebic dysentery cysts in their stools which were also full of Roundworm and Hookworm eggs, as I had expected.

At last the cause of all our illnesses had become clear and I had the opportunity to gain the cooperation of Miss Money-Kyrle in ensuring annual stool testing of the servants would be carried out, plus proper use of the double screen doors and sterilization (just in case) of salad vegetables in potassium permanganate. The latter turned the lettuce a pale purple which was not well received, but was accepted reluctantly by my colleagues. Gaining the confidence of the servants was a challenge to my basic Tamil abilities, especially explaining to them that the positive tests and treatment made their jobs more, not less, secure.

The dysentery rate among the students fell to zero, thus, happily ending the dysentery crisis. Miss Money-Kyrle and Mr. Moulton however, were never too happy about me afterwards. No word of thanks was ever spoken, nor letters of thanks from missionary organizations with regard to the thousands of dollars saved. This often, maybe always, happens when one solves a crisis which would not have occurred if the 'powers that be' had been on the ball in the first place. The unease of Miss Money-Kyrle and Mr. Moulton could be easily explained when one realized how many previous new missionaries who had passed through the Language School had been permanently disabled and even invalided home by their ignorance and inflexibility. I would be left with a permanent degree of colon weakness because of my bout of dysentery. There were a number of other health incidents which I attended to. I will not comment on these as they were about fellow missionaries and of a confidential nature. But another public health matter stood out which I will call 'The Milk Incident'.

QUALITY is all about standards, and standards are often set by those most likely to benefit from them. Such was the case in the matter of milk at the Language School.

Some time after arriving at the school, during meal times, there were heated discussions about 'Indian milk'. One American lady who was in the process of weaning her infant son, was particularly upset about what she said was the poor quality of the milk. Miss Money-Kyrle, dear old soul, immediately jumped to defend the honour of Indian cows. They were, she said just as good as any American ones, of this she was absolutely certain.

The young American mother, who was an American Congregational missionary was not to be dissuaded. Most of us agreed with her that the milk did seem a bit insipid. Miss Money-Kyrle and the cook, who received the milk every morning were adamant that the milk came direct from the cow, so it had to be of good quality. I suspected, as did others, that somehow it was being diluted. The question was how?

The American mother, a woman in her early twenties, somehow managed to procure a milk hygrometer. This was an expensive item and not one which we European missionaries had the funds to buy, even if we had known where to get one in the city of Bangalore. One morning, at breakfast she produced the said hygrometer with a flourish and 'hey presto' it showed that our milk was fifty percent below par. At last we had proof that appeared to show Indian cows were producing only fifty percent milk. Miss Money-Kyrle as a tried and true English woman, immediately questioned the accuracy of the American hygrometer.

This presented an immediate challenge to me as a scientifically trained person. I was quite sure that, as Miss Money-Kyrle had maintained, that Indian cows' milk was as good as any other, so there had to be some skulduggery somewhere. This occasioned another early morning sojourn around the Language School. Well before dawn about 4.45am, I crept from the dormitory, very slowly and quietly. The wooden beams easily creaked and might startle any one of a dozen or more sensitive and virginal lady missionaries, including Miss Money-Kyrle, to raise a hue and cry that there was a night prowler. Happily I made it out into the pitch black tropical night and, as I had previously planned, positioned myself behind a bush, precisely opposite the kitchen's back door, where I had been led to understand, the farmer every morning brought his cow to be milked directly into the cook's large milk can.

Soon I heard the unmistakeable breathing sounds of a large lumbering beast approaching. It was led by a diminutive boy and the farmer himself, towards the kitchen door. It was 'our' cow I was sure, even in the pitch darkness. It stood between me and the kitchen door where the cook greeted the farmer and agreed how much milk was needed. The little boy, who as was customary in hot South Indian villages, wore only a shabby gray shirt which just covered his bottom, held the cow by its rein.

The farmer knelt down, positioned the can and began to milk the valuable fluid into it. The squirts produced a regular and reassuring sound on the inside of the can. "Squirt-Squirt", "Squirt-Squirt" it went, I began to feel that I had misjudged the situation and that maybe these poor undernourished beasts somehow did produce dilute milk.

Then something about the little boy suddenly took my attention; a certain movement became apparent to me, a movement not related to the control of the cow's head and rein. I craned as close as was safe and as my eyes became totally dark adapted I realized that I was witnessing a highly skilled performance, which one had to see to believe. Working in perfect time with the farmer's squirts, the little boy was aiming a similar stream of fluid from a thin bamboo pipe into the milk can. This pipe came from a bulging bag which was concealed beneath the little gray shirt. The rhythmic squeezing of the bag projected a stream of what I was now sure was water into the can every time the farmer pretended to milk the cow's other udder. The timing and illusion was magical. I had to restrain a sigh of admiration. The performance completed, the little boy slowly led the cow away down the path and out of the compound.

I waited until the cook was safely inside and had shut the door. Then I crept stiffly away into the glimmering darkness, before the dawn light could reveal my under-cover activities. Later, after breakfast I mentioned my observations to some other students, including the American girl's husband. We agreed, rather than reveal the whole deception we would insist that the language school purchase a milk hygrometer and have the cook use it every day at milking time and then again when the milk jug was placed on the breakfast table.

That fixed the problem and from then on we drank a hundred percent pure milk, at least while we were there. I have little doubt that when we had all scattered to our work stations around South India that 'somehow' by an inexplicable accident the hygrometer would disappear and the milk would return to its 'true quality'. Ah, the magic and mystery of India.

The time quickly passed. We had six months full-time study before our First Tamil Examination. It was difficult, but knowing that success as a doctor would depend, to a great extent, on fluency in the language, spurred me on. Frances also studied the language, but I sensed she was not as enthusiastic. We both passed the exam. Of course for me it was only the beginning. I was expected to study on the job for a further period in order to take the Second Year Tamil Examination. Still lingering unanswered was whether I even had a job in South India and whether this language study would be used.

The Language School time presented us with many positives and some negatives, but in all it was a most enjoyable experience. During this time, as noted above, we contracted Bacillary Dysentery (Shigellosis), at least once. I also got Dengue fever (Break-bone Fever) for about a week, but managed to keep studying. I likely got it from one of the servants families that I visited and treated in their homes. Medical and nursing missionaries in those days inevitably contracted some of the diseases which they were treating, as they lived all day in an atmosphere of a variety of tropical infections and other diseases. Only by careful preventive methods and an attempt to maintain a high level of immune resistance, could one decrease the likelihood of infection. But there are occasions when it is not possible or politic to refrain from contact with ones patients. I discovered, many doctors in India, avoid touching patients often getting a nurse to do the touching or when having to touch, they had a fine piece of cloth placed over the patient's skin, as for example when examining the heart, by palpation or when using a stethoscope. As medical missionaries we touched our patients just as we would touch members of our own family, there were no distinctions. In my time the strict taboos related to so many simple actions in Indian society, were unacceptable to Christian missionaries, but I shall not detail them, as I am sensitive to the feelings of Hindus, who form the vast majority of people in India. As the six months came to a close we were pleased to have passed our language examination and to have weathered the various challenges at the school. Thus, it was a welcomed break to be invited for a brief visit with relatives in another part of India, prior to leaving Bangalore and being posted to a hospital on the Plains.

Aunt Pearl and Uncle Tommy sent their chauffeur all the way from their Rubber Plantation in Kerala on the west coast of Southern India where they had a beautiful hilltop estate. We had a wonderful few days visiting with them. Aunt Pearl and

Uncle Tommy were my favorite relatives. Uncle Tommy was the President of the Rubber Planter's Association of South India. His plantation was the only one in which the Moplas (Moslem workers in that area) did not strike against the unfair treatment of the European planters. They were also friends of Nawaharlal Nehru, the Prime Minister of India after Ghandi. I could write a book on what both of them did in a dedicated life of service to India from about 1910 to 1960. A truly remarkable couple. Our break was brief and it was time to get on with my missionary work, so we headed back to Bangalore.

As I focused on the fact that Dr. Azariah had been appointed to the position to which I had been sent in Kanchipuram, and that therefore an alternative hospital would have to be found to which I could be sent, the magnitude of my circumstances registered. The underlying question was whether my situation was created by the ineptitude of the Head Quarters in Edinburgh or whether Rev. Shaw had created the problem. It would transpire that it was Rev. Shaw. Without notifying the Edinburgh office, a deal had been struck by Rev. Shaw so that Dr. Azariah would become the superintendent of the hospital, a deal which supposedly would gain him political points in the region. The assumption was that I could be reassigned to something else. But that proved untenable when the Rainy Hospital would not accept a male physician. The Church of Scotland had no place to send me and, with no appointment, they did not have a mission house for us either. At that point, I felt we would soon be sailing back to Britain.

This process of indigenization (i.e. appointing Indians to former missionary positions) had begun seven years after India got its independence, just prior to my arrival. Such change was creating obfuscation on many fronts; senior missionaries did not want to face the possibility of an early retirement, Indians didn't want to lose the money that came with the missionary positions, and church headquarters were still living in the past and felt the young churches were not capable of being independent. As a result, there were the obvious miscommunications. I simply fell into one of the inevitable cracks. Nevertheless, I was not prepared to quit and kept hoping for a miracle, and one came.

The Church of South India had a medical advisory committee, which supervised the dozens of American, British, Swedish, Danish, Canadian, Australian and New Zealand mission hospitals in the five States of South India. Its chairman was Dr. Julius Savarirayan, the Medical superintendent of the Scudder Memorial

Hospital in Ranipet. Dr. Julius was a very fine doctor and Christian. His grandfather had been a convert from Hinduism, in fact one of the few Brahmin priest converts. His father had been a Christian Pastor. He had received his medical training in India and the United States, under the auspices of the Reformed Church of America (the American version of the Dutch Reformed Church).

It became obvious that Rev. Shaw had landed the medical advisory committee in a pickle of trouble, by his machinations in getting Dr. Azariah into the Kanchipuram hospital instead of me. I later learned that Dr. Julius was not at all happy with Rev. Shaw, who was politicking to improve his chances of being the next Moderator of the Church of South India. In my naivety, I never thought of politicking rearing its ugly head in a Christian missionary context. Alas, I would learn in time that there are as many ruthless Machiavellian clergy as there are in any other walk of life, maybe more, since they can more easily get away with it.

Dr. Julius was a stalwart man of Christian integrity and he offered to have me go to his busy hospital at Ranipet, and he would find a house for us for up to two years, during which time the Church of Scotland, and Rev. Shaw in particular, would have to find a place for me to work. Thus, it transpired that we left the relative coolness of Bangalore and travelled by train down to the hot, humid plains and the taluk (old Moghal word for an administrative area, used by the British) town of Ranipet, situated about a hundred miles inland from the Indian Ocean in the hot, dry upland plain, two miles north of the great river Palur. This was the area where the British army had defeated Tipoo Sahib, the great Mharata soldier, at the Battle of Arcot, one of the decisive battles which gave power to the Brits in India in the 18th century. My medical missionary work had finally begun in earnest.

Ranipet (Ranipettai in Tamil) was a market town for all the farmers in the area, comprising well over a million people scattered in thousands of little villages. There was a large Sulphuric Acid Chemical Plant in town, providing work to hundreds of men, and the inevitable Tannery, for processing the hides of the countless cows which died daily in a country which reveres the cow as holy. In time, more than sixty percent of Asia's leather production would come from Ranipet. The mixture of tannery, chemical plant and farmyard smells produced its own stimulating olfactory memories.

The Scudder Memorial Hospital was situated west of town and benefited from a south-west prevailing wind. It occupied a central location, as appropriate in a large compound , which also included a dozen houses or bungalows (Bungalow is the transliteration of the Tamil word for a free-standing house). All of these bungalows, we soon discovered, were fully occupied by Indian medical and other staff. Dr. Julius had commendably managed to totally indigenize the hospital staff, doctors, nurses, technicians and the host of other workers needed to run a busy 250 bed general hospital, with a 100-bed Tuberculosis (TB) isolation unit and a small Smallpox/Plague annex at the back of the property. The hospital had a well recognized School of Nursing. Decades before, it was founded by the Scudder family who provided family missionaries and financial support for the work of the American Reformed Church. For the next year and a half, I would basically be on loan from the Church of Scotland, joining the other three doctors to provide routine medical services.

Dr. Julius arranged the rental of an empty house, about half a mile from the hospital. The 'White House', as we named it, had been built for an assistant manager of the chemical plant. However, Mr. Briggs, the English manager of the plant had been unable to coax a Brit to work in post-independent India and eventually employed an Indian, who preferred to live in an Indian house nearer town. Unfortunately, the British architect contracted to design and build the White House, was not informed that it would be built in South India. So his European design was very different from the usual hot-climate requirements of deep verandahs, thick stone walls and shuttered, un-glazed windows. Thus, the sun beat relentlessly on the walls and windows, making the interior as hot as an oven. Air-conditioning had originally been planned, but that was out of the question on a missionary's salary. So, in our modern-looking, oven (home) we soon learned how to cope with day and night temperatures between 27°C (80°F) and 48°C (115°F) with 100% humidity all year round. We opened the windows, and with no shutters or mosquito-netting, a million insects, many bats and the occasional crow joined us at meal times and during the night.

Apart from the heat and the pervasive wild-life, the White House had its merits. It was after all 'out in the country' with a pleasant view of the nearby Yeri or lake. The lake was one of many irrigation reservoirs constructed as part of a thousand year old system used during the great era of the Pallava kings in Tamil Nadu.

These were developed for collecting the rain of the annual monsoon in October. It is probably one of the oldest, and still functioning, agricultural irrigation system in the history of the world.

We had to adapt quickly to the many natural challenges of India. Every morning one had to kick ones sandals to rouse any scorpions or large spiders from the toe-piece in which they like to spend the night. Snakes of course were common companions. The Cobra and the Krait are the two most poisonous varieties in South India. A most hair-raising event was when I almost tramped on a Krait as I stepped out of the front door. Another incident was when I came face to face with a cobra as I got out of the mission car, staring into its fanged jaws from an overhanging tree branch. In Tamil the cobra, which is sacred to Hindus, is called 'the good snake'. This is certainly a topic worthy of discussion on some dull wet day.

Then there were the pitiful shrieking howls of the pie dogs during the night as they slunk up to warm themselves against the walls of the house. Soon, I positioned two buckets of cold water on the little upstairs balcony wall, so that when the noise became unbearable I would creep out of my mosquito-netted bed and carefully peering over the parapet in the moonlight, aim a bucket-full right on top of several of these wretched animals, sending them howling in agony into the distant scrubby jungle.

There were also many colorful tropical birds to be seen and heard. The only one whose name I can still recall is the Hoopoo which makes a repeated, rather poignant "hoopoo" call, with emphasis on the first syllable. All I need to do is close my eyes and call "hoopoo-hoopoo" several times and I am back in Ranipet and India once again.

Not far from the house a dusty track marked the way to a distant village. One night not too long after our arrival, we were awakened by the sounds of a drunken brawl. Peering out across the moonlit scrub we saw the shadows of about a dozen men and women, shouting, laughing and screaming, as they lurched down the track towards their homes. Later we were told that they came from a 'drunken village'. Such villages are not unknown in India. No doubt for centuries some of the poor peasants sought temporary solace from the endless daily toil under the merciless sun, by imbibing lots of the beer which Tamils brew from the fruit of the noongoo palm.

Mrs. Shaw had arranged for us to have a servant lady, Jesumani, to do the cooking, marketing and cleaning. All Westerner people have to have servants in India. It is one way in which the so called wealthy Western people can subsidize the poor of the country. It's also a practical necessity as the servant ensures that you do not get cheated at the market. Jesumani was a large, pleasant widow, a Christian who, we discovered later, needed to escape from the sexual demands of her dead husband's brothers (an age-old custom in these parts). She worked reasonably well and she and Frances got along well, as far as I could discern, since I was only there at meal times. Jesumani always left to her little house in the late afternoon, leaving Frances to continue her knitting, sewing and endless reading.

A marriage that was in trouble three weeks after the wedding ceremony, began to flounder under the many challenges of India. My marriage had become little more than two people sharing the same house since our time at St.Colm's Missionary College in Edinburgh. In life, as most of us do, one just goes on, hoping things will somehow work out. I knew Frances was unhappy, a situation complicated by her silence.

Nevertheless, by the time we arrived in Ranipet, Frances was pregnant and came under the clinical care of my senior colleague, Dr. Julius Savarirayan. In February 1957, she was admitted to the Scudder Memorial Mission hospital to a private room on the upper floor. On the 10th she delivered a beautiful baby girl, who we would name Barbara Anne. She would later be baptized by the Minister in the local Ranipet Church of South India [1] in Tamil. She also had an Indian Birth Certificate.

Frances went through her first pregnancy reasonably well, but blamed Dr. Savarirayan for not preventing her from having any pain. This was unfortunate and unfair as no doctor routinely orders an anesthetic for a woman in labor, since it can jeopardize the baby by introducing unnecessary, and very powerful drugs into a normal process. The delivering doctor needs to give the mother the chance of having a natural childbirth, especially, if she is in excellent, robust health, which she was, but Frances insisted on an anesthetic. As it turned out, at the time of her delivery I had to administer a brief anesthetic.

Once home, Barbara, received much of her care from Jesumani, who did long hours of baby-sitting and became very fond of the baby.

In the mission field, it was customary for pregnant women to be relieved of any missionary activities six months before delivery and six months after. So, following Barbara's birth Frances had the luxury of having a servant to cook, care for the house and infant while she relaxed for six months.

For me, Tamil studies continued. I still had to pass the Second Year examination within the first three years of my service. I had to find, and pay, for a Tamil munshi (i.e. teacher) to come to my home several evenings each week for over an hour of study. My munshi was a Brahmin, Hindu, a science teacher at the Ranipet Secondary school, Mr. Venkatuchalam Ayyar. The Ayyars, the most prominent high caste Brahmin family of South India, had centuries old roots. They were partly Aryan and partly Dravidian, thus his thin, slightly pale features reflected the Hindus who, centuries before, invaded India from the north, gradually pushing south. The Hindus (Aryans) eventually, to some extent, subjugated the stocky, darker-skinned Dravidian Tamils.

Mr. Venkatuchalam Ayyar was a typical, polite, formal Brahmin gentleman, who cycled from town, joining me on the verandah, where we sat opposite each other on low chairs during these weekly classes. While the Indian custom was to sit cross-legged on the floor, the veranda concrete was too rough. We were both happier sitting on chairs. As the weeks progressed we steadily worked through the Senior, or Second Volume of a Tamil Primer. But I would learn more than Tamil from this fine gentleman.

Through our discussions I learned much about India and Hinduism, and he was interested in my Christian views in that very tolerant, charming and intellectual way, so delightfully typical of an educated Indian. I also discovered there were similarities. For instance I learned about 'popular Hinduism', which was similar to 'Rights of Passage' Christians; those people who see the church/temple as a social organization for Baptizing (or welcoming) their children into the organization, marrying family members, and providing burial services.

While Mr. Ayyar was expected to come on Mondays, Wednesdays and Fridays, some weeks he came unexpectedly on Tuesdays and Thursdays and sometimes he didn't appear at all. He never gave any explanation or apology and, I felt, he expected me to understand the reason. It was some weeks after we began that I came upon a book on Hinduism, called *Instrument and Purpose*. Written in English, by a Swedish missionary, it stated, in pain-staking Scandinavian detail, that in everyday Hinduism, everything, every act and every vagary of life, was or could be the instrument for a particular purpose. One had to be prepared to follow ones life according to certain rules which defined what one had to do and why. In one part of the book I found the answer to Mr. Ayyar's apparently unpredictable actions. I didn't quite get the hang of all his comings and goings, but enough to know that on certain days of the month, to do with the phases of the moon, it was inauspicious, that is, unlucky, to travel eastwards on a Monday or maybe westwards on a Wednesday. Mr. Ayyar lived east of the White House and so it transpired that on days in which it was unlucky to travel west he did not appear. I suppose that it would be rather like an Indian immigrant wondering why the mailman doesn't appear on a national holiday, except that in India such activities were individualized. Many Hindus believe implicitly in astrology.

This relationship with Mr. Ayyar was a positive one, but we would experience one of the negative features of life in India when a thief invaded our home.

One night we were asleep in the upstairs bedroom with Barbara in her little cot in an adjacent room. I awoke at some point and thought I heard an unusual sound, amidst the nighttime chorus, but since there was nothing more, I went back to sleep. In the morning we discovered that someone had broken in through the verandah door, not difficult to do in our British-type house, had made a meal of anything edible in our frig, and, I first assumed, left.

However during the day Frances realized that the intruder had stolen Barbara's little silver Baptismal mug, a gift from my parents. That was all he had taken, because that was all of any worth that we possessed. It turned out that the thief was a big criminal type from the underworld of Madras, who had been brought up in the Christian community, but had turned to crime. When he was back in Ranipet to see his folks he took occasion to steal whatever he could from all the missionaries' houses.

I should tell you that there were about ten American Reformed Church missionaries in the area, living in large bungalows. None of them worked in the hospital, but we met socially. They were mainly big tall Dutch Americans from Michigan and several from New England. In those days, these Americans each received twice the stipend of Scottish missionaries, the wives were also paid. This meant that each family had practically four times our income and, in addition, the generous American missionary societies sent out extra money for cars, children's education, camera equipment, projectors and other expensive equipment of various kinds. Our thief knew all about these people and their homes from his childhood days, and from his various relatives who were servants of their homes. There was much to steal, which was easily disposed of in the Madras Black Market. Someone must have told him about the new Scots doctor and, thinking that we would be as well off as our American colleagues, he included us in his night itinerary. What a disappointment, one small silver mug and a few bananas.

The next day, in the Outpatients Department I noticed a tall man appraising me and wondered why. I mentioned it to one of my Indian colleagues who confirmed that it was the thief. No doubt he had come to get a glimpse of this poor Scots missionary who hadn't had the decency to own more valuables. I later learned he had been caught in Madras, but none of the stolen items were ever found.

It was rather frightening for Frances, as he had been in our bedrooms and close to the baby. While I tried to ameliorate the incident by saying he wasn't a violent type, to ease her concern I arranged for, and paid, a night watchman to sleep outside, in front of the house. He was a Muslim, which was supposed to make him more fierce. I think he slept most of the night. I also had to be careful not to pour the cold water on him when I was scaring off the pie dogs. To his credit, we had no more thieves. Such help was essential as my full attention was now focused on my medical duties.

My routine now consisted of spending six days a week at the hospital with every fourth night on obstetric duty, and every fourth weekend on call. My day began at 6am and after Jesumani had served me a breakfast of Indian "cunji", I got on my bicycle and cycled down the dusty, cow trail to the hospital, in time for Morning Prayers in the hospital Chapel. From that time until I got home briefly at lunch and in the evening, practically everything was in Tamil. We sang hymns, prayed and had a Bible reading before setting out on Morning Ward Rounds at 7am, led by Dr. Julius.

The four doctors saw every patient, discussing their diagnosis, treatment and their discharge home. Ward rounds started in the Surgical wards, male and female, then moved to the Medical, Obstetric and Gynecological wards, then onto the Pediatric ward and finally the Tuberculosis isolation ward. It was thorough. I learned fast and first-hand all about tropical diseases and the differences in the presentation and management of many other diseases, in an Indian milieu. I could write a small treatise on Medicine in India.

The Outpatient (OPD) Clinic was conducted by two of us doctors until noon. Dr Rajendra Sunderaj (His first name was after one of the most illustrious Chola kings of South India), was always my colleague. He was Dr. Savarirayan's second in command and had been in the Indian Army, mainly north India, prior to coming to Ranipet. As a Tamil and as a Christian he was happy to be working in a

Christian (mission) hospital and back in his native State. He had recently married and was hoping to have a family. As is usually the case in countries in which missionaries have brought local people to a belief in Jesus Christ, even after they become Christians they retain many of their cultural customs and loyalties. This was also true in Western countries, centuries ago, although most European Christians have long forgotten that some of their day-to-day traditions are actually holdovers from a pre-Christian era.

In South India most Christians were converts from the outcaste level of the Hindu caste pyramid. Some were from a Sudra background (i.e. the lowest of the four castes) and a very few came from Brahmin priestly family backgrounds. The two main Brahmin families in Tamil Nadu were the more superior Ayyars who were paler, indicating their stronger genetic connection with the light-skinned Aryan invaders from the north, who ruled in South India from about 300 C.E. onwards, and the darker Nadars, who were of purer Dravidian blood. These matters were of course never talked about, but I learned from observation and reading. Dr. Sunderaj as a Nadar felt somewhat self-conscious about his darker Nadar color, and most particularly about his wife's complexion. She was a very beautiful woman, but whenever there was a photograph being taken she contrived to get into the shade and was thus able to blame that for her being so much darker than the Ayyar and/or Western missionary women. In addition the Sunderaj's house was at the opposite side of the hospital compound from the Ayyar members of staff, as if by chance. The Nadars always stated it was their preference. Such is the strength of centuries of caste distinctions in India. The word for caste in Sanskrit provides the clue to the problem. It can be written as, "runge" and means color.

The higher the caste the paler, the lower the darker. Happily I have never suffered from color-conscious racial prejudice and so had no difficulty dealing with people of any color, but this was not so for higher caste Indian people and also for many Caucasian 'white' people. Such bias is the fruit of ignorance and is always to be found in the less educated members of the human race.

Returning to our Outpatient Clinic, I can still see the lines of patients. Picture two long lines, male, female of all ages stretching out of a large room and along the side of the outside wall, in partial shade, all standing, or sitting cross-legged on the ground. There were no chairs, except for the two doctors. There was no privacy. The whole process of history-taking, examination and prescription of treatment was carried out with everyone listening. If a patient needed admission, then we would arrange it immediately, having previously discharged some patients during the ward rounds. If medicine was required, we wrote a prescription and told the patient to go and get it at our hospital Dispensary (i.e. Pharmacy), down the hall. Most of our medicines were very, very cheap and for those with absolutely no money, they were free. The same medicines down in downtown Ranipet, cost several times more.

It took me a day or two to get used to examining all my outpatients standing up, but that was the custom. As I indicated, more serious cases were admitted and could be examined at the bedside. In this way we saw up to a hundred patients by noon, when we closed down until 3pm, during the hottest hours of the day, which averaged 32°C (90°F) to 40°C (105°F) in 100% humidity eleven months of the year.

From 3pm until 5pm the clinic continued, but there were fewer patients, as most came from the many surrounding villages and had set out on foot at dawn and needed the afternoon hours to walk home before darkness fell around 6 pm. There were no street lights and robbers were always a danger at night.

The two doctors not at the Outpatient Clinic were in the Operating Room from about 9am until the list was finished, usually around 1pm. They would be operating on surgical, gynecological and pediatric inpatients, interrupted by any emergencies which arrived at the front door of the hospital. The surgery covered a full range of General Surgical and Gynecological conditions, all kinds of trauma as well as Phrenic Crush, an introduction of air into the pleural cavity, for Tuberculosis patients. We had Nitrous Oxide inhalation anesthesia, due to the generous donation of anesthetic machines from the American Reformed Mission. Two men had been trained in basic anesthesia technique and that made surgery easier and safer than the old Ether anesthesia which I would use later in North India. I benefited from an immense amount of learning and experience in surgical procedures, with three sessions a week plus emergencies around the clock, personally operating at the rate of about one thousand operations a year.

Every fourth night one of us doctors was on duty, sleeping in a cot in the hospital. Night work consisted of mainly carrying out obstetric deliveries, usually about five to six per night. At that time in India a baby was born every few seconds.

I never liked Obstetrics because of all the pain which the women experience in order to give birth. The Birthing Room at the Scudder Memorial Hospital was a large bare area with few windows, with about ten to twelve beds. Every night all or most of these beds were filled with woman in labor. South Indian women, like Italians, believe in the loudest possible shouts of pain and so the room echoed continuously with their multiple tortured cries of pain. One night in four, delivering these little peasant women, many just girls, put me off Obstetrics for ever. I preferred surgery where I could anaesthetize my patients and relieve their pain.

In addition to the above routine medical activities, we held outdoor Leprosy Clinics once a week in the compound and once every three weeks, we travelled out into the countryside, at the hottest time of the day. We would stop the hospital van at the roadside, then walk into the scrub jungle for about twenty yards to a small clearing. There we set up a table for the records clerk. Once set up, the 'clerk', a male nurse, shouted out a number (i.e. "One"). Within a few moments, a figure would appear from among the trees, often hiding his/her face with their vaishti or sari , and slowly approach us. The clerk noted who number 'One' was in the Treatment Record Book. I would talk quietly to the patient, finding out how they were getting along, examining them and prescribing the needed Sulphone pills which had recently been developed for treating leprosy. The clerk then gave them a bottle of pills and the person quietly, furtively disappeared back into the jungle. The treatment and drugs were, of course, free.

We then waited for several long minutes to give them time to get away, then the next number was called and the process repeated. We saw about ten patients at each of five or six roadside/jungle stops during the afternoon. Unlike the other patients the excessively hot time of the day was best for these poor secret leprosy patients, because most other people were not about.

These, what I will call 'Jungle' patients, were people who had contracted leprosy which their family members or co-workers had not yet recognized. Maybe a small patch on the skin or a numbness due to nerve damage. They knew that inevitably once their family and community realized that they had leprosy they would be cast out of their family and village, for ever. Such is the fear, the terror of the disease. The leprosy patients whom we saw openly at the hospital in a clearing about a hundred yards away from other people, were those who had been cast out of their communities and were living in the jungle, begging for food whenever they could. Many just died.

It was no different in Europe in past centuries. Britain gradually got rid of the disease by throwing out of the island anyone with leprosy. Prior to that a leper was ostracised from all communities and had, on pain of death, to ring a bell as s/he walked past any habitation. We in the West are not immune from this disease. The last leprosy hospital in Canada only closed in New Brunswick in the 1930s and there are always a few leprosy cases being treated in isolation wards in hospitals in the southern states of the United States.

What is perhaps not understood is that unless one has long-term close skin contact with a leper, or actually touches an open leprosy sore with a finger which has an open cut, and/or if one sticks that finger in ones eye, it is perfectly safe to touch a leprosy patient. I saw hundreds of lepers during my years in India and shook hands or otherwise touched them so that they felt cared for and not outcastes of society. Of course, I strictly observed the rule of not exposing a cut finger or rubbing my eye during such clinics. This latter was the biggest danger, as in the excessive hot and humid climate of India, one was continually sweating and beads of sweat constantly dripped off ones brow into ones eyes unless wiped away. I developed the knack of wiping my brow on the upper part of my short-sleeved shirt.

It was for this reason that Christian missionaries also developed Leprosy Hospitals or Leprosaria in different parts of India. In these special hospitals lepers could stay for the prolonged periods needed to treat the disease and, before the advent of Sulphones in the 1950s, many had to spend the rest of their lives in such facilities. Dr. Cochrane, a missionary of the Church of Scotland, whom I mentioned above, started the first leprosarium in South India at Chingleput. He later was honoured and appointed as the first president of the World Leprosy Association. The Church of Scotland also developed a Leprosarium in Kalimpong.

In addition to our medical duties, the four doctors 'tucked in' lectures for the nurses and technicians who were trained at the hospital. The lectures were given in basic English and that is when I developed a simplified practical surgical nursing course. Later when I went to Kalimpong in the Eastern Himalayans, where the nurses had less English and all lectures had to be in Nepali, I made written copies of that surgical nursing course, which the nurses could commit to memory. Upon receiving such written material, I was pleased to note that all the nurses were able to pass their All India surgical nursing exams, for the first time.

Thus my days in Ranipet were full of worthwhile service, healing the sick and poor of one small part of India. That was why I had volunteered and it was an immensely satisfying, if often difficult life, as a doctor. It was what I had expected and what I looked forward to continuing for the rest of my career. However, as has been often truly said, life is full of change, nothing lasts for ever.

In the course of my work, there were occasional visits on business, to the cities of Madras, Vellore and Madurai. Visits to Madras were mainly to Mission or Church of South India meetings. Visits to Vellore were regarding medical matters, as the Christian Medical College was our tertiary care referral centre. I visited

Madurai twice; once in search of a driver's license for India. I could go on at length about such visits but will confine myself to the first Madurai trip.

When I had arrived in India I held an International Driving license. This, I was assured in the United Kingdom, by Indian Consular officials, covered India. However when I visited the Taluk government license office in Vellore, the Police Superintendent of Motor Vehicle Licenses, informed me that this was not recognized in the state of Tamil Nadu. Despite my showing him a statement from the Indian authorities he was adamant. We looked across his large office desk at each other, his expressionless face and large black eyes staring unblinkingly gave me the impression that he might be under the influence of some narcotic. I knew that many Indians habitually took Bhang (Marajuana). I was trapped. It appeared he held all the aces. Next he quietly and slowly extended his right hand, palm upwards across his desk, in the age-old gesture seeking a bribe. Searching for something to say, I said, "What are you suggesting ?" In reply he answered, "fifty rupees". Gathering up my apparently useless papers, I stood up and turning on my heels, left his office.

In the outer office I asked what I had to do to apply for a driving license and sit a driving test and was given an application form and told to join a very long queue outside in the mid-day sun. It was about thirty-five degrees Centigrade in the shade and in the full sunlight and 100% humidity of a South Indian day, I was soon soaking with sweat.

The queue, snailed along as the afternoon wore on. All of those in the line-up were short, slim Tamils of the servant or message-boy level. I quickly understood that no person of position would ever choose to be there, nor have the time to do so. Stubborn and determined to do things 'the proper way', I endured. Eventually, after about two hours, I reached a dirty little office in which a bored-looking, sweating, middle-aged Brahmin official sat cross-legged behind his table.

He said curtly in English, "What do you want ?" I passed him my application form. He smiled with a sneer saying, "You are foreigner. You must get a permission letter from a High Court Judge, before I can process your application". I answered, "Where is the High Court ? . He replied with a gesture, pointing vaguely, "In the city". Then ignoring me shouted "Next". That was that.

I asked a bystander in Tamil, the location of the High Court. He explained that it was about a mile away in another part of town. By this time 'the day was far spent' and I knew my drivers license would have to wait until another time. I returned to Ranipet after wasting a whole day. There I explained my problem to Julius, but it was obvious from his reaction that he could not help me. I knew he understood I had not given the Superintendent the expected bhaksheesh (i.e. bribe). So the matter was left until a later date when I could find time.

About a month later I set out for the Taluk High Court in Vellore. It was another hot dusty, humid day and there was a large crowd of people milling about in front of the steps up to the entrance of a rather imposing, pillared building, a legacy of the British Raj. Making my way up the steps and into the large forecourt through jostling crowds of anxious people, all no doubt seeking their own bit of justice, I reached the door into the Court itself. The armed police guard asked me in Tamil what or who I wanted. I explained. Looking almost apologetic, he opened the door ushering me into a large, stiflingly hot court room and pointed towards an official sitting near the raised platform, saying, "See him".

I walked rather awkwardly down the centre aisle more or less straight towards the judge, who looked at once surprised and irritated at my intrusion. Trying to avoid his gaze, I hunched over and soon reached the official who heard my whispered query. He gave me a helpless glance and told me to wait at the side of the court until he called me. I sidled over to the relevant shadows of the side aisle and stood waiting, a tall young white man trying, without much success, to be inconspicuous in this large hall of dark skinned Tamils, many carrying on whispered conversations about their case or petition. I had the sinking feeling that I was in for another long wait.

Much to my surprise and even shock after several minutes in which the judge asked a flood of questions to a petitioner, this being a civil court and thankfully not a criminal one, he shouted out to me in English, "Who are you and what do you want ?" I hustled over to stand beneath his imposing presence and explained briefly my predicament, that I had been told by the Drivers Licensing official to present myself at his court. He exploded in anger and shouted that I had no business coming there and that he would not under any circumstances help me, rounding off his salvo of invective saying, "Now, get out of my court !". Needless to say I did and quickly.

If I had been in any doubt that the days of the British Raj and British power were over, that would have convinced me. But as one who completely sympathized with Indian independence, I understood his right to treat me in any way he pleased. After all this was but one very small indignity to a white man soon after this judge and millions of other Indians had spent years suffering worse insults from so many members of the occupying British authorities, just recently terminated. However I was still no further on in my quest for an Indian driving license. There was some urgency for me to get a license, as Rev. Shaw was wanting me to use his mission car when he was off on furlough expected to start in the very near future.

Thinking over a possible strategy I needed advice from a friend. Immediately I thought of Bishop Leslie Newbiggin, a Presbyterian missionary from Barrow-in-Furness, who I respected and had talked with several times. I contacted him by telephone at his office in Madurai, half-a-days journey by bus south of Ranipet. He reassured me that he could help and to come to his office at a convenient time.

Being a man I could trust, on an agreed day I set off very early, arriving in the late morning at Madurai. I was soon at the Diocesan Office. Bishop Newbiggin was a man of average height and build with a warm, outgoing personality. His greeting calmed my concerns over my drivers license. He took my application forms and invited me to have a cup of tea, saying something quietly to a servant, before joining me.

We had only begun to chat when he rose as an elderly South Indian pastor entered the room and was graciously invited by Leslie to join us at tea, which the elderly, white-haired pastor did. Leslie introduced him as the once, now retired, Collector of Madras State. He had been the chief administrator for the State and the most powerful official in all Tamil Nadu since the British left eight years before. He was also a Christian who had chosen to train and serve as a lowly village pastor in the Diocese of Madurai in his retirement. He looked over my papers, wrote a few words and signed his name saying that my application was now complete. All I had to do was have a brief driving test back in Vellore. This took about two minutes. We talked pleasantly for another few minutes then quietly he excused himself. Leslie's response was "now you'll be able to drive in India".

He being a busy man, after tea I excused myself and returned to Ranipet by bus, sandwiched on the long journey between Tamil villagers and others, packed into a large Mercedes Benz bus, travelling at about seventy miles per hour along the dusty roads of Tamil Nadu. After India got its independence the Germans got a huge contract to supply thousands of beautiful, powerful Mercedes-Benz buses, which could be seen from one end of India to the other.

A few weeks later I made my way, for the third time, to Vellore in search of a driving license. I had great trust in the retired Collector's signature, but was still wondering what would transpire as I entered the licensing office. The policeman looked at my form, looked at me with interest and a quiet smile, stood up and asked me to follow him out to a car. He told me to get into the driver's seat, while he got into the passenger's seat and said "Drive". I had only just started the engine and gone about twenty yards when he said, "Turn left" (India drives on the left side of the road as in Britain), which I did. Then a small block further on he again said "Turn left". This was repeated twice more in short order and I found myself back in front of the licensing office, where he turned to me, gave me my license, shook my hand and said good day. Months of waiting and numerous trips and it was all over in a few minutes. It is true to say that it is good to know people with influence. That is, for better or worse, true anywhere, but most certainly in India.

At last I could drive Ellis Shaw's mission car until he would return after his year of leave. Driving the car was a saga in itself, since the car was a virtual wreck and due to be replaced. Mr. Shaw's plan, which he did not discuss with me, was to get me to keep this wreck functioning for a year at my own expense, so he could, under mission rules, get a brand new one on his return. Many times it broke down and I had to find ingenious methods to patch it up and keep it running.

Shaw's car, being so unreliable, was only used for short trips. Fortunately, I was able to use the hospital van and travel with Dr Julius to other hospitals in Tamil Nadu, Andra Pradesh and Kanada (old Mysore) state, about which I could talk for hours.

In the nearer vicinity to Ranipet I visited the great Palar River, which for almost eleven and a half months of the year is a huge dry river bed about a mile across. In fact about seven feet down it runs as an underground stream all year. This fact allowed Dr. Julius to take me one day in the Kattiri Kalum (phonetics for the season when the heat cuts you) with his wife and daughter to the dry river bed where a pipe brought cold almost ice-cold water from the underground river, in that period of hot 40°C (105°F) plus 100% humidity from May through September. The feeling of that icy water flowing over one is exquisite and we all took a turn getting soaked. Of course only Dr. Julius and I stripped off into our already donned swimming trunks. Mrs. Julius and her daughter just got soaked, in their saris, but in the heat they dried quickly.

Another time I visited Arcot a few miles from Ranipet, where the British defeated the powerful Marhatta Moslem king, Tipoo Sahib, which marked the beginning in earnest, of the British occupation of India.

On a hottish day I took three of the young men from the Scudder Memorial Hospital, one lab. technician, Balasundaram and two male nurses to Sion Malai and a little village church which they wanted me to see. The village church was, architecturally Christian at one end and Hindu at the other. The hill was another example of the indigenization of Christianity into India. As one climbed up a steep path, the ten commandments were written in large letters on placards at intervals up to the top where a small church (or rather a shrine) was built with both Western and Indian architectural components. This was where I understood the truth about the indigenization of Christianity during the centuries since its inception.

Finally, the day came for me to return Shaw's mission car when his year-long furlough was over. As I turned into his driveway in front of his bungalow, the car gave a final death rattle and would not move another inch. Shaw was not at home. So I mustered about twenty servants and nearby farm workers and with much persuasion, we lifted and carried the old Standard all the way up the driveway and deposited it at his front door. I heard later that was its final, ignominious resting place. What happened after that I do not know. Shaw never mentioned the car again. My time at the Scudder Memorial Hospital in Ranipet with Dr.Julius Savarirayan was coming to a close. The agreement was that within the year Rev. Ellis Shaw would find a hospital location for me, in lieu of Kanchipuram. The question was where?

As the time approached, Julius asked me if I would stay on, but I felt that my loyalties and responsibility lay at a place designated by the Presbyterian Church mission. I also indicated that I believed wherever possible an Indian Christian should be filling the positions in mission hospitals, schools etc. While surprised by my reply I could see he was pleased, as most missionaries wanted to hold on to whatever position and power they already had. We agreed that he would look for another doctor. A few months later, Dr. Jimmy Selvanayagam arrived to learn the ropes from me prior to my departure. Jimmy was a delightful guy and I was sorry that I would not be working with him. It was the right decision for me, for Dr. Selvanayagam and the hospital. Jimmy went on to take his F.R.C.S. in Edinburgh and in time became the Medical Superintendent of the Scudder Memorial Hospital.

Thus, the time came for our departure to Kilpauk, a suburb of Madras. Dr. Julius arranged a pleasant farewell party and off we went to live temporarily at the mission house in Kilpauk, a suburb of the city of Madras, where I would wait until Rev. Shaw found a position for me. I would keep busy studying for my Second Tamil Examination.

MISSION TO INDIA

THE Scots Mission House at Kilpauk was a huge old colonial mansion, built and originally occupied years before by some senior official of the British Raj in Madras. After Independence, the building was sold to our mission 'for a song'. It stood in acres of park land, had a wide driveway up to an imposing arched doorway like an aristocratic house in Britain. The imposing two and a half storey building was stretched out in two long wings. We entered the huge front porch and walked through the large double doors, wondering silently how the Church of Scotland could afford the upkeep of such a grand edifice. It was not long before we understood.

We were met by an aged Indian servant who showed us into a vast almost empty room and directed us to two very old and ordinary wooden chairs. This room proved to be most of one wing of the ground floor. It had no other furniture, no drapes or curtains. The tropical sun, with no barrier, poured through the iron barred windows creating an intensely hot environment.

Presently an elderly, slightly stooping, lady appeared and said in a matter of fact, rather gruff accented voice, "You must be the Robertsons ?". Without waiting for a reply, she continued, "I am Miss Hermansen, this is my house. You will stay upstairs in one of the bedrooms". Thus said, she beckoned us to carry our things up a large stairway and into a suffocatingly hot and stuffy room in which two small cot beds sat adjacent to a small table and two chairs.

She said, in her Danish accent, "You vill be fine heer and you (meaning me) vill stoody at ze table". Finally she announced that dinner would be served at 5pm, as she went to her bed early in the other wing. With that she turned and left, clomping her way down the wooden stairs.

Miss Hermansen, a Danish missionary, had somehow come to be in the Church of Scotland mission. After running a craft school for children and young women for many years, she was within months of her well-earned retirement after about forty years as a missionary. As we got to know her a little over the succeeding months we found her to be a woman of sterling character with a quiet, dry sense of humour. She had a very strong Danish accent which somehow added to her interesting ambience in that austere and almost empty building.

We ate at one end of a long table, the only furniture left in the other ground floor wing. She sat at one end, so that, she said, she could see who was coming towards her in the huge dark room. The old servant had found two chairs for us next to her and a kind of cradle in which Barbara lay. As was the custom in such colonial houses the kitchen was set back about twenty yards from the rear of the building, so that the smells of cooking and the chatter of servants would not disturb the tranquility of the Sahibs dinner table conversation. What this meant was that the old servant had to carry the food on a tray all the way across to the house then all the way to the other end of the huge table where Miss Hermansen had chosen to strategically place herself. Her assessment of the meal was reflected in her comment, '"Zee soop iss aalvays colt, by zee toim it arrrifs". It was something out of the past and yet it spoke volumes of the end of an era.

On Sundays we went in Miss Hermansen's small cramped British car, to the Scots Kirk. The Kirk had originally been established to serve the spiritual needs of the large population of Scottish businessmen and civil servants in Madras in colonial times. It had been decided in Edinburgh to continue to supply money and a minister even though there were by then no Scots left, except one or two elderly missionaries. The majority of the small congregation which scattered itself around the spacious sanctuary were Anglo-Indians, clinging to their 'British' heritage. It was all rather sad. Miss Hermansen preferred to go there and worship in English, rather than worship in a Tamil church with its increasingly different music and order of service, as Indian Christians proceeded to indigenize their places of Christian worship.

She sat next to the central aisle, with us next to her. I shall always remember with a smile the young Scottish minister, called Henderson, who made his processional entry down the central aisle wearing only a pair of boxer shorts under his flimsy black cassock, which was never properly tied at the back. At every service, as Rev. Henderson passed by her pew, Miss Hermansen would say in a loud hoarse whisper, "Again, no trouaserrs !" Shorts were, in her opinion, totally out of place and I had to agree. However, from another point of view, it did seem to fit the general air of unreality. Here was a Scots Church service being conducted as if it was in Glasgow or Edinburgh, with no acknowledgement of its Indian setting, and with only two Scots present. Getting someone for such a position must have been extremely difficult. Rev. Henderson later told me he came out for a three year stint 'in the Tropics', aware of the good golf course nearby and prepared with three years of sermons in his suitcase.

The days upstairs in that stifling hot room passed slowly as I crammed for my exams, while Frances, now without a servant, had to look after Barbara.

Kilpauk shall be memorable for two happenings, one good and one bad. First it was where one day I stretched out my arms towards Barbara, saying "Walk to Daddy" and with a smile and a chuckle she took her first steps. She was a happy wee girl with dark brown hair and green-brown eyes. She was like both of us and neither of us, as any good child should be, contriving to be her charming self.

That was the happy memory. The not so happy event was an unexpected bout of illness. What occurred, I realized in hindsight, was the culmination of months of stress to which I had been subjected, but had studiedly ignored.

At night, as it was unbearably hot indoors, we set up the mosquito-netted cots on the flat verandah, to catch the slightest whiff of breeze. So one night when I went to sleep with, as usual, my lungi loosely covering my groin area, I dozed off enjoying the slight breeze at a midnight temperature of 42°C (106°F). However, that particular night the temperature fell as I slept, to about 27^0 C (80'F). Now everything is relevant and although 27°C (80°F) might seem comfortable for those in the west, that fall of 15°C (26°F) gave me a severe chill in the kidneys. About 6am I awoke shivering with acute pain in my lower abdomen and a desperate need to pass urine. I arose and went to the bathroom, but could not under any circumstances pass urine. The pain became steadily worse and I had to waken Frances to phone the Rainy Hospital (our mission hospital in Madras, albeit only for women) and ask Dr. Anderson if she would send the ambulance to pick me up as I had developed an 'acute abdomen'. The ambulance was not available so I went in a taxi, with only a shirt and a pair of trousers which I painfully put on. Frances stayed behind with the baby. She would have no contact with me for the next three weeks.

At the hospital Dr. Anderson gave me an injection of morphine and without further discussion, arranged for me to be transferred to Vellore hospital about 130 kilometers (i.e. 80 miles) away. She was emphatic that no man would be admitted to her hospital under any circumstances.

The hospital ambulance arrived about 8am and I was bundled into the back on a stretcher. The two attendants and myself set off trundling through the heavy Madras traffic, slowly reaching the western suburbs by about 9am, when suddenly there was a loud bang. One of the rear tires had gone. We were right in the middle of a busy shopping area with dense traffic and people crowding around while the driver slowly took off the tire and walked off to the nearest service garage to get it repaired. There was no spare tire. Dr. Anderson wouldn't allow the extra cost, he said. His mate stayed with me.

A hour later, the attendant returned and by the time the tire was replaced it was nearly 11am. By this point the pain in my abdomen was extreme, the morphine having long worn off. The attendants had no additional medication to give me. So, off we went again and trundled out onto the bumpy main road to Vellore. Roads in India are often bumpy and there was no shock absorption in the ambulance. Feeling every bump made it a gruesome journey. In my initial calculations, under the best conditions, including a lunch break for the drivers, we might reach the Vellore hospital around 2.30 pm, but that calculation had long passed as we were still far from our destination.

The old vehicle which usually crawled around the slums of Madras a few miles at a time picking up women in labor to take to the Rainy Hospital, croaked and bumped its way along the highway going west through open countryside with miles of paddy fields stretching out on both sides. It was a familiar sight to me, but one I hoped would soon pass as every bump produced increasing pain. While I was familiar with sport injuries this was entirely different, and from a medical point of view I was concerned about just what was happening internally.

We travelled on until we reached a small farming village, where my two attendants went for a bite to eat, leaving me in the vehicle. Returning later, by which time I had lost all track of time, we resumed our journey. All the while the old engine kept protesting in the heat. Suddenly there was another loud bang and we again lurched to a stop. The driver and his mate, after a quick assessment, informed me that another tire had blown. The driver then indicated that Dr. Anderson, memsahib, absolutely refused to have new tires bought and that even in the city, they often had to get a tire repaired. However at this point we were in the middle of nowhere and the driver would have to walk back to the nearest village about five miles back, carrying the tire. This time his mate went with him leaving me alone in the old tin-can-of-an-ambulance. Time passed and I sweated buckets in the heat, laying as still as possible, and in continual pain. I had no watch, there had been no time to put one on when I left the house in Kilpauk. I was becoming slightly delirious. Vaguely, I reckoned that they would take about two hours to reach the village, an hour for the repair, and another two hours humphing it back. In my delirium I calculated about five hours from sometime in the early afternoon.

Eventually the two ambulance attendants returned, refitted the tire and we set off again. It must have been late afternoon. I lost interest in anything but trying to hold myself still to ease the pain as we continued our journey. We jolted along for what seemed like hours until at last, after dark, we crawled into the old city of Vellore and finally made it to the hospital where I was admitted. It was about 8.30pm.

Vellore Medical College is a missionary hospital, one of the finest in the world, which was founded by the famous American Missionary doctor Dr. Ida Scudder. I never heard what my two driving companions did and, as it transpired, never saw or heard of Dr. Anderson again.

The receiving surgeon was another Scot, Dr. MacPherson, a surgeon, working as a missionary in Vellore Medical College Hospital, the largest mission hospital in India. He examined me with great care before ordering more morphine and putting up an intravenous drip. I was in a state of acute intestinal obstruction. He said that the most likely diagnosis was, he thought, an Acute Volvulus of the small bowel and that he would observe me while I rehydrated over night. He expected that by morning he would have to do an exploratory laparotomy.

In a small upstairs private room with a little Tamil nurse coming and going through the night to take my pulse and temperature, I began to reflect on my recent life, trying to identify what could have contributed to my condition. I dozed off and the next thing I remember was the dawn. Soon, Dr. MacPherson returned and was pleased that my condition had not worsened. We talked. I told him of all the stress to which I, in retrospect, had been subject in recent months and wondered if this had upset my autonomic system and produced a malfunction of both my bowel and bladder.

He was immediately interested in this line of diagnosis, because, like me, he could see nothing in my history which would have definitely led to a diagnosis of Volvulus.

Finally he seemed to accept my analysis and said that he would have me X-rayed by Barium meal. The X-ray was done by an English Radiologist from Birmingham, also a missionary.

What the X-ray showed was remarkable. A loop of my Jejunum was completely flaccid and grossly dilated, while distal to that no barium had been able to reach. My diagnostic intuition proved to be correct. It was a case of complete autonomic dysfunction. There was no mechanical blockage, a large loop of my jejunum had just stopped contracting. Without going into clinical medical details I had fallen into a rare type of intestinal obstruction, which was undoubtedly due to the combination of the chill and the underlying build-up of psychological stress from the problems of my marriage and the quagmire of the confusion and mismanagement to which I had been subjected for almost two years. This was exacerbated by Rev. Shaw publicly blaming me for his inability to find a suitable position for me, a situation for which he was totally responsible. It had been a very difficult period in my life.

Dr. Macpherson then prescribed a conservative regime of treatment with which I totally agreed. I escaped 'the knife'. I would have numerous Barium Meals and enemas as the doctor assessed the progress of my illness. The rest was also therapeutic. After three weeks my bowel suddenly returned to normal and I was discharged back to Kilpauk, with some anti-spasmodic pills to take daily. For the rest of my life I would have to take such medication from time to time to counteract a recurrence of this problem. My condition was written up in the Medical Missionary Journal of India, which was at that time quite a prestigious magazine.

Having lost over ten pounds, I was down to 160 lbs and looking quite thin and gaunt. Frances and Barbara were both in good fettle when I got back. I returned to the upstairs room at Kilpauk and to my Tamil studies for the Final Tamil Professional Examinations which were to be held in Kodaikanal in a month's time.

We were supposed to move to Kodaikanal (we called it Kodai) just before I fell ill in February, but we did not get there until late April. Kodai stood atop a range of ex-volcanic mountains at a height of 7,000 feet. When 'The Plains' temperature reached over 38°C (100°F), it was only 16°C (60°F) at Kodai. For this reason, missionaries in South India had for years escaped the intense summer heat on The Plains by spending several weeks at Kodai. In the 1950s there were at least twenty different missionary organizations whose missionaries visited and took short holidays in Kodai from the April to September period. Most were from the United States, who sent about 2,500 missionaries to India, while the remaining 1,000 came from Scotland, England, Ireland, Wales, Germany, Sweden, Denmark, Norway, Holland, Canada, Australia, New Zealand. Scotland had about a hundred missionaries in India.

Frances, then pregnant, went ahead of me and spent six months in Kodai from April until September. This was because as a wife she did not have to do any mission work for the six month before and after the child's birth.

When I arrived in Kodai, I was informed that the chairman of the Language School Examination Board, Rev. Inge Frykholm, a Swede, had cancelled the exams because there were too few candidates. Having worked for months preparing for these exams, I wrote to him expressing my disgust over his decision. Fortunately, in responding to my letter he stated the exams would be held as scheduled. So, I sat the exam and passed with Distinction. Such achievement, however, did not solve the main problem as I still had no idea whether I had a medical position.

This was a very complex time since Rev. Shaw, our senior missionary of the Church of South India (CSI), could not find a permanent hospital assignment for me in South India. It was becoming transparently clear that I should probably never have been sent out to South India in the first place. In the summer of 1957, this disastrous state of affairs came to a head when I was preparing and then passing my Second Tamil Language Examinations. Having passed the exam. and therefore having surmounted all the hurdles required for me to spend the rest of my working life as a medical missionary in South India, there was no place to which I could be sent. Dr. Julius had already appointed an Indian Christian doctor to the position which I had temporarily filled at Ranipet. It was a mess, and one that I had not created. It was only with great patience, tact and skill that I avoided being blamed for the whole shimozzle. Authorities do not like to take the blame for their mistakes. By the grace of God, Bishop Leslie Newbiggin, my friend, was up in Kodai just at that time and he advised me to hold on, if it was God's will a solution would appear. Simple though that sounds it is usually the best advice in such situations in life; masterly inactivity. But I wasn't entirely inactive.

I not only prayed a lot but focused on other activities while I waited. I spent some time singing in the missionary choral union as a tenor soloist with two ex-professional singers, also missionaries. This musical interlude was recorded and later played on All-India Radio. I also joined, by invitation, three English missionaries, who liked to sing Elizabethan madrigals, but were lacking a tenor. Besides this musical interest, there were other diversions.

I joined a group of South Indian Bird Watchers led by Dr. Krebs from Denmark. Dr. Krebs, in addition to being a missionary, was also a world authority on the unbelievably tiny birds which live up in the Kodai Hills and spend all their lives flitting from branch to branch under shrubs, never more that three feet above the ground. These diminutive birds such as the Tickel's Blue Flycatcher birds are no larger than one and a half inches in length. I can still see Dr. Krebs whispering the Latin names of each bird he identified, in his very thick Danish accent, and the sight of him crawling on all fours through the bushes, holding his huge pair of binoculars in front of his eyes, until he was less than three feet from one of these wee birds.

Frances and I took little boat trips on the Kodai Lake, which fills the crater area of a bygone volcano. We had a single occasion of a Church of Scotland Missionary Tea, meeting some of the other Scots missionaries in South India. Of course we went to church every Sunday, and attended, as was the missionary custom, all the churches of the other denominations in the area, to demonstrate that we all believed as one.

As the days passed, I had an increasing sense that something fairly momentous was about to happen. Just before I was due to go back to Kilpauk, I received a telegram from the Church of Scotland in Edinburgh, requesting that I consider a six month appointment 1,600 miles north to the Charteris Memorial Hospital in Kalimpong in the Eastern Himalayas, to replace the senior medical doctor, Dr. Craig, who had to take a medical leave. The offer presented problems. It meant leaving South India with Frances pregnant, expecting twins, packing for six months and travelling by train, an old Boeing plane and a Land Rover from Madras to Kalimpong in the foothills of the Eastern Himalayas. A long journey to a very different climate among people who spoke at least five different languages, none of them Tamil.

I wrote Bishop Newbiggin, since by that time he had returned to Madurai. He replied that this was the guidance of God for which I had been waiting. After a day of thinking and discussion with Frances, I sent a telegram to Edinburgh confirming my acceptance. In the mean time, Dr. Jimmy Dick of our Church of Scotland mission to Nepal had agreed to stand in until I arrived.

It was another busy time. I realized there was no place for me in South India which the Church of Scotland Mission could finance. They were already having difficulties finding money for missionaries, as Scots Presbyterians were losing interest in helping the Third World now that The Empire had ceased being in control.

In September 1958, we left Kodai, returning to the upper room in Kilpauk to begin the complicated business of preparing to go temporarily to the other end of India. This would be an entirely different culture, ethnic area, languages, climate and, as anticipated, an entirely different medical situation. All my South India learning would have to be tucked away, while I prepared myself for another round of learning.

Because of the six month secondment, not everything would be transported north. So, I had to pack our belongings in a number of large packing cases 3ft x 3ft x 4ft, raising them up on large cans filled with water to keep out the ants. The ants would otherwise devour all the paper, resulting in books being demolished and wrapped items breaking without paper covering. Miss Hermansen allowed me use of one of the empty ground floor rooms in the big old mission house for the storage of our items until we returned. Then there were the travel arrangements. In India it is necessary to book early especially in light of the various transportation systems to be considered; the train journey from Madras up to Calcutta, the DC plane flight to Bagdogra and a Land-rover 'taxi' up the ghat (steep winding road) to Kalimpong. Kalimpong, called the gate-way town to Tibet, stood at 5,500 feet up in the Eastern Himalayan foothills, not far from Sikkim, Bhutan, Tibet and Nepal.

As our journey time approached, I had an intuition I would not be returning to the Plains, and so I gifted my bicycle to George, the younger servant of Miss Hermansen. My bicycle was a light, modern British type, which was much easier to ride than the old heavy (ex-British) type provided by the mission. He was delighted.

We made our rather subdued goodbyes to Miss Hermansen, since she fully expected us to be returning in six months, she being left with the responsibility of our packing cases. It did not happen that way. After our taxi to the railway station drove out of the compound, we never saw or heard of her again. We were heading to the other end of India where new challenges awaited.

S. India: Missionary Language School students and staff 1956. Frances Robertson, 3rd from the L., Back row.

S. India: The lake at Kodaikanal, up in The Hills. An old volcanic crater.

S. India: The Yeri (artificial lake) as seen from the 'White House'

S. India: 'White House' amidst palm trees, 1956

S. India: Rice Paddy planting near the 'White House'

S. India: The Scudder Memorial Hospital, Ranipet

S. India: Indian medical colleagues at Scudder Memorial Hospital.

S. India: Some of the nursing staff at the Scudder Memorial Hospital.

S. India: Missionary colleagues at Ranipet. Frances Robertson, 2nd, Bill Robertson, 3rd from R, top row.

S. India: Dr. Bill Robertson conducting an outdoor medical clinic in the Kodai hills.

S. India: A water tap in Madras City, 1957

S. India: Farmer's market, Ranipet 1956

S. India: Christian church with Golden Mohar trees.

S. India: Architecturally indigenized Christian church, 1957

S. India: Sion Hill (Sion Malai), about 20 miles from Ranipet.

S. India: Stairs up to Sion Malai shrine with Lord's Prayer phrase.

S. India: Christian shrine on top of Sion Malai.

S. India: Ribbon seller at Ponnai festival.

S. India: The bangle man at the Ponnai festival.

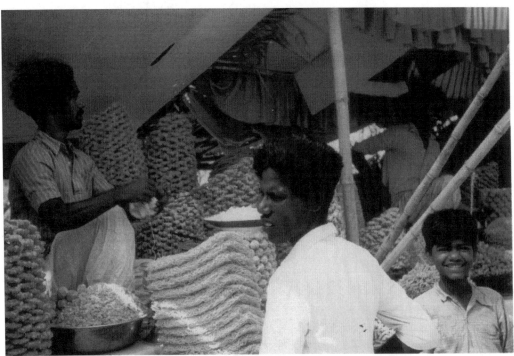
S. India: The candy seller at the Ponnai festival.

S. India: Evangelist selling Bible portions at the Ponnai festival.

S. India: Hindu temple and temple wall at Kanchipuram.

S. India: Hindu temple goporams at Kanchipuram.

S. India: Hindu temple and temple tank at Tillivilicumdram.

Chapter 5

NORTH INDIA

That evening Frances, Barbara and myself settled into our booked train suite consisting of a small but adequate room with an adjoining bathroom. The long train ride would take us up the east coast of the Indian peninsula, through Tamil Nadu, and on to Andrah Pradesh, and the states of Oriya and Bengal.

At night the beds were pulled down from the walls, and, as needed, I jumped out at the many stops, for coffee and/or bananas, to augment the prepared food we were carrying with us. By this stage, Frances was about six months pregnant with what turned out to be twins. Barbara travelled easily, happily glugging on her bottle. It was a long, sometimes interesting journey, and not really uncomfortable, since by this point we had become somewhat acclimatized to the heat of India.

Reaching Calcutta, travelling by taxi, we encountered the rather broken down, disorganized metropolis, which had been the first great centre of British power in India. It had been a great city for centuries before the Europeans. We stayed at the Salvation Army Hostel, the cheapest place we could find with basic European standards. I'll always remember, although the building was in the city centre, being awakened in the early hours of the morning by a chorus of cock-crows, followed by the lowing of cattle wishing to be milked. This was India, country sounds in the middle of a city.

Calcutta, during the 1950's, was experiencing the problems of a rising population caused by the influx of refugees with the expected shortage of space. From a gracious and leisurely city, Calcutta in the fifties became a noisy, crowded and a melancholy city. It was a city of shortages, especially of food grains and housing. The middle fifties saw the city in the midst of strikes, and mammoth political rallies which were led by tram workers, bank employees and students organized by the Communist Party of India. The disruption that these caused, together with the squalor and disease -both results of the refugee problem- were beginning to give Calcutta the global notoriety which would become an integral part of the city's identity in the second part of the 20th century.

The next leg of our over one thousand, six hundred mile journey would be by plane. Again, we travelled by the inevitable rickety taxi out of the city to a little airport where we boarded a small plane, one of the original small Douglas aircraft, a sturdy DC 9, a wonderful and reliable passenger plane.

The flight was interesting and not very long. We landed uneventfully at Bagdogra air field, near the town of Siliguri, at the base of the Himalayan foothills. To the north-east was the country of Bhutan, to the north-north east Tibet, to the north Sikkim, to the north-west Nepal and to the south East Pakistan (later called Bangaladesh).

Travelling with limited baggage, as we were only supposed to be going for a few months, we quickly transferred to a hill taxi, a typical Land Rover. This was the preferred transportation as it was a strong, reliable vehicle able to accommodate an unbelievable number of passengers, and negotiate the winding hair-pin mountain bend roads (called ghats) for hours on end. Frances and I sat at the back, awkwardly holding onto Barbara's basket, as we rounded the hair-pin bends, one after the other, endlessly climbing from the hot, humid plain up to the cooler air of the hill town of Kalimpong at over five thousand feet. We travelled for about four to five hours. Climbing, we put on sweaters as our bodies shifted from the tropical heat of South India at 30°C (88°F) to 40°C (104°F) to the mountain temperatures of 15°C (59°F) to 25°C (77°F). We would relish the mountain climate, as Kalimpong was a rather idyllic place to live. A fair number of European and American people came there to enjoy the fall and winter beauty of the Himalayan foothills, and the view of the highest mountains in the world stretching across the horizon from east to west. The nearest mountain was Kanchenjunga. 'The Snows' as we called them, were an awe-inspiring and unforgettable sight. I never got tired of gazing at Kanchenjunga (in Tibetan it means 'the five sisters'), when my days work was over and before darkness fell, just before my evening and night duties began.

It was the middle of the afternoon when we piled out of the Land Rover at our destination. We had come to a stop on a narrow little road which wended its way up a steep hill with tall trees and buildings on either side to the Charteris Memorial Hospital. It was, to us from the Plains, cool fresh and very different. As the taxi reversed, turned around and disappeared down into the town below, we looked around. In minutes, a small, fair-haired woman in a white coat, appeared and welcomed us with a friendly smile and in a clear North-East Scottish accent. This was Dr. Janet Duncan, from Thurso, who would be my medical colleague for the next few years.

Janet pointed to a little wooden bungalow adjoining the road and beckoned us to follow her with our luggage. We walked up steps to the back of the house, then a flight of stairs onto a verandah and on through the front door into an apartment-sized, living room, bedroom and kitchen, which she identified as 'The Anderson Flat'. This would be our temporary home in Kalimpong. Then, excusing herself due to the pressure of work, she disappeared up the winding road to the hospital, which was out of sight from the Anderson Flat.

That quiet, unfussy little welcome is all that I recall of our arrival. In retrospect I realize that Janet was under the clear impression that I was only seconded to Kalimpong for a maximum of six months and that, accordingly, she was not anticipating that we would be colleagues for what turned out to be several very busy years. On this initial greeting, I too was unaware that I would be working there for the next three years, not just six months.

The next day, a Sunday, I spent with Dr. Jimmy Dick, who had been standing in for several weeks awaiting my arrival. Jimmy was from Eastern Nepal, but had begun his missionary career in Kalimpong. He took me on a quick, but thorough tour of the Male and Female Surgical wards, the TB wards, as well as showing me round the Operating Room, the Outpatient Emergency room, the General Outpatients, the little X-ray room and the Laboratory (for which I would be responsible), and a look round the rest of the two hundred and fifty bed hospital. I was to share the On-Call work with Dr. Duncan for all the wards including the Medical, Surgical, Obstetric and Pediatric wards and visits to the two hundred and fifty bed Leprosy Hospital for which, with the administration, she was now responsible, while Dr. Albert Craig, the senior missionary doctor, was on sick leave in the United Kingdom. In addition, we would share the nursing school teaching between us, I on surgery, internal medicine, and tropical and other infectious disease, she on Obstetrics, Gynecology and Pediatrics.

That evening my mind was crammed with the responsibilities which lay ahead, the demands of a new environment and the realization I still hadn't learned a word of Nepalese, which was the lingua franca of that Himalayan ethnic cross-roads. I fell into a deep sleep. The 6am alarm heralded the beginning of my north Indian medical duties, which began, as it would for every weekday, with 7am prayers at the Nursing School, as was the custom in all mission hospitals.

After prayers, I was briefly introduced to the rest of the staff of nurses, compounders and technicians then whisked away by Jimmy Dick to the operating room to watch and learn from him how to do Cataract Extractions. As Jimmy said, "You must learn to do these, as there is nobody else within three hundred miles to do them. The local hill people will not go down to the Plains and anyway they can't afford it as they have to pay". That occupied Monday morning.

In the afternoon we went on a private consultation to see a visiting American lady who had taken ill. Such consultations were an important source of income for the hospital and though often tedious, they none the less had to be done. That lady was a visiting CARE agent, who we both soon diagnosed as more in need of men than medicine. Jimmy and I were only too glad to be together, for protection. This was the agent on whom we wanted to make a good impression in the hope of getting additional free and much-needed medical supplies and books for the hospital. It was a delicate consult, but we managed to maintain a proper medical decorum without upsetting the woman as 'Hell has no fury like a woman scorned'. A key fact that all doctors must realize, yet find ways to circumvent.

We also did ward rounds and an outpatient clinic and, later in the evening, another ward round to see that the cataract post-operative patients were comfortable and all was well. Around 11 pm I tumbled into bed and did not spend valuable sleeping time thinking about Tuesday when Jimmy would leave to return to Nepal. Incidentally, I have never heard or seen anything of the good doctor Dick again. Such is life. How many times the people to whom we are most indebted turn out to be like ships passing in the night, or angels sent by a beneficent God. I had just entered a beautiful, but politically dynamic environment, which held many unknowns.

In the late years of the 19th century the British Raj, which ruled the Indian subcontinent, became troubled by unsettling political conditions along the north-eastern border, where the State of Bengal met the Himalayan kingdoms of Nepal, Sikkim and Bhutan and the key ancient trade route from Tibet wound its way over the 19,000 feet Nathu La Pass, then south through Sikkim to India. It is likely that, as with the military actions of all powerful nations, the underlying reason for the British concern about the local quarrel between Sikkim and Bhutan, was trade, specifically the rich Tibetan wool trade. It is a fact of history that the fine wool of goats, sheep and yaks, which protects these mountain animals from the bitter cold found in the over 10,000 feet plateau kingdom of Tibet, had been found to make the very best 'pull-throughs' for rifles in the world. As you may know, the muskets and rifles of recent centuries have to have the inside of their barrels regularly cleaned to maintain their efficiency. To do this a plug of wool is passed through the barrel. In the late 1940's when I did my military service, we all had to keep our rifles clean by using pull-throughs, so that the sergeant-major could inspect the shining walls of our rifle barrels. It was a regular drill. I have no doubt that the British Army had long been aware of the military benefits of using Tibetan wool and that they were the principal buyers of that wool.

No doubt concerned that the trouble between Sikkim and Bhutan would upset the Tibetan Wool trade, the British Army engaged in what were called the Anglo-Sikkimese and Anglo-Bhutanese Wars and soon came to occupy the wedge of Himalayan foot-hill territory, half of it from Sikkim, half of it from Bhutan, between Tibet and Bengal, thus ensuring the untroubled passage of the valuable Tibetan wool into India. The occupied territories were then called the Darjeeling District of Bengal and remained so after Indian Independence in 1948. Later in 1975 India advanced its army further north and took over all of the kingdom of Sikkim. That latter take over was to better secure India's northern border with Tibet, which had been brutally invaded and taken over by Communist China in 1959, while I was working in Kalimpong.

The town of Kalimpong is situated in the eastern part of the Darjeeling District, its Bhutanese name meaning 'the Summer Palace Place'. It had been from time immemorial, the cool, pleasant and picturesque site to which the Bhutanese Royal Court moved in summer to avoid the oppressive heat of the central valley of the mountain kingdom. In winter, when hot, wet, humid weather arrived in Kalimpong the court returned to the cool, dry weather of the central valley. It was a little town of 12,000 people of nine ethnic origins, perched on an escarpment, 5,500 feet up in the foothills of the Eastern Himalayas. To the east the steep slope falls away into a valley, beyond which is the border of Bhutan; to the north, the most southern tip of Tibet and to the west, Sikkim. To the north-west lay Nepal with the spectacular sight of the five peaks of Mount Kanchenjunga, at over 28,000 feet in altitude. To the south lay the northern plain of India and a little further east what was then East Pakistan (now Bangaladesh). An unbelievable location, a veritable mountain cross-roads, a strategic centre and the doorway to Tibet. In the late 1950s it was also known as the 'city of spies'.

The town of Kalimpong lay further down the hill from the Mission compound, straddled across the steep ridge. The crowded main street was narrow and threaded its way more or less along the crest. The mainly two storey buildings caused deep shadows in which a variety of traders and shopkeepers vied for the attention of passers-by and depending on their appearance, in Nepali, Bengali, Marwari and broken English. The trickle of tourists attracted not only the shopkeepers but also a few poor, sad and tired-looking Tibetan refugees who were already begging help, having lost everything.

The Bhutanese royal family had chosen well, for the town sits astride a steep escarpment, providing magnificent panoramic views of the Himalayan mountains to the north and the Plains of India to the south. Truly in it's hey day it must have been a veritable Shangri-La. The British wisely allowed the Bhutanese royal family to continue owning the land of the town and, in my time, the Queen Mother of Bhutan, the Rani Dorji, still maintained the palace in some style and was the wealthy landlord of the whole town of Kalimpong, including the considerable piece of property on which the Church of Scotland had established its mission over a hundred years before.

The Rani Dorji was the wealthiest person in the eastern part of the Darjeeling district and she maintained an official Bhutanese presence in what had become India. At that time, Bhutan was officially and by its own decision, a closed country. The Rani Dorji's home thus constituted the official connection of Bhutan with the outside world. In this role she was well chosen, having been educated in a Swiss finishing school and being fluent in both English and French as well as being the most influential person in the town and its environs. The Rani, as we called her, was a devout Buddhist, a lady of great intelligence and peaceful composure, who without exception conducted herself with a truly royal dignity, unfailing politeness and quiet good humour. In that isolated corner of the world she was in her own way very like the British 'Queen Mum'. I have spent some time talking about the Rani, since she was not only the landlord of the Scots mission, but also the generous benefactor of the hospital and leprosarium. It was also my pleasure to provide medical care to many of her servants and staff and even her personal Buddhist priests and on one occasion her special pet dog.

When I first thought about the Darjeeling District after my arrival, I wondered why the Scots had chosen to set up their mission headquarters, hospital, university and primary and high schools in Kalimpong, rather than in the larger town of Darjeeling in the eastern part of the district. A brief review of the history of the British presence in the area, showed that Darjeeling was, and still is, a more attractive site, standing, as it does at 7,000 feet, commanding the very best view of the towering mount Kanchenjunga, and enjoying an even cooler, fresher and, in summer, less humid climate. It was for that reason that the British authorities in India, particularly in Calcutta, chose Darjeeling as its favorite hill station, to which thousands of British sahibs and memsahibs all flocked during the hottest and most humid months in the Plains.

In the days of the British Raj, white people would not have countenanced the presence of a Missionary hospital, leprosarium and educational facilities, for the local natives anywhere near Darjeeling and its holidaying ruling class, especially facilities run by lowly 'missionaries', always pronounced in a disapproving tone. The British authorities in the Empire, strongly disliked the presence of Christian mission work as, to them, it " gave the natives ideas above their station in life and fomented their revolutionary tendencies". The British had their own white medical doctors, nurses and chaplains, to keep them safe from any contamination with natives, and seriously ill white people were transferred home to 'England'. Under no circumstances would a member of the British Raj permit themselves to be treated in the same hospital as "a bunch of damned natives".

In the early months of 1959 Kalimpong was a hive of activity. The Chinese Communists had committed the brutal genocide of half of the Tibetan people and thousands of refugees fled across the mountains into Sikkim and on into India. Many were sick and arrived at the Charteris Memorial Hospital. They suffered from war injuries, wounds which were the result of torture by Chinese troops, starvation, exhaustion, and various infectious diseases, including tuberculosis and most appalling, leprosy. The Chinese routinely expelled into India, all Tibetans found to have leprosy.

This was the year in which the Dalai Lama was expelled from Tibet. I saw him as he paused briefly in Kalimpong on his way to his long exile. He was several years younger than me. Most of the Tibetan refugees had no money, let alone energy to go any further than Kalimpong. I treated many of them. As I reflected on the plight of these refugees and the uncertainties of the Missionary enterprise, one evening I wrote the following poem, reflecting for me, my fellowship with those refugees as transitory beings pausing awhile in the age-old continuity of Mother India.

No Resting Place

The winds blow cold and chill through the town, tis' winter
Tattered prayer flags flutter hopefully from the house tops
An evening sun imparts a golden brilliance to their faded glory
In the narrow streets lamas, muliteers and tired, lonely women
Ebb and flow slowly, indecisive.

Where shall they go those exile wanderers from the past?
There is no resting place for them, only stops among strangers
On a road going down.

They came with questioning faces and sad hearts
Where shall we go? Is all their tragic mime
But one blessing theirs, they have no sense of time.

And we urgent minions of decaying foreign missions
Restless progeny of a Western church,
Striving, straining with outmoded tools, the Faith supreme
To spread
Our future too, does it not all uncertain lie ahead?

We too like them are strangers in a foreign land
Escapees from the turmoil of the 'wind of change'
Though they must go while we may stay,
"Tis we are sad and happy they, if subtle truth be told,
Not they, but we at twilight stand, indecisive.

THE lady from CARE, whether or not she knew it before her arrival, brought with her the much needed additional antibiotics to enable us to cope with the sudden influx of refugees. As the newly arrived surgeon, I operated on many bullet and shrapnel wounds and fractures as well as some plastic surgery for the torture mutilations. One of the saddest procedures which a surgeon has to do on occasion, is to carry out limb amputation. Too many of the leprosy patients who had been forced to march for many days across the over 18,000 feet mountains from

Tibet to Sikkim. The rough journey usually destroyed at least one of their feet and ankles, which was presented to me as a filthy mess of festering pus, already well on the way to septicemia and death. Immediate below knee amputations were frequent. It was a credit to the immense toughness of these Tibetans that they survived to reach us at the hospital. Those with more advanced leprosy were admitted to the Leprosarium where they would spend the rest of their lives, since no leper was welcome in the general Indian population.

The arrival of the Tibetan refugees added to the already numerous local population of people, reflecting the multi-ethnic mix of this border trading town. The majority were Nepalese, to whom the British government had given land when they retired from the British Ghurka Regiment. Next were the Lepchas (or more correctly the Lapchees), the native people of Sikkim, who had spilled over into the previously Bhutanese area. They also constituted the majority of the Christians. Most of our excellent nurses were Lepchas, who normally spoke Nepalese which over the years had become the lingua franca of the area. Then there were the various wool traders, rich Marwaris from Rajahstan; some Punjabis; the Bhutanese staff and servants of the Rani; Bengali civil servants and soldiers, since we were in the State of West Bengal; a small number of American 'intellectual' Buddhists, mainly from the American population in Paris, who wanted to live and meditate in the Himalayas; last the Chinese in the Chinese Trade Agency, plus those who said they were shoe salesmen, but were later shown to be spies awaiting the anticipated Communist Chinese invasion of India. A challenging and intensely interesting polyglot group, all of whom I treated at one time or another.

By 1959 the pace of trade in the streets had been reduced due to the Chinese invasion of Tibet and the resulting stoppage of the wool trade. But the other industry to which the town owed its life was the Church of Scotland Mission, with its MacFarlane Memorial Church, the Charteris Memorial Hospital, the Tibetan Craft Industry, a University and Girls and Boys High Schools and Primary Schools, all of which provided the health, education and welfare services for the town and most of the Darjeeling District. Further up the ridge from the Mission compound the Church of Scotland had later established Dr. Graham's Homes, which provided excellent education and caring homes for the Anglo-Indian children born of the many casual sexual relationships between Bengali and Nepalese young women and British businessmen and tea planters down on the Plains. Dr. Graham, a former doctor at the Charteris Memorial Hospital, had redirected his time and energy to the school as a responsible Christian response to the irresponsibilities of many of his British fellow countrymen.

Truly, the Scots missionaries had done an excellent job in answering the varied needs of the area and was still, in the late fifties, leading the way. However, I am happy to say, as the years passed all but one of the teaching positions, were filled by well-trained Christian men and women from the Indian Christian community. Likewise all the nurses and technicians and support staff of the hospital were local people, some Christian, some Buddhist, some Moslem, some Hindu, only the two medical positions had not yet been filled by indigenous people and, in harmony with my own views on missionary work, these two should, I felt, be filled by Indian people, as soon as possible. Even then I was aware that with the Chinese threat to India, things would inevitably change, and they did.

Although it was obvious that Dr. Duncan and the absent Dr. Craig were both happy and set in their positions as the 'white' leaders of the hospital, I foresaw and admitted to myself, what they either did not see or did not want to see, that we would be the last western missionary doctors at the Charteris Memorial Hospital. All during 1961 before I left on a furlough which proved to be final, the grinding sound of military vehicles in low gear, labouring up the Teesta Valley to the border with Tibet, filled the night air. The Indian Army moved regiments of Sikhs, Dogras, Mahrattas and Ghurkas, their crack troops, up to the Tibetan border to face the forty-five thousand Chinese soldiers who were, at that time poised to flood into the Indian plain and overrun West Bengal and, it was rumoured, all of India. Local defeatist gossip was that one Chinese soldier could defeat six Indians. Whatever the reason they did not have the chance to prove it. My own view is that the Indian soldiers would be more than a match for the Chinese peasant army and history seems to agree with me, for their generals thought better of it and came to a halt at the mountainous border between Tibet and north-east Sikkim. This then was the historical and political atmosphere in which I found myself. These were critical times for India, and a changing world also for missionaries.

The Charteris Memorial Hospital was named after a generous Scottish Presbyterian philanthropist and built in the early years of the 20th century. It was situated, like most of Kalimpong's buildings, astride the ridge, on which the original Bhutanese royal family summer court had met. The Church of Scotland Mission had been able to rent the land above the town and had through the years, built from below upwards, the Mission Industries, then a number of houses for the missionaries, the Girls High School, the MacFarlane Memorial Church, the

Hospital, (in five separate parts, straddled on either side of a narrow, winding little road) the Boys High School and the University, then more mission bungalows, as we called them in India. (Bungalow, a Tamil word meaning a free-standing house, pronounced like *bungala*).

As one climbed up the little road from The Anderson Flat, where we lived near the bottom of the Mission Compound, the Tuberculosis Wing was on the left, a newish 20 years old, but cheap two-storey block, built in a hurry as TB had spread into the area. It housed about eighty patients who had a wonderful view down the steep slope to the mighty Teesta River, 2,000 feet below. On the right was the Nursing School, where I gave Surgery and Medicine lectures and where we had daily morning prayers. A little further up on the same side was the rather shabby wooden Outpatient Building, where we saw many patients every day. The road then leveled out for about a hundred yards. On the left the ground fell away very steeply down into scrubby jungle all the way to the Teesta River. On the right stood the main hospital two storey building, well built in stone and brick, a central arched entrance led to open wards on each side and, stairs added at one end led to the upper wards. The ground floor wards accommodated up to twenty-five Surgical beds each. Upstairs were a mixture of obstetric, medical beds and several private rooms. In addition at the south end were the operating room suite and the obstetric suite.

The Operating Room, was a large corner room with high windows on two sides, its walls painted white. An old operating table gifted by the Edinburgh Royal Infirmary in 1905, stood at one side, above which hung a naked one hundred watt bulb. In fact most of the useful illumination came through the windows. The remainder of the space was filled with instrument cabinets and treatment tables, all of venerable vintage. I spent many long, busy hours in that Operating Room, helped by the Nurse Supervisor, Gracie Mary Rai, a tough half Nepali, half Tibetan girl in her early twenties. I often thanked God that He had arranged for her to be there, for she was the first nurse they had, trained in operating room nursing. Apart from arranging all the instruments and other equipment pre-operatively, she organized and trained her team of ever-changing student nurses, all of whom were tough little Hill girls, Nepalese or Lepcha, from the Darjeeling district's many hill farms. All were between 4'10" and 5'1". Later one or two Tibetan student nurses came along for their training stint. They were bigger girls as most Tibetans are quite tall. Some of the Khamba tribesmen, who were fighting the Chinese and slipped across the border for treatment of their wounds were well over six feet tall and tipped the scales at over two hundred pounds.

The Medical and the Pediatric wards and the Pharmacy lay about fifty yards behind and below the main building on the east side of the ridge. There was also the small government outpatients building, staffed by two Bengali government three-year doctors, one of whom, was Dr. Kharmakar. Part of the complex arrangements of the Charteris Memorial Hospital, in addition to renting from the Rani of Bhutan, was an agreement with the West Bengal Government that the Mission would allow accommodation for the two doctors to carry out weekday clinics for non-acute complaints at minimum charge paid to them directly. If they encountered a patient whose condition was beyond their resources then they referred them to me or Dr. Duncan, as appropriate, at the other Outpatient area, for which the patient had to pay the Mission. (I should note that we as missionaries made no money from any patient, but the nurses asked the patients to make a small donation to the hospital if they were poor, but requested a moderate fee for better-off patients. All of which went into special locked steel boxes, only opened by the Medical Superintendent and the Hospital Treasurer once a week. All the money went to support the hospital.)

The key rooms on the ground floor of this main building were, the Emergency Room in which I treated many walk-in and carried-in patients, at all hours of the day and night. The Laboratory was at the front, in which basic blood and urine and other simple diagnostic tests could be done. At the back of the building was a small windowless room in which a very basic X-ray machine and Dark Room had been recently set up. These two recent additions were at the simplest level in radiography and laboratory services, but were a godsend to the surgical and tuberculosis work in which I became immersed. For these improvements, Dr. Craig should be credited.

Further up the ridge from the hospital wards was another Nursing Residence, outside which the Nurses Graduation Ceremonies took place at least annually. Further up was the Medical Superintendent's large bungalow looking out over the Teesta and beyond to the magnificent sight of Kanchenchunga. About another hundred yards up the ridge were the homes of the technical and other support staff. Beyond this, quite a bit higher up, were the Boys High School and then the University and the houses for the professorial and teaching staff.

This considerable out-lay constituting, as I have said, the health care, school and university facilities for the District, was something of which the Church of Scotland could be proud and of which I was, even for a few short years, immensely happy and fulfilled to be a part.

At this point I should explain that within months of my arrival at the Charteris Memorial Hospital, the Mission Headquarters in Edinburgh, Scotland, notified us that Dr. Craig's illness was proving chronic and that he would, in all probability, not return for at least a year. Accordingly, the Church of North India, Darjeeling District authorities, under which the hospital had come to operate, negotiated with the Church of South India, to which I still officially 'belonged', my transfer to work 'permanently' (in fact only until Dr. Craig returned) in the Charteris Memorial Hospital. With this transfer I now had to arrange for the transportation by rail and road of all our possessions, such as they were, which at that time lay in packing cases in Kilpauk, Madras. That took some effort, but at least I had been given the foresight before I came north to pack properly, so that they were safe to move all the way up the Indian subcontinent. As soon as the church in Kalimpong saw that we were going to stay, we were offered the vacant Guild Mission House to live in. Now confirmed in my position, my days began to fall into somewhat of a routine.

My day began at 6am with a hurried breakfast and a quick, hundred foot climb up to the hospital and Morning Prayers. This was followed by a short discussion with Dr. Duncan, my colleague, and then on to my Surgical ward rounds. At least twice a week I also did a ward round at the TB unit for which I was also responsible. After the ward round it was usually to the Operating Room (OR) for the morning's operating session. I did all the surgery including Caesarean Sections and Gynecological Surgery as Janet did not like doing surgery. I worked alone in surgery with the assistance of the nurse trainees and Gracie Mary Rai, the OR Supervisor.

Dr. Albert Craig, the former medical administrator, apparently did not like doing surgery and avoided it in every way possible. For example, Janet told me at the outset that "There wasn't the need for much abdominal surgery and the trauma cases were usually so severe and late in coming that there wasn't much one could do to help". Indians, she said, never had Acute Appendicitis; Dr. Craig had strongly maintained this. Thus, I very soon understood that the Charteris Memorial Hospital had been operated largely as a place for medical treatment by injection, pills or masterly inactivity. It was not long before I encountered a return case of a man who complained of lower abdominal pains and an old history of what seemed to me to have been a case of acute appendicitis. His case had been treated conservatively by Dr. Craig, involving weeks in hospital until the worst pains had subsided, after which he had been discharged home, but he never really felt better. The proper treatment of such a case at that stage, as any doctor knows, can be complicated. It took time and a lot of work. After that, I vowed that I would keep an eye out for acute abdomens, even if they were not supposed to occur in the Himalayan foothills.

It is a difficult thing to have to think ill of a medical colleague, but there was no room for sloppy sentimentality in the remote situation in which I was working. There was no possibility of referral of patients to Calcutta, three hundred miles away and absolutely beyond the financial means of our patients, even if they had been willing to go. Surgery should have been carried out on a routine basis for many patients and had not been. I merely proceeded to do what surgical work came to me but in doing so I faced three critical problems; anesthesia, staffing and lighting.

The only anesthesia in use was Ether inhalation, which had been discontinued years before in the West and replaced by a range of expensive methods involving the use of special anesthetic machines, the simplest being one which provided Nitrous Oxide. This was the type we had used in the Scudder Memorial Hospital in Ranipet, which benefitted from the wealth of the American based Reformed Church of America. I was left with a dilemma, I could not simultaneously do the Ether inhalation and the surgery so had to find another option.

Dr. Duncan declined to be involved. Dr. Kharmakar, the Bengali government doctor agreed to give ether for only short procedures, such as tooth extraction or wound debridement. I could have asked one of the little Nepalese nursing students to give the ether with me supervising, but that was not allowed and all the qualified nurses were too busy to be spared to help.

At that time in the United Kingdom, Spinal Anesthesia was frowned upon as potentially dangerous and I had not been trained in it. Nevertheless, I decided that if I could master the technique it would allow me to give the anesthetic, re-scrub-up and then proceed to operate.

With Gracie Mary Rai I set up a team procedure to ensure the necessary strict supervision of the patient's condition throughout the operation. In two years of using Spinal Anesthesia every week I had no problems and was able to perform much major abdominal and lower limb surgery by its use. I have no doubt that

God was with me, if only because I was working with great care. But what many do not understand is that the unexpected can occur even with faith in God. Its then that one, whether they believe in God or not, cries out, "Oh God help me !". Unfortunately very few of my generation and later Boomer generation of doctors in the Western world believe in God.

Thus, to ensure that I could carry out efficient and safe spinal anesthetics I had to study medical text-books. I also wrote away for other current information on the technique. Next I had the vials of the anesthetic bought, assembled the other equipment and set up a strict regime for both the nurses and myself to follow. The first one was an exciting occasion. All went according to plan and the procedure was then available for my routine use. Next I went on to study Regional anesthesia for the upper limb, using the Brachial Block method. In addition I used, as I had been trained in Glasgow, Local anesthesia for small localized procedures. I had and have always loathed to cause any pain to a patient and always took every possible measure to provide painless surgery. The staffing problem presented different challenges.

Since we had few staff and a Nursing School, the trainee nurses were rotated through the operating room for six-week periods. So I was more or less always training one how to assist me. Most were willing and very conscientious though some couldn't last the pace and Gracie Mary Rai had to change anyone she saw was wilting under the strain of the heat and the physical effort of holding on to retractors, handing instruments, cutting with scissors etc,, This worked very well and they all got excellent experience.

One little trainee nurse was a skinny girl who was the daughter of Geng Singh the campus gardener (mali). Matron Karthak told me that she was having great difficulty keeping up with her studies, in fact was at the bottom of her class which resulted in her class-mates calling her a "latti" (in Nepali meaning 'dumbo',' dumkoof'). When the day came for her to assist me, she was obviously very nervous, but my teaching method was to speak slowly, quietly and clearly in Nepali telling her how to carry out each new maneuver necessary to assist with retractors, forceps, scissors, holding and swabbing bleeding capillaries and so on. To my great joy and to her classmates amazement, she learned every action first time and with deft care and efficiency. Very soon she proved to have nerves of steel and strong tireless hands; nothing perturbed her, whether the sight of blood, the heat, the pressure or the need for absolute dependability. I knew we had found a 'natural' OR nurse. I'm happy to say that her studies immediately improved and that in due course she passed her All India Nursing Examinations with flying colours. No more "latti" she! I'm sure she would go on to be an OR supervisor of super efficiency and iron will.

The third problem was OR lighting. It was challenging to work in the peritoneal cavity with only the illumination of one hundred watt bulb dangling four feet above my head. That problem had to wait for a year for its solution and it turned out to be initiated by Dr. Kharmakar who as I said, occasionally assisted me by giving ether anesthetics. He had talked with his supervisor and ultimately the Minister of Health for West Bengal got to hear of my lighting problem. One day the Deputy Minister of Health, himself a medical doctor, visited the hospital and without warning arrived at the OR and asked to see me operating. Of course he was admitted suitably gowned and masked. He watched me in silence successfully perform an abdominal operation. When it was over he congratulated me and expressed admiration mixed with concern that the only lighting available was a hundred watt bulb. He then said that he would see what he could do about it. Several weeks later a lovely new universally adjustable OR light arrived and was installed at no cost to the hospital. I entered a new era in my surgical experience, with its help. In retrospective I realize that the Deputy Minister's main objective was to ensure that when the Indian government inevitably took over the Charteris Memorial Hospital some years later, that the OR would be fully functional for the Indian Army surgeons. It is often an ill wind that blows nobody any good.

With the help of the operating surgery textbooks which I had brought with me and the excellent training I had received at Glasgow Royal Infirmary, I was able to successfully carry out a wide range of general, abdominal and gynecological surgery, caesarean sections, cataract extractions, tendon repairs, numerous fracture and dislocation reductions, many other traumatic injuries, including bullet and shrapnel wounds and a great volume of chronic wound treatment. Last but not least I learned leprosy surgery at the Mission to Lepers hospitals at Purulia and Bilaspur from a Tamil surgeon Dr. Thangaraj who had been trained by the missionary surgeon Dr. Paul Brand the surgeon who invented the operations which were and still are, used to correct the awful deformities of hand, foot and face which typify this dread disease.

Successfully performing surgery to help all these poor people in need was, for me the greatest joy and fulfillment of my life. Little did I know that, within six years, due to circumstances beyond my control, I would be out of surgical practice, never to return. One day I hope God will explain to me what still seems to me to have been an awful waste of my training and experience.

But in 1959, 1960 and 1961 I was wonderfully happy with God's help. All my patients survived and without complications. I was reminded of the Biblical passage of 'the blind see, the lame walked, those sick unto death were made well'. This was what I had hoped to do as a medical missionary and at that time, I was hoping to go on doing that for a life time. But it was not God's will that it should be.

I soon realized that my arrival at the Charteris Memorial Hospital coincided with two major changes in the hospital's clinical workload. First, greatly increased operative surgery, partly due to my decision that what surgery could and should be done, but mainly due to the stream of Tibetan refugees and guerilla fighters, seeking treatment for wounds. Secondly, the influx of Tibetan refugees with no resistance to tuberculosis, caused a flood of new cases at our outpatients, thankfully at a time when for the first time, successful treatment by Streptomycin and Izoniazid, had become available.

The practice of successful surgery in the hill-top Charteris Memorial Hospital up in the foothills of the Himalayas, was at once fascinating, rewarding and challenging. Like all surgical practice it revolved round Outpatient Clinics, Surgical Ward Rounds, Emergency and Elective Operative Surgery Sessions in the OR and related teaching duties, which in my case were in the Nurses Teaching Unit. Key to all this was the diagnostic services provided by the lab and x-ray services

After the morning operating session, a quick lunch then back up to the Outpatients Clinic, then nursing Lectures, visits to the Tuberculosis wards and the Leprosy Hospital, I was kept busy until my final post-operative ward round at around 11pm.

In addition to the many local hill people, I was fortunate in having the presence of a young man of half Tibetan, half Nepali background, just several years younger than me, Rakam Singh Yonzam. Rakam had but recently taken basic training in operating the small X-ray machine and in developing the x-ray plates, in doing blood counts, blood typing and the preparation of microscopic slides of sputum specimens. I helped him expand his knowledge and we formed a good team. Almost every day in these years, a new case of pulmonary tuberculosis arrived and I was able to make a definitive diagnosis and start immediate antibiotic treatment. A high percentage of these patients had extensive bilateral TB cavitation, but even so, many lives were saved. The worst cases we held in the TB wards for as long as possible. I carried out Tube Thoracostomies for Pneumothorax and

Phrenic Nerve Crush procedures on a number of these patients with good result. For most Western doctors, Tuberculosis is a rare condition, but I had seen many treated in the large TB hospitals around Glasgow, which in the forties and fifties were overflowing with up to ten thousand patients.

Beyond the Main building and down the east side of the ridge, as I have mentioned, were the Medical and Pediatric wards which Dr. Duncan looked after, the Pharmacy, headed by Asa our Chief Compounder (as pharmacists are called in India) and the West Bengal Government Clinic, staffed by the two licensed doctors from Calcutta. Initially I could not quite understand why we needed the government clinic. Later, I learned that since the area was part of West Bengal it was required to provide some medical care there. In return for being allowed to set up the clinic in our compound, the Mission got much needed West Bengal government funds to augment its meager budget. Patients who attended the government clinic had to pay a small sum for an attendance. This money was taken by the two doctors to add to their modest income. Soon after my arrival Rakam told me that the other Indian government doctor, was illegally charging patients extra for referrals to me. I had it stopped but it probably recurred later as I had no time to check up on it and patients wouldn't admit it anyway.

The outpatient clinic was a one-storey wooden building about fifty yards down from the main building. Between us, Dr. Duncan and I saw about thirty ambulant patients every week-day. Most were walk-ins, a few of the wealthier made appointments. This was a private clinic, meaning in the Mission hospital jargon, that patients had to pay a moderate fee for our consultation services, all of which went to the hospital funds.

The patients at the Clinic came with a wide variety of medical problems which were usually of a chronic nature and after they had gone to a number of other doctors in the town without success. The complaints ranged through every kind of disease in males, females and children and were at all times a diagnostic challenge, especially since the patients were of varying ethnicity and language. Most spoke Nepali or Hindi, but some spoke Tibetan or Bengali or Marwari. A few, like the American Bhuddists from Paris spoke English.

Although neither Dr. Duncan nor I were too keen to spend much time away from the many acute patients in the wards, seeing the OPD patients, who were relatively wealthy, either rich or middle-class and sometimes not very sick, the clinic was a major source of income for the hospital and thus demanded our attention. When not in the clinic or operating room, my daily routine always included visits to the wards.

Every morning I met the surgical charge nurse, usually Elizabet, a capable young Lepcha woman, whom I feel sure would eventually become a senior member of the hospital nursing staff. At the outset she helped me communicate with the patients.

All medicine begins with history-taking, without which proper Diagnosis, Examination and Treatment is impossible. Since I had initially no knowledge of the Nepali language, on my first day there I asked her in English to ask a question in Nepali then translate it back to me and so on. It is a time-consuming process, but Elizabet was very patient. Soon I took notes, phonetically, of her questions and the patients answers. In a few days I amassed over fifty key questions, from "Good morning", "How are you ?", "I have severe pain", "Where is the pain ?", "It is here", "Take a deep breath", "Lie flat", "Turn over", "Bend your arm" etc. etc. to "You are doing well", "How do you feel ?", "I feel much better" and "You will soon be able to go home", etc., etc. Later on, as I took Nepali lessons in the evenings from Mr. B.C. Simick, I wrote all the phrases in the Nepali script and, of course, added many more until I passed my Nepali Language Examinations. At the same time I collected the same phrases phonetically or using the Devanagiri script, in Tibetan, Lepcha, Hindi and Bengali, with the help of the nurses of these ethnic groups. It took a little time. I would here comment that it always pays to learn at least seven words or phrases in other people's languages, such as; "Good Morning", "How are you ?" "Yes", "No", "Excuse me", "Thank you", "Good Bye". When you use these few words and phrases, people immediately come alive, feel respected and are happy and friendly. I speak from long experience in over a dozen languages. As my language proficiency improved in the multi-lingual clientele of Kalimpong, my rounds took less time.

The leprosarium was situated on an isolated lower ridge separate from the rest of the mission compound, about half a mile distance north of the Charteris Memorial Hospital. It was the ideal site for the care of leprosy sufferers, a fact that earlier missionaries had wisely foreseen. It was approached by a narrow dirt road from near the hospital. Dr. Duncan came with me on my first visit as she was in charge of the hospital in the absence of Dr. Craig.

We followed the road as it curved out of sight around the shoulder of the steep escarpment and then, quite suddenly one caught sight of a white building, perched atop a steep bluff which jutted out from the hillside, its white dome shining brilliant in the sun. The adjoining main church building was built in the beautiful and characteristic Tibetan architectural style, its roof sweeping upwards from curved eaves. The dome rose out of its outer end and could be seen for many miles, even as far as the southern tip of Tibet, less than thirty miles away as the crow flies. Its style was particularly appropriate as so many of the residents came from the Himalayan countries of Tibet, Bhutan and Sikkim.

Leprosy was not uncommon in the locked and virtually mediaeval culture of Tibet, ruled by a benevolent Buddhist ecclesiastical autocracy, with the Dalai Lama at its head. Although many in Western countries think that leprosy has been eradicated, this is a mistaken belief. Leprosy is a disease which has existed for thousands of years, it's origins shrouded in the mists of antiquity. Some historians believe that the cradle of the disease was central India and that it spread via trade routes to Egypt, China, south-east Asia and later to Africa and Europe. Columbus is thought to have taken it to the new world where it spread through South and Central America. Over the centuries and in most countries lepers are ostracized, rejected and expelled from their homes and communities once their disease is recognized.

In 1869, an Irish Presbyterian school-master, Wellesley Bailey, from Dublin, established the Mission to Lepers in India. Tibetan lepers had heard that missionaries had built a leprosarium near Kalimpong in which they could find refuge if they had the strength to reach it. For them, the only way to reach Kalimpong from Tibet was south over the 19,000 foot Nathu La Pass into Sikkim and from there into the Darjeeling District of India and Kalimpong.

As these lepers reached Nathu La they could see, thirty miles away to the south, the gleaming white dome of the little Leprosarium church, a shining symbol of hope in the misery of their suffering, outcaste lives. When I later talked to those who had made this journey, they told me that many had died of cold, starvation and exhaustion on the punishing trek over the mountains. With no transportation they had to walk long distances to reach the Nathu La Pass, after which they had another thirty mile trek down to the Leprosarium. There was no telephone or bus service, so we only knew they existed when they arrived. The Rani Dorji of Bhutan, was a devoted benefactor of the Charteris Memorial Hospital and the Lepsorarium. She was particularly concerned with the plight of the lepers and her donations included money to decorate and embellish the little church, as it stood like a shining light on that Himalayan hillside.

Before the development of an effective drug, leprosy was a life-long sentence and so missionaries had set up isolated homes or colonies for lepers, particularly in Asia and Africa, where they could find refuge and kindly care until their inevitable untimely death.

The first ray of hope in the fight against leprosy appeared in 1872 when Armauer Hansen, a Norwegian doctor, discovered the germ (mycobacterium leprae) causing the disease. Later it was shown that leprosy was contracted through the skin, the bacillus having an affinity for the sheaths of the nerves particularly the ulnar and lateral peroneal nerves, with early lesions appearing on the face, trunk and arms. The organism thrives in the insanitary and overcrowded conditions found in the poorest areas of the world.

It was not until 1941 when the sulphonamide drugs, particularly the drug Sulphone, were developed, that a treatment for the disease was possible. Leprosy patients, if treated early, can be cured. While millions of lepers have been treated, the disease persists. The reasons for this are that there is often a great fear in seeking early treatment, it can be prolonged and costly, and often unpleasant due to severe side effects and drug reactions, deformities and disfigurements require extensive reconstructive surgery for which there is a lack of resources and, even when the disease is treated, there is great difficulty in being accepted back into their communities.

Even if the leper is cured of the disease and the germs killed, s/he may be unable to get a job as no employer believes that the disease is cured as long as the deformities exist. Leprosy deformities are due to damage done to nerves in the arms and legs and to infiltration of the skin of the face. Such deformity is accompanied by a loss of sensation, so the numb fingers soon become damaged and mutilated. It was the great medical missionary, Dr. Paul Brand, who in 1950s in India developed a number of reconstructive surgical operations to restore the limbs of the leper to a normal position and shape allowing them to find employment and rejoin society. I had the opportunity of learning these operations and was able to set up reconstructive surgery at the mission hospital and treated many patients successfully. I hoped that an Indian doctor would be trained to take over and continue this work when I left.

As Dr. Duncan and I drew nearer to the leprosorium, we could see the lines of separate houses or group residencies, strung out in tiers and clinging to the steep hillside. I wondered about the danger of mudslides, common in the Himalayan foothills, but the site had been well chosen. Jutting out from the main slope it would avoid the torrents of water and mud which could come from higher up.

Like other leprosaria, the Kalimpong one began as I have indicated, as a refuge for diseased outcastes. Thus they were often called colonies. As early treatments became possible the colonies developed treatment centres which in time became hospitals within the colonies. In addition the missionaries encouraged the residents/patients to engage in various crafts which could be sold to augment their very basic living standards. Thus the three elements (i.e. colony, hospital and industry) gave birth to the concept and reality of a Leprosarium. Dr. Craig and Dr. Duncan saw it from the medical point of view and persisted in the use of the restrictive term 'The Leprosy Hospital'. I did not argue with them, for this was an incomplete description.

In 1959 the leprosarium was full to capacity. This was due to the fact that the Communist Chinese knew of its existence and herded all Tibetan lepers who had survived their initial invasion and genocide, to the border with Sikkim at the Nathu La Pass and expelled them. Only the strongest survived, as I have indicated, to reach Kalimpong. On arrival they joined their Tibetan brothers and sisters along with a smaller numbers of Bhutanese, Nepalis and Bengalis.

In the houses and along the walk-ways, they spent their time, between treatments, talking, playing games and in weaving and embroidery. As is often the case, it was the women folk who did most of the work.

I soon discovered that many patients required surgery to clean up the horrible sores which developed on their hands and feet, due to a loss of sensation. For some the only possibility was amputation of diseased fingers, toes, feet or legs, to prevent secondary infection leading to septicemia and death. Amputation is always one of the saddest surgical operations. My work with the lepers was primarily to do with these surgical interventions.

Thus, my routine workday went from 6am to 11pm, with meal breaks, and frequent night calls to emergencies or post-operative cases. I had a bell installed under my pillow so that it would not disturb Frances when a call came to the front door. Due to the fact that Dr. Duncan would not be involved in any surgery I was often called out even on my alternative week-ends off. During those years in Northern India I seldom was able to sit through a full Sunday morning church service without being called out. It was a busy time and a completely worthwhile one. While often lacking the sustenance of Sunday worship, I never failed to read God's Word and to pray.

I should not fail to mention the composition of the Kalimpong missionary community in 1959. The most senior missionaries at that time were Mr. Scott and his wife, the Principal of the College which he had worked hard to build up over his thirty and more years of service. The Scotts were scheduled to retire after a life in that idyllic Himalayan community. They were to be the last Western members of the college staff. After they retired the college was run by local Nepali or Lepcha Christians. This was truly an achievement in indigenization.

Then there was Miss Scrimgeour, the headmistress of the Girl's High School. She was middle aged. The teaching faculty consisted of Miss Wallace, a young high school teacher, full of vim and vigor; Martha Hamilton, a vivacious and talented young missionary who was very active in Christian youth activities including leading evangelistic hymn singing with her guitar. Miss Hamilton belonged to the wealthy family who owned the P & O shipping line. She would later retire from the Mission and became the headmistress of the most expensive and respected girls private school in Scotland. Later a young couple, Tom and Betty Brunton arrived to help in the Boys High School.

In this life we all make choices. I chose to be a medical doctor, while most of my missionary colleagues were school teachers whose daily lives were less arduous. For them their working day began with classes at 9.30am, finished at 3.30pm with Wednesdays and week-ends off, a month off at Christmas and Easter and three months holiday in the summer.

In contrast, in the hospital, the staff was headed by Dr. Albert Craig, who was on sick leave with his wife; the young Dr. Janet Duncan and an English Nurse, plus me. We worked from 6.45am to 11pm most days with alternate week-ends off unless there were emergencies. The only holiday I had in four years was when I was sick, once. It never occurred to me for a moment to complain, I volunteered to work in India to help sick people and they needed help every day. To any would-be medical missionary my advice is, "If you don't like hard work don't volunteer as a medical missionary".

With our arrival there were fourteen Church of Scotland missionaries working in Kalimpong. In addition, there were two American fundamentalist female missionaries, several Swiss Jesuit priests in a boys high school on the other side of town, a group of Seventh Day Adventists, a group of Belgian Nuns in nearby villages, and a small Jehovah Witness Church with its missionaries. About thirty Western missionaries had been 'called' to spread God's Word in that small community of about fifteen thousand townspeople plus over one hundred thousand people in the Darjeeling District. In reflection, I noted that in the hot plains of India there were about ten missionaries covering a population of several million. You might ask why the difference in numbers? I realized that all those missionaries who had been directly sent to Kalimpong from Scotland, were people who had 'pull' in their home churches, and had asked specifically to be stationed in that delightful hill station area. Others without 'pull' or, who like me, did not know what 'pull' was and wouldn't have used it anyway, were sent into the heat, dust, dirt and trials of the tropical plains of Asia or the steamy jungles of Africa.

I may sound slightly disillusioned, but no, I am simply a realist. This of course does not mean that one is not aware that some people will try and stack the deck in their favour. It was by chance or, as I believe, the Will of God that I was moved temporarily to Kalimpong, which turned out to be over three years, almost half of my missionary service.

I should mention that all these different missionaries, when in the field mixed together regardless of denomination, because we knew that we were there for the same reason, to help our brothers and sisters in the Third World in the name of Jesus. Back home in our respective countries we separated into our own churches again. Later, I used to say how great a pity it was that the churches did not all join together around the world. Then people would believe our message that God wants everyone to love one another. It would defeat the power-mongers who promote separation. I believe in a fellowship of believers in One God, a viewpoint that is rarely mentioned as groups strive for their own territory. While in northern India, my time was mainly in the Presbyterian Mission which consisted of several components.

In the town, the Presbyterian Mission, established from the late 19th century, had three church congregations, the main one being the MacFarlane Memorial Church, which stood just down the slope from the hospital; the Tibetan Church, which was situated about half a mile up the ridge from the hospital; and the little white-domed church in the leprosarium. The MacFarlane Memorial Church was built on the edge of the solid rock ridge, its tall stone steeple could be seen for many miles around. The main hall or sanctuary was of stone with a corrugated iron roof, as were most of the buildings in the town, and it had weathered many torrential showers of monsoon rains. The church could accommodate several hundred members and with its high vaulted ceiling, was cool and airy even in the hottest, humid weather during the rains of July into August. Apart from our missionaries, the local congregation was entirely Nepalese or Lepcha. Since the British government offered retiring Ghurka soldiers (Nepalese) land in the area they soon outnumbered the native Lepchas of the country of Sikkim. Thus, while many of the congregation were Lepcha they had to accept Nepalese as the language of the church. This, despite the fact that the clergyman, Pastor Peter Targain was a Lepcha as were about half the Kirk Session. When I worked there, the Lepchas were entirely bilingual, although I never heard any of them speaking their own tongue, until I specifically asked a Lepcha nurse to teach me phonetically, a few sentences in which to talk to Lepcha patients coming in from the villages. It was quite a different language from Nepali. Nobody knew where it came from and most were too shy to use it in public, but I did.

Pastor Targain was a very fine man. He would later baptize my twin daughters, Christine and Marjory, in Nepali in the local MacFarlane Memorial Church. One of his sons later married Ongmeet Karthak, who was the excellent Matron of the Charteris Memorial Hospital during my time in Kalimpong. Many years later the couple moved to Gangtok, the capital of Sikkim, the native country of the Lepchas and their son went to Scotland to study as a medical doctor.

The church services, in Nepali, were always a great test of a missionary's language knowledge, yet these were easier than Tamil, to which I had been accustomed in South India. It can be a bit lonely sitting through a church service if you don't understand what is being said. The hymns were sung to Nepali or North Indian folk tunes, much as we in the West have used folk tunes for hymns. The accompaniment was either to a bajan or a guitar and the singing was loud and enthusiastic. The Nepalese, quickly adopted the guitar, and seemed familiar with the instrument from their past. As you probably know, the people of Nepal are, in the historical, ethnic sense, called 'The Hun', (pronounced '*Hoon*'), as they belong to the same people as the Huns who invaded Europe. Like the Germans, they make excellent soldiers. The Nepalis who fought in the British Army, called themselves 'The Ghurkas', (a Nepali tribe) and are to a man, fearless fighters.

After it had been confirmed that we would be staying in Kalimpong for more than a six months secondment, we moved, as previously noted, to the Guild Mission House which marked our official status as Church of Scotland missionaries to the Church of North India. We were now accepted into the missionary and Indian Christian community of the area.

The Guild Mission House was a large two-storey nineteenth century, wooden house of about nine rooms, of which we occupied about half. It was provided with a minimum of furniture, as are all mission houses; beds, a few tables and cupboards, not much but sufficient. It was situated on the edge of the khud, overlooking the Teesta valley several thousand feet below, and above, in the distance on a clear day, a magnificent view of Kanchenjunga.

Our house staff included Pratap, a cheery Ghurka cook and Jaitee, a stolid Nepali housemaid. Frances only had to order the food and Pratap did all the marketing, cooking and cleaning up in the kitchen while Jaitee cleaned the house. Geng Singh did the gardening, such as it was, but he was paid by the Mission. Frances, who continued to refuse to get involved in any mission work, had lots of time to play with Barbara, knit baby clothes for our expected twins, or just read.

Barbara, a delightfully mischievous little girl, used to play games on Geng Singh the mali (gardener). One of the mali's duties was to water the Guild Mission House lawn, or what was an excuse for a lawn, as it swept rapidly down and over the edge of the khud (steep slope) and into the jungle. It was one of his chores to water it with, in our impoverished Mission, an ancient hose, probably over fifty years old from the halcyon days of richer times. The hose, or what was left of it, had become a series of non-leaking pieces cleverly joined by the adept Geng Singh by foot long tubes of dried bamboo. Barbara's antics would be to run around when Geng Singh was out of sight and uncouple, first one piece then another piece of bamboo, immediately stopping the flow of the vital fluid, to the mali's puzzlement. He took quite some time to credit Barbara with the knowledge and ability for such mischief.

As mentioned earlier, Frances was pregnant with twins as we travelled north to Kalimpong in the fall of 1958 and the final months of her pregnancy were difficult. She was a month overdue, a fact that worried her more and more in the last four weeks. She read everything she could about inducing labor from my medical text-books and repeatedly pressed me to have Dr. Duncan induce her labor. I discussed this with Janet several times but she insisted that as she, having post-graduate qualifications in Obstetrics and was in charge of Frances's case, her opinion should stand. Unfortunately Frances did not agree and, as the days passed, she became more and more apprehensive and had a serious hysterical fit. The complexities increased as when she went into labor and needed some anesthesia, I as the only other qualified doctor in the area, would have to administer the anesthetic. Frances, was terrified at this possibility as she had read the anesthetic outcome statistics from my textbooks. What she did not fully know, was that in the event of a complicated delivery and the need for a Caesarean Section, I, as the only surgeon would have had to operate on my own wife. This was an unmentioned risk of missionary life. Sometime later, I learned of one such case in Africa, in which the medical missionary had prided himself on providing all the medical care to his wife and family. One day, he was out in the Bush far from any other medical help. In the mission van was his pregnant wife, three small children and his African driver. Unexpectedly, his wife went into labor. While he had delivered his other three children with no problem, this time his wife had great difficulties. The baby was delivered successfully but his wife died. He had no alternative but to bundle his dead wife and his four children into the van, drive many hours across the Bush to the nearest railway station , and travel by train a days journey to Cape Town. He was admitted to a mental hospital, completely insane. He never recovered. A tragic but sobering tale of missionary life.

As it turned out, I did have to administer an anesthetic to Frances during the delivery as one twin arrived two hours before the second. Fortunately, she did not require a Caesarean Section, which was what Dr. Duncan had correctly forecast.

Just prior to the twins birth, my parents arrived and were there for the twins birth and later baptism at the MacFarlane Memorial Church and the Baptismal Party in Guild Mission House. The twins were baptized as members of the Church of North India, while Barbara had been baptized into the Church of South India. Unknown to me my father went to South India and talked to my former colleagues before travelling to north India. He was well aware of the many difficulties I had been facing in India, but said nothing. Since my work schedule did not alter with their arrival, they spent most of their visit with Frances and the children.

After the twins were born we employed a middle-aged Nepali lady to feed and care for the babies from 8pm to 8am every day for six months. When those six months were over, Frances, voicing no comment on her intended action, bundled up the three children, and returned to Scotland. As I look back, her actions should not have been a surprise. I was aware she was not enamored of missionary life, our relationship had been under immense strain in India, and the Chinese government had amassed 45,000 troops just inside the Tibetan border with India with the possibility of them overrunning India a viable concern. It would have helped if there had been any prior discussion. We would be separated for the next two years.

On the day of her departure, when I arrived home late in the evening, Pratap told me that almost as soon as I had left the house that morning at around 6.35am my wife had ordered a taxi (Land-rover) and disappeared with the children. Under such circumstances, the Guild Mission House always had mixed memories for me. Weeks later, my thoughts were expressed in the following poem:

Kalimpong –1959

It was totally unexpected, but surely I should have known.
Walking quietly down the compound hill
A days work done, but never really over,
In the motley collection of aging buildings
Dignified by the name of "hospital".

Autumn leaves were gently falling as I pass the church
The familiar, well-worn path welcoming me home,
Sweeping round the corner, the beauty of the Teesta valley
Always made me momentarily pause, breathing in its refreshment.
Up the verandah steps, through the open door
The sound of my footsteps on the polished wooden floor
Contrasting with an eerie silence.
No babies' cry or gurgle, no friendly creaking of a mother's step upstairs
Only utter silence!

Quickly sensing something different, through
to the dining room and on to the kitchen at the back.
A kindly, quiet, steady look on Pratap's face,
His laconic, "Memsahib gayo, Nanihuroo gayo"!

They're gone, where to, when, why, the questions
shrieking in my head, but only the brief queries answered,
"This morning, just after you left for the hospital
in a garry, all four left, going with much luggage,
to Siliguri, maybe Calcutta? Who Knows?"

Supper alone, silent except for the little clattering of dishes
and cutlery and the sound of my own chewing, loud in my ears.
"More bhat sahib?" "No dhanyabad, not hungry".
Why the screaming in my head, the dizziness?
A thousands reasons milling around, a rare pain in the back of my head,
What does it mean? ... Life will never be the same again.

Back in Scotland, Frances arrived on my parents door-step with three young children. My father, in his seventies, unknown to me, was already ill with pancreatic cancer. My mother at sixty-four, had not looked after small children in many decades. Nevertheless, they did all they could until circumstances forced my father to arrange to pay the rent for an apartment for Frances and the girls first in Gourock, and later, in Largs. He also provided additional funds to augment the small allowance coming from my mission salary directly from Edinburgh. Frances never wrote or made any effort to communicate in the two years. I learned snippets of what was happening to my family from my mother's letters. Family relationships were such that I did not want to burden my parents with the apparent breakdown in my marriage, even if they could have assumed such. This episode initiated the inevitable ending of our marital relationship, however long we kept up appearances after I returned to Scotland. I was left with no alternative but to dive into my work. Thankfully, my colleagues never brought up the topic and I had plenty of surgical challenges to keep me focused.

My lonely existence at the Guild Mission House was rarely interrupted in the next two years except for the brief stay of Patrick Hamilton. Patrick was a young newly qualified Scottish doctor, the brother of one of my colleagues, Martha Hamilton. He was hoping to learn some Nepalese, before he did his military service in the Ghurkas, which in those far off days was still a British army regiment. He was tall, slim and faired-haired and spoke with a pronounced Oxford accent. I invited him to help me in the medical work at the hospital, he preferring the medical wards to surgery. Some evenings we had long chats about medicine, India and the world in general. All in all it was good to have his company for a few months. Interestingly enough I followed his career to know that he eventually returned to University, took several degrees in Tropical and Preventive Medicine and some study in Africa, becoming a Professor at the London School of Tropical Medicine, an academic job with research which would suit him perfectly. Other than this my daily routine continued as my surgical practice grew. In addition to the leper reconstructive surgery, my practice included both routine and complex surgical operations, some unique to India. There were so many special patients which became part of my life. The following is a snapshot of a few cases during these years.

A young Bhutanese girl about nineteen, who had come to the Leprosarium for treatment, appeared one morning complaining of abdominal pain. Many diagnostic possibilities immediately ran through my mind, the last thing being an Acute Appendicitis, as Dr. Duncan had firmly asserted that such a condition 'did not occur in the Hill People'. However, as I completed the medical history through one of our Tibetan nurse trainees who spoke Nepali and a smattering of Bhutanese, I found pathophneumonic signs of a very acute appendicitis. I then arranged for the operating room to be readied immediately for a laparotomy. After suitable pre-operative preparation and under ether anesthesia, I speedily removed a very inflamed appendix which contradicted the premise of no appendicitis in Hill People. The patient made a rapid recovery avoiding the potentially fatal complications which would have occurred by ignoring surgery and hoping that the abdominal mesentery would wall off the offending appendix. In my years at the Charteris Memorial Hospital, there were several occasions when I had to treat returning patients who had received 'prospective' treatment at the hospital. They had never fully recovered and required difficult surgical intervention to finally remove the appendix and undo the damage of multiple adhesions. That is always a sad type of surgery to have to perform, but it is better than doing nothing. Another case was that of a boy with a hare lip.

One of the realities of missionary medical practice in a relatively remote and poor area of the world, is that since there was no adequate government-subsidized medical care, most surgery for the poor in India is mainly for severe emergencies, caused by road or other accidents. Elective surgery for a host of conditions is available only to those who are able to pay large sums of money to specialists in whatever field of surgery is involved. Only Mission hospitals provide, as best as they could, elective surgical care for the poor.

Thus, it came about that one morning at the Out Patient Department (OPD) I met a young Nepali boy with a severe Hare-Lip congenital deformity with his parents asking if there was anything I could do. Since my arrival at the Charteris Memorial Hospital I had been able to help a few people with previously untreated conditions and this had encouraged others to come hoping something could be done for their family member. I had not performed any plastic hare-lip surgery before, nor had I seen it done in a teenager. Back in Scotland such cases were routinely corrected in early childhood, which entailed a much simpler operation. I had brought with me to India excellent surgical text-books, but did not at that moment recall whether they covered hare-lip surgical correction in any detail, so I temporized my reply by asking the family to return the next day, when I would confirm whether or not appropriate treatment could be provided. This may sound very legalistic and it was deliberately so, as, contrary to Western doctors beliefs, one has to be even more careful treating patients in the Third World where malpractice can be fatal, not just expensive.

That evening I read up all I could find on the surgery needed to correct a harelip and felt guided that I could help this boy to a fully satisfactory outcome. So the next morning I offered to operate with the promise of a satisfactory result, provided that they realized that a perfect result might not be possible. They went away to think about it. The next day they returned asking for admission for the operation.

As with all surgery in Mission hospitals, it is preceded by prayer for the surgeon, that he/she be skilled, that the assistants be able and that the patient be healed. The operation, performed under carefully administered local anesthetic, which I gave just before the operation, was a complete success. The little boy and his parents were so happy. I told the parents that if they wished, they could put a donation into the box. I think they did, but cannot remember. What mattered most was that the surgery was successful. I liked that quiet, cool type of surgery involving great attention to detail and remembered thinking that if it were ever possible I would like to pursue such painstaking surgery. Another case, far more complex, was the surgical correction needed following a bear attack.

Some time later, a tough stocky-looking young man appeared, unable to speak properly, pointing at his face which had been badly mutilated by a bear up in the wilds near the Bhutanese border. The attending nurse said he was a Bhote, which was the local Nepalis' way of saying he came from the wilds and might be Tibetan, Bhutanese or maybe a Sherpa; we never found out. His distorted speech was because the bear had torn away most of his nose and lips, leaving an ugly hole which had healed up months ago, leaving bad scarring and contractures. After a detailed examination I realized that it would be possible to loosen up the cheek tissue and close the gaping hole of his nose, as a first stage. Then later after some weeks, when the initial surgery was well healed, it would be possible to reconstruct his lips, sufficient that he would be able to eat and drink and maybe learn to talk again, intelligibly. The operations were long and difficult for me, but happy to say they were a success and he did manage to eat, drink and speak again. He was not beautiful, but not monstrous as he had been. He remained in Kalimpong, having given up life in the wild. He got a job and occasionally appeared at the hospital smiling with a happy, if wry, smile. It is a great satisfaction to be able to help such a person. As noted previously, the Tibetan conflict was ever present, with their many surgical challenges.

One morning a small, crumpled little Tibetan woman, who looked over fifty but was actually in her twenties, was admitted to the surgical ward. I found her lying in bed on her side, with her face turned away into the pillow.

When I approached the bed she cowered even further into her pillow and put her hand over her cheek. With the help of one of the Tibetan nurse students we managed to get her to sit up and tell me what was wrong. I didn't need to ask her *what*, but wanted to know how it had happened.. What was wrong was obvious. The right half of her forehead and orbit were depressed into an ugly scarred hole, which had partly healed. She told me that Chinese soldiers in Lhasa had beaten her and then, as they had done with many Tibetans, had hung her by a rope round the ankles from a pole, then kicked her head, causing her to spin around, all the while kicking her on the body, arms, face and head, until they had exhausted themselves. Somehow she had survived this and other bestial acts and was left for dead. At night, fellow Tibetans came and took her secretly to their home. Eventually she managed, along with others, to escape from Lhasa and reach the Indian border, from where she finally reached Kalimpong.

Her story could be repeated for many other Tibetans during the period from 1956 to 1960 . To their undying shame all the civilized nations of the world turned a blind eye to the Chinese aggression, counting on nobody knowing anything about the closed land of Tibet. Half the population was massacred, all the youth were taken to China and subjected to compulsory brain-washing, then brought back to Tibet and used to betray their parents on trumped up charges. Most of these parents were then imprisoned, tortured and executed. The remnant who survived either escaped to India via Kalimpong, as the young Dalai Lama had done, or betrayed their country and their Buddhist religion. The true story will not be told for many years, because the Dalai Lama and his followers in the free world do not wish to bring further troubles to those who remain. What China has done to Tibet is one of the foulest untold genocides of history.

The little woman I found was only a young woman in her early twenties. I won't go into a lot of medical detail, but simply say that she stayed at the hospital for several months. First we had to help her get her strength back by providing a good diet, at the same time making sure that her wounds were fully healed. It was only then that I operated, correcting the depressed bone of her forehead and around her right eye, which had been miraculously saved. Skin had to be moved so that the gaping hole was covered and her appearance returned to as normal as possible. During the months that she stayed with us, she became quite at home. When she eventually left we all hoped that friendly Tibetans would look after her. The next incident, while a minor procedure, showed the strength of some Tibetans.

One day I had to extract a very large carious molar tooth from a Tibetan tribesman (there were no dentists in the Hills, I was it). We only had ether anaesthesia and as the large Khamba tribesman lay stretched out on the OR table, I had elicited the help of Dr. Kharmakar a Bengali government three-year trained Calcutta graduate to carry out the short anesthetic, his first one. I instructed two nurses on each side to gently hold the patient's forearms while I tussled speedily with the reluctant molar. As soon as the patient was under I proceeded with the extraction. We had three old tooth extractors, as old as the OR table and one of these was for molars. I was making rapid progress, but when I had nearly completed the procedure, I told Dr. Kharmakar to reduce the anesthetic, which he did. At that moment the patient began to come round and raised both his arms from the shoulder, lifting the four little nurses, two on each side, who with great courage and determination held on like grim death, until his arms were vertical. They must have weighed up to two hundred pounds on each arm, an impressive demonstration of strength, which all of us except the patient remembered. Moments later the tooth was successfully extracted and this mighty Khamba slowly lowered his arms and lay in a peaceful slumber. These kind of Tibetans were not only tough and strong but also were lusty drinkers. Our ether was small beer to him. Besides Tibetans, there was also a Moslem community.

One afternoon I was called to one of the private rooms in the hospital to see a wealthy Moslem trader from the Punjab, who was visiting the town. I'd have to say it was not his lucky day, because the Chinese invasion of Tibet had closed the border and the lucrative wool trade was suddenly at a stand-still and now he had developed extreme abdominal pain. The gentleman before me was a man of average height, of spare build and about forty. He was in obvious distress, but like most Moslem men he was stoically bearing his pain. I sat by his bed-side with the nurse standing at the top end and took the best history I could. He spoke Punjabi and a few words of English. The nurse and I spoke Nepalese, English and a few words of Hindi, which is similar to Punjabi. Slowly it appeared that he had been neglecting a long-standing right inguinal hernia, which some days before had suddenly become very painful. He had a high temperature, a racing pulse and extreme tenderness over the right inguinal area. It was obvious to me that his hernia had become encarcerated and was in urgent need of surgical relief. I explained, as best I could, what was wrong and the attendant risks, stressing that immediate surgery was needed.

As a lone surgeon I was confident that I would be able to release the bowel which had become trapped in the tight hole of his inguinal opening. I put up an intravenous drip of Normal Saline, which was all that we had in those days and asked the OR Nurse Supervisor, Gracie Marie Rai, to prepare for major abdominal surgery. I stated that initially I would be administrating a Spinal Anesthetic and then re-scrub to proceed with the surgery. The skin and underlying tissues were stretched thin over the mass of the incarcerated knub of herniated bowel. The bowel which protruded appeared, as is usually expected, like one small loop of small intestine, compressed into a purplish mass. I carefully released it from the tensely stretched tissue surrounding it and, still holding it, awaited the hoped for return of a normal blood supply and return of its colour to a healthy pink. But to my dismay it remained badly discolored. Very gingerly teasing the loop out of the abdomen I discovered, to my horror that the loop was in fact two loops. Under the poor illumination of the hundred watt bulb, I could discern two thick trunks of swollen, deeply purple bowel, of at least thirty-six inches in length, descending into the abdominal cavity. At that moment, I knew I was in deep trouble and that the patient's life was in danger, since all the dead bowel would have to be excised. The incarceration had been addressed which would relieve his most severe pain, but I envisaged the need to perform some major surgery under a spinal and with only a student nurse to assist. Later, if all went well, more surgery would be needed for an inguinal hernia repair.

After we got him closed up, appropriately sedated, on an intravenous drip and back in his bed, I had to explain to him that further major surgery was imperative. He seemed to know without me going into details, that it was a matter of life and death and only asked "When"? I replied, " Tomorrow morning". I held his hand and said a short prayer which he seemed to appreciate and wished him a good night's sleep. Then I walked slowly down the hill to the Guild Mission House. It was late. Pratap, my faithful cook was still waiting for me and served a gratefully received meal before quietly leaving for his home. He seemed to know that there was something on my mind. After my meal I looked out my trusty volume on Emergency Surgery, as I had a feeling that I had read something special about incarcerated inguinal hernia and sure enough at the bottom of a page was a brief footnote in minute print, precisely describing what my patient had; it was a dreaded Meidle's hernia. It made sobering reading. By now certain that my patient would have a length of dead bowel in his abdomen which must have been there for some days, at least, I realized that I would have to perform a resection of a long length of his small bowel, followed by an anastamosis and so I went on to read all

I could find on such potentially complicated operative procedures, remembering that there would have to be very careful hemostasis, since we had no blood bank. A blood transfusion is something which in most of India and, certainly in a remote hospital in the Himalayas, is difficult, due to the racial and religious problems and prejudices; but that is a story for another time. I retired to bed in the empty house, prayed for my patients, especially the Moslem trader, and prayed for sleep and strength for the following day.

Early the next morning, after looking in on my patient I went to the OR and discussed with Gracie Mary Rai the needed preparations for a bowel resection and anastomosis. She had no experience of these operations and wasn't sure of what instruments I would need. She also added that to her knowledge nobody had performed such operations for many years, if ever. We did find a set of abdominal clamps which had been sent out from the Edinburgh Royal Infirmary, she thought, before WWI. We collected as many instruments as we could find and she took them for sterilization, mobilizing pretty well all the abdominal surgery equipment we could amass. I set the operation for mid-morning, knowing that time was of the essence. I knew that back in Scotland my patient, in his condition would have been under the care of a complete medical and nursing team with every kind of technical support. Lone major surgery is an exacting practice and greatly concentrates the mind.

As ever, we began with prayer and if ever there had been a time when it was most needed for the patient and me, that was it. The spinal anesthetic and resection and anastomosis which followed, took me, with the assistance of one student nurse after another, ably organised by Gracie Mary Rai, over four long and grueling hours. It was probably the most challenging surgery which I have ever done. I know that it was only with the help of God that all went well.

Slowly over the next weeks, my patient recovered and with the constant attention of myself and successive nurses, slowly gained strength and very importantly began to feel that he was going to live. After several weeks of convalescence in his private room I had to explain that he still needed his hernia repaired to prevent a recurrence. He took a few days to digest this news, but eventually agreed and we set the date for yet another spinal anesthetic and the needed hernial repair. Happily the day came and all went well. The repair needed to be quite extensive, but was fully satisfactory. I told him that he would have to be watchful and plan to take several months to fully get his strength back. Finally after all kinds of medicines and diet to help him regain his strength, he began to be his old self again and prepared to return to his home in the Punjab. On the day of his departure we all wished him well, then just before he took his leave, he presented me with a very generous cheque for thousands of rupees for the hospital. Then we both made our final salaams to each other and waved him away in a large taxi which would take him down the ghat to Siliguri airport, then on to Calcutta and eventually to the Punjab. Our prayers went with him. As expected, in time I would also have dealings with the Queen Mother of Bhutan.

One afternoon during an outpatient clinic session, a nurse arrived and informed me that the Rani Dorji of Bhutan would like to talk to me. Now, as I have mentioned, the Rani was not only a very charming senior lady, but she was also one of the main financial supporters of the Charteris Memorial Hospital. So, such a call was more or less a Royal Command. Fortunately, I was readily able to go and meet her as she stepped out of her limousine. The limousine was a rare sight in these hills, but a Queen Mother had to travel in style and comfort. She obviously had something special on her mind and drew me aside, so that we stood apart from the patients and visitors coming and going near the main hospital entrance, humble though it was. In that idyllic site, the Rani quickly came to the point telling me that her personal Buddhist priest had become completely blind and could I help. News had reached her that I had performed Cataract Extractions with some success and she wanted to know if I would help her dear spiritual advisor. The Rani was a devout Buddhist and had been daily waited upon by this priest for many years. He was now, she said, in his mid-eighties and as far as she could ascertain was otherwise in good health. Of course I said that I would be very happy to see him and would then be more able to give a considered opinion. She informed me that he refused to go down to the Plains to an Ophthalmic surgeon in Calcutta as he was adamantly opposed to leaving the hills. This was in fact true of most of the Hill people, who often said to me they would rather die than go down into India for any reason whatsoever. I understood the Rani's difficulty, either she take the risk of my modest ophthalmological surgical skills, or have her beloved priest retire totally blind into some remote monastery and end his active life as her spiritual attendant.

Several days later the limousine drew up at a prearranged hour and out stepped a tall, aristocratic looking Saffron-robed Buddhist priest attended by two massive Bhutanese Chowkidars (body guards), who in their turn were attended by two large Bhutanese wolf hounds, well known for their savage ferocity in the defense of their master. It was a dramatic spectacle and attracted a small crowd of curious, but respectful onlookers. I greeted him as one always does in the East with the raised salute of two hands pressed together in front of ones face, which as most people know means 'Peace be with you'. Then I gently took his hand and led him into the examination room and assisted him to sit down. Of course the two chowkidars came too. I indicated that the dogs would have to remain outside, which they accepted with some reluctance, but they no doubt had been told by the Rani to cooperate with the Doctor Sahib as necessary. So there we were, the four of us. A rather odd little group.

I examined the old priest's eyes with the Chowkidars standing immediately behind him, so close that I could hear their deep breaths as they became affected by the importance and, for them, the strangeness of the occasion. As I brought my ophthalmoscope close to the old priest's eye, they quivered noticeably, concerned as to what this strange weapon might do to their precious charge. Altogether this was not the easiest examination I had ever carried out, and it became evident that it was only the beginning of this unusual relationship. Both the priest's eyes had very advanced cataract opacity and they were fully ready for extraction. This was good, because many times one has to turn the patient away for some months until the lenses have become solid and able to be easily removed in their entirety. A long delay would not have impressed the Rani or the body guards. Fortunately, I thought, the dogs opinions did not need to be sought. Through one of the nurses who knew a little Bhutanese, I gently indicated to the old priest that I would be able to operate on his eyes with what I said was a very good chance of recovering much of his sight. Of course nothing is guaranteed in surgery and I had to gently indicate that sometimes the result was unsatisfactory. This is true for even the best of eye surgeons. I had also to help him accept that only one eye would be operated on at first. All being well, the second eye would be operated on in about six months, once I was sure that the first eye had fully healed and he had regained sight with the addition of spectacles, as necessary. This kind of explanation is not easy to make to people with, what was in those days a medieval understanding of Western Medicine.

On the appointed day, early in the morning, I scheduled the operation on the first eye, while my hands were in their steadiest state and after I had spent time alone praying for God's help. The limousine arrived and out stepped the priest, his two attendants accompanied by the two wolf hounds and then finally the Rani Dorji herself. This I could see was going to be an interesting morning. I explained to the Rani that normally attendants or friends were not allowed into the operating room, for reasons of sterility and to avoid disturbance, especially during the delicate nature of eye surgery. She smiled a little smile, but said with all her usual charm that she was sure that I would not mind her presence with the two attendants, though to my relief she said that the hounds would stay outside. After all, she said, that she was intensely interested to see how the operation was done, especially as she had never seen one being done before. I whispered to Gracie Mary Rai our OR Supervisor, that we would just have to accept this situation and asked her to try and keep the chowkidars, who were both over six feet tall and about two hundred and fifty pounds each in weight, away from my elbow during the operation. Good cataract surgery is not a lengthy procedure. The little crowd which included the Rani, the two chowkidars, Gracie Mary Rai and myself, now stood round the head of the operating table. Gracie had forcefully put OR masks on the chowkidars. I judged that the chowkidars and even the Rani would not keep still or quiet for long. All of which impressed on me the absolute need to do it well and with dispatch.

I was, as was my custom, about to begin with prayer, then instead invited the Rani to offer a prayer, which being in Bhutanese would be a comfort to her priest. The Rani gently obliged with a quiet little prayer. I hoped that God would realize just how fervently we all needed His help. Then, concentrating all my mind and hand, proceeded to cut into the cornea with our one little Graefe cataract knife and in a few seconds I was gently guiding the opaque and solidified lens out of the eye, as the Rani and the body-guards craned their heads forward to catch a glimpse of events. Gracie eyed them with threatening movements of her head, as I stitched up the incision using those wonderfully tiny and effective needles which skilled engineers have developed, to enable very fine sutures to be inserted to close the cornea. Then on went the large eye pads and it was over. At that point I asked the Rani to explain to her beloved priest that he would have to remain lying quietly in one of our private rooms for a day or so. She spoke to him for a minute or so in rapid whispers. Then I realized how good it was that she and the body-guards were there, for they easily helped carry the old man to his room, as the Rani gave firm instructions.

The next day before anyone had arrived, a nurse and I removed the bandages over the operated eye and "Thanks be to God" he could see. His smile of gratitude and gentle, firm handshake I have always remembered with infinite happiness. I had by now successfully performed a growing number of cataract extractions, but this gentle old Buddhist priest had such an air of spiritual tranquility that we were all enveloped in the heavenly peace of the Spirit of God. It is the same Spirit which is experienced by all believers in the One Creator God as there is only One Great Spirit.

Six months later I was so happy to successfully operate on the old priest's other eye. I don't know for how many more years he survived but I have the satisfaction of knowing that he was able to see and continue to be the Rani's personal priest until the end of his noble life. The next case was quite different.

I was called one day to the home of a rich Marwari trader called Rameshwar Ishwar Prasad. The Rameshwar, as he was generally called by everyone in Kalimpong, came from Rajasthan in north-west India. Like most of the other traders in the town, he had come to make money in the rich Tibetan wool trade. In early 1960, that trade had come to a stand-still due to the Chinese invasion of Tibet, but the Rameshwar had made a lot of money and like other Marwari businessmen he was content to wait and see what the Chinese would do. Later the Chinese re-opened the border to trade. Business is business and in India there are few others who can equal the Marwaris in business acumen. Originally farmers who had to struggle to eke a living out of the largely dry and infertile desert lands of Rajasthan, many became money-lenders providing capital to other Indians. It is of note that there are few Jews in India. Those who came in the various diasporatic incursions seem to have integrated with the local Hindu, Buddhist and Sikh communities in what became Kashmir, the Punjab and Kerela and were not forced into money-lending as they were in Europe.

As a high caste Hindu, the Rameshwar lived in a large house in which all the members of his family lived, including his parents, brothers and sisters, uncles and aunts and all their children and grandchildren. It was a typical Hindu joint family residence and was situated down in the main business section of the town. There, space was at a premium. Buildings had to huddle together to find a firm footing along the ridge on which the town had been built. For this reason most of the houses were several stories high and seemed to lean towards each other across the narrow main street, joined here and there by power and telephone cables. Colorful washing hung out to dry in the mid-day sun and over all was the loud, dominating yet sedating, dawn to dusk sound of Hindi film music, helping people forget their troubles in an often harsh world.

The big Mercedes car which brought me to the Prasad's home stopped outside a tall grey building and I was ushered into a dark corridor which led into a hall occupying the heart of the house. In the warmer climes of India it would have been open to the sky, but in the cool Himalayan foothills it was roofed over. The hall-like space was filled with, I reckoned, as many as fifty people of all ages, no doubt members of the extended family. Everyone seemed to be talking. The noise even blocked out the loudspeaker Hindi film music from outside. As I entered, I was aware that every eye was turned towards me and an expectant hush fell on all. This must be, I felt, what great actors or singers must feel as they come on stage. This was the practice of medicine on a grand scale and I had to perform.

In the middle of the 'hall' was a raised dais, with a bed on which lay a very elderly-looking gentleman who was groaning in obvious discomfort. His long white beard straddled over his bare chest and his gnarled old hands hovered protectively over his lower abdomen. I climbed up onto the dais and spoke to him gently in Nepali, which he understood, asking him what was wrong. He quickly let me understand that he could not pass urine and was accordingly in extreme pain. A brief examination confirmed that he had a very severe retention of urine, due most probably to an enlarged prostate. I had come prepared and opened my doctor's bag and laid out the necessary equipment to perform the simple catheterization procedure. You could have heard a pin drop in the pervading deadly silence. Not even a dog barked. Then gently uncovering the old man's genitals and cleansing them appropriately I could feel that all the onlookers eyes were riveted on his most private part. But this was India and one could sense the sympathy of everyone present who were after all caring family members intent on the relief of any suffering to their beloved grandfather and household head. Quickly I inserted the needed catheter and as the relieving flow of fluid trickled into the awaiting kidney dish, an audible sigh of relief was expressed from over fifty mouths. The muttered thanks of the old man had hardly been emitted when the Rameshwar ushered me quickly out of the hall, down the dark corridor and into the awaiting taxi. In five minutes I was back in the hospital almost wondering if it had ever happened. The kidney dish and its contents had been spirited away, as they say, 'never to return'. What I had been participating in was the relief of the pain of the respected and beloved elder member of a loving family, who was in his last hours of life. The next day the Rameshwar came by to thank me, pay the bill and inform me that his dear father had passed away peacefully during the night. It is a truism to say that Hindus know how best to help their dying relatives enter the next world. Another case involved the Chinese Trade Agency, a presence all too apparent in the late fifties in that part of India.

As noted previously, Kalimpong was the main town on the route from Tibet to India and, as such, was the location of a key Chinese Trade Agency. Such agencies were equivalent to embassies in most other countries. In fact, it was a centre of spies located there in anticipation of a Chinese invasion of India. The town had a whole street of Chinese shoe makers who did not seem to sell any of their wares except to an occasional American tourist. All these Chinese reported to the Chinese Trade Agency, which relayed the intelligence back to headquarters in China. The local Indian population seemed to know what was going on but felt powerless to do anything about it. It was reliably confirmed that there were thousands of Chinese troops on the Tibetan side of the border with Sikkim, just waiting for the order to move.

My association with the Chinese Trade Agency began some months before when one of their 'agents' appeared and asked if he could tour the hospital. He said he was a tourist with an interest in health facilities. I gave him a very brief tour, during which I quickly realized that his queries were to confirm the medical capabilities of our facility in handling wounded soldiers, when/if the Chinese army occupied the area. My replies were terse and without useful detail and he soon took his leave in that truculent way in which communist agents, or for that matter agents of any fascist state, tend to behave in situations in which they believe they are in control. Subsequent events were to prove him wrong as the resolute Indian Army shortly arrived and took up defensive positions. My other experience with members of the Chinese Trade agency in Kalimpong was however, quite different.

One morning a Mercedes Benz car from the Chinese Trade Agency, complete with Communist Chinese emblems, appeared at the hospital. An official from the agency asked for me and said that the head/Communist Commissar of the Agency wanted me to give a medical consultation at the Agency ASAP. Fortunately I was able to answer his call immediately, as it was not one of my operating days. Taking my trusty stethoscope I was whisked away down into the town then up the winding and dusty road to a bleak, concrete, three-storied building standing well away from any other habitation. The front entrance was protected by steel mesh gates with two guards with Tommy guns slung from their shoulders, standing at the ready. The steel mesh gates eased back enough for me to enter and I was immediately led up to the second floor into a large bare room furnished with a simple wooden table, chairs and a bed against one wall. A very tough middle-aged man in a communist uniform rose to greet me and was introduced by a young Chinese interpreter who spoke fluent English with an American accent. We sat down and the Commissar took off his jacket as it was hot and stuffy, revealing a very badly scarred forearm, obviously the result of war injuries. He asked about me, where I came from, where I had been trained as a doctor and how I liked it in India. I avoided the latter question by confirming that as a missionary I had been sent here on a mission. This he understood as he too was here on a mission, however different. I pointed at his mutilated arm and asked what had happened. I suspected that he had been on the Long Journey with Mao Tse Tung. He relaxed and enthusiastically recounted his experiences in the fighting which led up to the communist take-over of China. In short, he was a hero who had been rewarded with this position in the idyllic foothills of India.

The interpreter turned out to have been educated in an American Presbyterian mission school and university and was comfortably fluent in English, which greatly helped our conversation.

By this time I began to feel that I was not there to examine or treat either of these gentlemen and sensing my query the Commissar called to someone who had been standing just outside the door. A few minutes later a well-built, slightly over-weight, but not unattractive Chinese lady of what I assessed as peasant stock, appeared and was introduced as the Commissar's wife, whom he told to get up on the bed. Somewhat sullenly the lady acquiesced and leaned rather stiffly against a pillow ignoring me and staring stonily at the opposite wall of the room. She was not a happy camper, as the saying goes.

The four of us sat a trifle uneasily in our respective places. I broke the silence by asking, "What is the problem?" I did not feel at that moment like asking the lady, "What is wrong, from what are you suffering?". My question was made to all three, somebody had to explain why I had been called. With an audibly unhappy sigh the Commissar launched into a long story about his wife's complaint, which had by the time of my being called in, begun to give him considerable frustration. The young interpreter was visibly uncomfortable translating this rather personal information about his boss's wife, especially in such a tight little community, isolated and in a foreign country. Beginning in a rather hesitant style, which grew more confident as he realized that only he and I could understand what he was saying and more so when I asked him questions for clarification which he felt able to answer without going back to the Commissar, he unfolded the following little history of the commissar's wife' complaint.

About six months previous (about the time that the Chinese army moved up to the Sikkimese border and threatened India) the Commissar's wife began to complain of stomach pains. She went, or rather was taken, to consult a local Indian doctor in the town and he diagnosed gastric acidity and prescribed antacids. That seemed a very reasonable diagnosis and treatment. However the lady's condition did not improve, so she went to another doctor in the town. He said that the first doctor was completely wrong in his treatment and he ordered a battery of blood tests which showed, he said, that she was anemic and needed iron therapy. Again, a reasonable diagnosis. But still the lady was unhappy and didn't follow these doctors' advice. Next she visited yet another doctor in the town, who decried the diagnoses of the previous two and again not unreasonably diagnosed, stress. He prescribed a tranquillizer, but after a week on that she became very unhappy with how the drug affected her. Her husband was becoming irritated and said that he didn't trust any of these blankety-blank Indian doctors and they were charging him too much without positive results. He then stated he needed to see someone whom they could trust. That opinion was not entirely fair to the Indian doctors as their advice was collectively quite reasonable. However, it would also be true to say that they would not be overjoyed at treating the wife of a Chinese official whom they would undoubtedly be aware was the chief honcho of the Chinese spies in the area. Indians are very patriotic when it counts. And so it was that the Commissar was told that the only non-Indian doctor in Kalimpong whom someone had recommended was me.

Having given me a moment to consider the story from the translator, the Commissar turned to me and asked what I thought. I had already made an initial presumptive diagnosis, but indicated that I would make a clinical examination of the patient, followed by some tests. I hoped that I would be allowed to carry out the physical with only the lady and a female attendant present, but that was brushed aside and I was urged to get on with it. I was not unaccustomed to such situations in villages where there is usually little if any privacy. It's a community affair, not a personal affair. The lady was not very cooperative and it was with some difficulty that I made the examination. I found nothing of clinical significance, except that the lady was very unhappy and at one moment when her husband could not see her face, she gave me a look of helplessness. I completed my visit by ordering several tests which in all fairness would confirm or otherwise the opinions of the Indian doctors and quietly took my leave, saying that I would return once I had the test results. The armed guards at the steel-mesh gates let me out and I returned to the hospital in the Mercedes. It was a little awkward as I knew that passers by would let it be known in the town that the Missionary Sahib was treating someone in the Communist Agency. I pondered the problem of the lady I had been seeing and felt pretty sure that she was physically fit as a flea, mentally normal and level-headed, emotionally stable and stoical, but nevertheless 'unhappy'.

A week later I returned and the four of us again met in the upstairs room. The tests had been, as I had suspected, negative. On hearing this the Commissar looked surprised and asked, through his translator, "Now what do we do ?". I confirmed that in my opinion his wife was in almost every way a fit woman, but that something was bothering her. The Commissar turned to his wife and in a moderate shout asked her what I imagined would be, "What in the name of goodness is troubling you, woman?. His wife continued to stare stonily gazing at the window.

Her expression was stubborn and uncommunicative. It was time for me to intervene, before we had a real barny on our hands. The translator was looking acutely embarrassed and the Commissar was at the end of his fuse, thinking, I judged, that he had done everything possible to make his wife happy. He had got her out of the very restrictive atmosphere of Communist China to a quiet, tranquil haven in the Himalayan foothills. The climate was pleasant, she had her own things and was the top lady in the Agency. She even had some jewelry which would be uncommon for women in Communist China, certainly in that era. Although she had not uttered a single word in my presence, I felt that I understood her predicament. Here she was, thousands of miles from her own people and family, cooped up in the Agency in a country increasingly anti-Chinese and probably with nothing to do. There was no evidence of children, and last but not least, it was well-known that the Chinese government was seriously considering invading India from the nearest border crossing which was only twenty minutes away by Jeep. Whatever was troubling her she no doubt felt that her tough, veteran husband would not understand or be sympathetic and so she just sat there hoping for a miracle. With these thoughts in mind I turned to the translator and asked him to put the following question directly to her, not to the Commissar, "Would you like to return to China ?". For the first time she spoke, looking directly at me. From his look of amazement she had said an emphatic "Yes". The translator confirmed this to me and I followed up with a second question to her. "Are you homesick for China ?". To which she made the same response which I now understood was, "Yes". So that was that. My presence was no longer needed, for obviously the problem was not medical and would be solved between husband and wife. The Commissar and his wife now launched out into a voluble conversation, which one could easily guess included the husband's comment, "Why didn't you tell me sooner ?" It was all very natural and human.

I indicated to the translator that I should now take my leave. He found a gap in the conversation to tell that to the Commissar. He turned to me smiling and thanked me asking how much had to be paid. I told him fifty rupees for all the tests and the two calls, which was our basic rate for private patients. He exclaimed that it was only a fraction of what each of the Indian doctors had charged for doing nothing. I shrugged and said that I had really done very little and in the mission we only charged basic fees. He smiled and looking sincerely into my eyes spoke with some feeling. The young translator gave me the gist of it, saying that the Commissar is exceedingly grateful for my honest assessment of his wife's problem and that he felt at home with me as I was open and, like the Chinese, did not beat about the bush. He paid the fee and shook my hand warmly, leading me out into the corridor, down the stairs and we said goodbye at the front door. Later I heard that he had arranged a transfer back to China for himself and his wife. I was happy. The next case I will mention was a bit closer to home.

As I noted before, Jaitee was the Guild Mission House housemaid. She was a small Hindu Nepali woman about twenty, with an expression at once, stubborn and impassive, reflecting her sturdy peasant roots. Nepali girls from poor hill farms have tough lives from an early age, constantly working under the total domination of their male relatives, until they are married off to continue the process under another macho male. Such is their life and I doubt if it will change much in a hundred years. Jaitee worked well enough around the house as far as I could gather before going to her home in the late afternoon.

One day as I was about to rush off to the hospital she accosted me in the hall and coming to the point said, "Doctor Sahib, my sister has bad sore throat, will you take out her tonsils?" This, as the first time she had ever really addressed me, came as a surprise, but her direct question was as clear as could be and of course demanded an equally clear reply. I replied, "I will have to examine her first. Tell her to come to the Clinic and then I will let you know". This satisfied her and she turned away with a hint of a smile dawning on her usually firm features.

In due course her sister appeared at the outpatient clinic and I waved her offer of the usual fee as she was the relative of one of our servants and therefore of one of our household. Jaitee's sister, was a younger woman who looked very much like Jaitee but much happier looking despite her complaint. In a very hoarse voice, she launched into an explanation of her problem which in summary was that she was plagued by constant recurring severe sore throats and that she sometimes felt as if she was going to choke, such was the constriction in her throat. On opening her mouth I could easily see that the poor woman had indeed the largest and most infected tonsils I had ever seen. Her breath was offensive in the extreme and I knew that without removal of her tonsils that this otherwise nice little woman would end up married off to some nasty old farmer, since no other man would have her.

Jaitee's little sister badly needed a tonsillectomy, not just for her general health's sake, but also for her future life. I thought for a moment as I completed a general examination to confirm that she was otherwise in robust health. Apart from assisting at one Tonsillectomy as a student in Glasgow five years previously, I had no practical experience of the procedure. I recalled that in the pile of old instruments I had found in a drawer in the OR there was a guillotine and snare specifically for tonsillectomy. These, as with the other instruments had been donated from the Edinburgh Royal Infirmary sometime in the early years of the twentieth century. In other circumstances I would have referred this patient to an Ear Nose and Throat specialist and that would have been the end of it for me. But the nearest such doctor was hundreds of miles away in Calcutta, and anyway she would never be able to afford the travelling expenses let alone the specialist's fee. Like most of our patients either we could help them or that was it for them. Being Jaitee's sister made my decision somewhat more difficult. My treatment would have to be not only adequate but a resounding success. I decided that with such large tonsils using the Snare with accompanying very careful dissection would be the method of choice, since, as with all tonsillectomies, bleeding from the tonsillar arteries is the most life-threatening risk, due to blood pouring into the lungs. In addition my only available general anesthesia was ether and out of the question. ENT surgeons, at least in those years, had an anesthetist put the patient under briefly, before a rapid removal of the tonsils; always a risky procedure preferably demanding a steady nerve and a swift technique. I reckoned that for Jaitee's little sister, it would have to be sedation with some local anesthesia for me to use in this case. When I told her that I agreed to operate, she beamed gratefully. My responding smile was more cautious as I knew the potential problems which I had undertaken.

On the next morning Gracie Mary Rai and one of the student nurses helped the patient onto the operating table. Gracie helped me explain the procedure and what we wanted her to do or not do and that it wouldn't take long. I had not given her such info the day before as it might have frightened her from agreeing to the operation which she very much needed. We prayed and then I proceeded. I won't give the gory details of the operation. A Tonsillectomy is always a messy, bloody and unpleasant operation, as well as potentially dangerous in an adult. This is the main reason ENT specialists prefer to remove childrens' tonsils, using the guillotine method, which is completed virtually in seconds. Frankly, I would never recommend it. Most children/people do not need their tonsils removed. Tonsils are their for a reason, which is to intercept germs as they enter the mouth and reduce the chance of respiratory and/or lung infection. But Jaitee's sister's tonsils were too large to leave untreated. They were indeed a significant challenge, but I succeeded in removing them and in securely ligating the bleeding branches of the tonsillar arteries. If you can excuse the analogy, they were about the size of ping pong balls and almost as hard as golf balls.

She made a good and rapid recovery and I never saw her again. Later, Jaitee confirmed that she was fine and so happy to be rid of her problem. Another case was the result of a human relations controversy unique to northern India.

Late one afternoon, as is often the case, I was called to the Outpatients. A young Nepali hill porter had been attacked, by a colleague who claimed that he was having an affair with his wife. That day I learned the accepted punishment among hill porters for such an offense was to take a chukri (the lethal weapon of all Nepalis) and chop the offender's calf through below the knee. This, among other things would destroy the man's career as a hill porter. Hill porters, if you have ever seen one, can carry huge loads up to two hundred and fifty pounds or more up many thousands of feet. They are a main form of transportation of goods from the valley towns up into the hill villages and their leg muscles are probably the most developed of any, certainly that I have seen.

So, as I discovered, this poor fellow had been well and truly chopped. At first I thought it would mean a complete amputation, which is no doubt what the assailant had intended. However, a faint hope presented itself as the larger bone, the tibia, was not completely severed and by good fortune, the chukri had not severed the posterior tibial artery and vein. The foot with the lower leg was twisted round and lying in a bloody mess. I was presented with another unprecedented surgical challenge. I gave the poor chap an injection of morphine, to relieve his pain and severe shock as he had been carried by friends up a long mountain path and then transported by Land Rover to the hospital. After the nurse and I made him warm and comfortable, I addressed the leg.

Without going into detail, I managed to carefully bring his foot around to its proper position and then check whether there was any evidence of a pulse in the foot. There was a faint pulse at the ankle, partially due to the contraction of blood vessels second to shock, but it was a pulse. I decided to try and save the leg. It was a long and laborious process. After the initial surgery to clean and suture what was left, I immobilized the whole leg and foot in a plaster shell. The reconstruction required several OR visits over a period of weeks to reassemble the leg.

I am happy to say that he did walk again and was able to return to his demanding physical job, which I am sure was as much due to his robust health and outstandingly tough bodily strength, as to my ministrations. I have no doubt that he would avoid any further advances to his colleagues' wives. He had survived a rough but effective deterrent to further dalliance.

My medical practice not only involved the local population but also members of the missionary community. The Rev. Ewan Traill was a redoubtable figure and the accident involving his wife is but one unfortunate incident in his colorful career. Ewan was the Principal of Doctor Graham's Homes and School for Anglo-Indian children.

I first met Ewan when he sought my medical advice for a minor surgical problem. I learned that he had been a much decorated infantry soldier in WWII, following which he had been called to the ministry of the Church of Scotland. After some years in various churches he had accepted his current post and was thoroughly enjoying the job with its very comfortable perks. I believe that he had been bending his elbow rather too much and this was the reason for the catastrophe which occurred one dark night as he drove his wife back from Darjeeling to Kalimpong down that dangerous ghat road, involving dozens of tight hair-pin bends, down 6,000 feet to the Teesta Valley and then up to the Dr. Graham's Homes at over 6,000 feet.

It was the early morning when I was called to Emergency, to see someone injured in an accident, the little nurse said. She explained in breathless Nepalese that Traill sahib's wife was in a bad way. The scene in the gloomy outpatient room with its poor lighting was not good.

Mrs. Traill, whom I had met socially at a dinner in her home, was a tall, blond, athletic lady, who had been a physiotherapist by profession. The patient whom I then was examining was critically injured and in a state of severe shock. Before any attempts at detailed examination of her condition she needed and got treatment for shock.

The sad story which her husband told as we stood over his wife was that as they were driving back late that night, Ewan had driven their Jeep over the edge of the narrow winding road and the car plunged down the very steep slope into the jungle towards the mighty river Teesta. Ewan and his wife were thrown clear and hurtled down at least a hundred feet through the trees and dense tangle of jungle trees, shrubs and plants. Ewan apparently had been only moderately injured in one shoulder and for which he disdained any treatment. He said that he had climbed down the jungle slope and eventually found his poor wife unconscious and badly injured. He gathered her in his arms and somehow climbed back up through the dense tangle of the jungle and reached the roadside, at what must have been around one or two in the morning. This must have taken all his considerable strength and determination. There they waited until he was able to wave down a late night Land-Rover 'taxi' returning from Darjeeling. His wife owed her life to Ewan and his heroic strength. However, I have sometimes wondered how she balanced his gallant rescue of her against the grim fact that the accident was all due to his drunken driving.

In the foothills of the Himalayas there was no police investigation of this white sahibs' tragedy, especially as after I had completed my clinical examination of Mrs. Traill I recommended that she be immediately transferred to the United Kingdom. The details of her injuries would take several pages to describe, but suffice to say that she had sustained multiple fractures of her cervical, thoracic and lumbar spine, multiple rib fractures, a broken collar bone and extensive bruising and lacerations. In short the fact that she was still alive was credit to her considerable strength and fitness. I made her as comfortable as possible in a kind of plaster sling arrangement which I reckoned would be the safest method of transporting her. I heavily sedated her and gave her husband a further supply of pain killing medicine and sent them off on the approaching long, difficult journey to the best orthopedic hospital in London, England.

I later learned that Mrs. Traill had survived her injuries, but was left with many disabilities including the fact that, not surprisingly to me, she had to wear a special body brace for the rest of her life. But one thing was sure, Mrs. Traill was one tough lady. In the aftermath of the accident the Traills did not return to Kalimpong, their children and possessions being forwarded back to Scotland in due course. The whole episode was a tragedy, especially overshadowed by the fact that the Rev. Traill had been about to be removed from his post at the time of the accident for unknown reasons. The next case may only be found in a Third World country, but was one to be remembered.

Among the new inpatients who had trickled in to the surgical wards one morning was a little Nepali boy, accompanied by his parents, who complained of acute abdominal pain. Although nine years old he looked more like seven. This was not all that unusual in Indian villages. Grossly anemic, almost cachectic in appearance, his miserably thin hands and arms protectively clasped his tightly bulging tummy. His general symptoms indicated some kind of intestinal obstruction which needed immediate attention. I put up an intravenous solution and we prepared him for an operation.

I performed an exploratory laparotomy, not knowing what I would find, but expecting some kind of bowel obstruction. After a careful but rapid examination of his small and large intestines I found a loop of jejunal small intestine, distended and as solid as a bicycle tire. In palpating the mass I suspected some kind of worm infestation. After isolating the loop I opened the bowel and was able to bring out a tangled mass of horrible white round worms, which on release began to writhe and twist on the operating towels. One of the student nurses began to faint and the other nurses made sounds of disgust as I withdrew more and more of the foul infesters. Eventually over a hundred of these vile worms were removed. I asked Gracie to have them suitably destroyed, after showing them briefly to the boy's parents. In India seeing is believing and the wise surgeon always shows what had been causing the problem, whenever possible. In the West, doctors have managed to fend off the interest of patients' relatives in such things, which I think is a mistake. After sewing up the little boy's gut, and checking that there was nothing else of concern, I closed his abdomen and he was returned to the ward, still on his intravenous. I had never before seen, or at that time heard of such a cause of obstruction.

Once he had fully recovered from the operation I treated him with appropriate medicine for round worms and he went from strength to strength. After several weeks he had become an active, strong little boy, running around the ward and getting in the way of the nurses. One day his parents appeared to take him home, finally assured that he was going to survive.

My memory is of so many faces and patients with conditions similar to western medicine and others quite distinct to India. My skills were needed for them at a point in time, and it was my privilege to have served this purpose. But time was moving on and with Dr. Craig's return from his medical leave, it was time for me to leave. But before closing this chapter, I wish to note two stories which were somewhat outside my usual medical responsibilities.

The Rameshwar, a man in his late forties, was a devout Hindu and a Marwari tradesman in Tibetan wool, who came from the State of Rajasthan. My dealings with him were solely in the area of health services. I treated his wife and children, his father (as noted above) and also himself. Our main contact had to do with the need for extra private beds, for the treatment of his and other well-to-do families in the town. Since the Mission had no money for such construction, the Rameshwar decided to pay for the construction himself at a cost of many thousands of rupees. We discussed the size, location and general design of the proposed 'private wing'. One day his building contractor arrived and work on the new building began.

Late one evening while visiting the wards, I heard a noise coming from the construction site. So, in the pitch dark, I walked over to check on the sounds. Suddenly a familiar voice rang out of the darkness, "Good evening Doctor Sahib". It was Rameshwar. I asked him if everything was alright and he said all was quiet for the present. I then asked why he was there. He answered in a hoarse whisper, that he was keeping a watch against thieves. He then explained that all builders in India are cheats; that the contractor never delivers all the agreed building supplies, taking his cut before handing them on to the site foreman; who in his turn also takes his cut before apportioning the supplies to his team of workers. Finally each worker arranges to steal hand-fulls of cement as he mixes the concrete. He does this by having an old family member, maybe his mother, sitting unobtrusively on the ground among the supplies, ostensibly to give the workers their lunch at break time. She has a sack hidden beneath her sari and between her crossed legs, into which the stolen cement is deftly dropped. At the end of the working day the workers carry off this sack and share the profit gained among themselves. The upshot of this multi-level thievery is that the buildings in India are usually substandard in quality and results in the periodic and inevitable collapse of buildings, dams and bridges at some later date. The Rameshwar was grimly determined that such thievery would not occur in his donated building, so he did night duty there throughout the construction and arranged for one of his sons to prevent the thievery by day. This was a measure of the character of the man. It resulted in the construction of a first-class new Private Wing, which bore his name.

Later as I was preparing to return to Scotland, I made lists of all my packed belongings, carefully stored in large packing cases and deposited in the loft of the Lal Kothi bungalow, to await my supposed return after a year's leave. I had to leave these belongings in Kalimpong, as the Mission assured me that I would still be needed there even after Dr. Craig had returned from sick leave. As things transpired Dr. Craig reminded Mission headquarters that they only paid for two medical missionaries at the Charteris Memorial Hospital, he and Dr. Duncan who had also returned from her leave. Thus, I was going to be supernumerary and would have to be assigned elsewhere. I had returned again to the uncertainty of my missionary assignment.

Knowing the uncertainties, I decided to seek the help of the Rameshwar and asked if he would be kind enough to arrange, if it proved necessary, to send my packing cases to me in the West when I was able to afford it. He agreed, and true to his word, ten years later sent the cases to me in Canada. How I got to Canada is another story. The next situation was entirely different.

Not too long before I was due to go home on furlough, I arrived at the hospital to be told that Rakam Singh had *bagiyoed* (in Nepali, this means he had taken off, disappeared without explanation). This was an immediate blow as I depended on him to take the X-rays and do the lab work and, in addition, we had become very good colleagues as I respected his work ethic and abilities. But it was apparent from the attitude of the nurses that there was something not quite right about the situation, but no one would talk.

Rakam was the eldest son and contributed considerably to the family upkeep of his widowed mother. All I knew was that a teen age brother was studying at the mission school in Kalimpong. I felt intuitively that money had something to do with his disappearance. Nobody in these hills was wealthy. All were trying to survive as best they could. I knew I had to act quickly. It not being an operating day, I left a message that I would be back in a few hours.

I high-tailed it up to the staff houses, where I found Rakam's younger brother and asked about Rakam. I soon told him to take me to his home in the hills as I expected that is where Rakam would go. As we walked, or rather half-ran, I had to keep a very firm hold on the boy's arm as several times he attempted to struggle free. I held very firm and hurried him to the bus station in the market place.

We arrived in a few minutes at a land-rover stand and soon found ourselves in the tightly packed back of a Land-Rover on the way, I hoped, to his village one or two hours away. Well into the afternoon it got scorching hot and I began to notice Rakam's brother getting fidgety, which I knew meant that he was thinking of jumping out and running for it at the slowest corners. As the land-rover nobly, if reluctantly ground its way up and up the mountain road, I felt it was nearing the time to get out and the driver presently shouted and came to a brief halt and motioned us to alight.

It was already late in the afternoon as we climbed down from the garry I released my hold on the boy and in a flash he ran off along a narrow path between the water filled maize fields. I took off after him as fast as my ex-rugby wing three-quarter legs could take me and, to his obvious surprise, I quickly caught up with him. We slowed to walking pace and I told him that he had better go to the right village and the right house. We must have stumbled along for about a mile, until we entered a little cluster of houses, in one of which I hoped to find my erstwhile colleague Rakam. I told the boy to be sure to go to the front steps of his mother's house. Presently he stopped at one house, pausing briefly, then ran off into a nearby grove of trees. I paused, then slowly mounted the four wooden stairs to the verandah of the little house. I stood for a long moment hoping someone would come out to see who it was. After maybe a minute of silence a shy little middle-aged Nepali lady appeared around the door and looked at me questioningly. She looked just like Rakam. I greeted her and then asked "Is Rakam at home?" In answer she nodded and beckoned me to enter. Like most of such hill village houses, there was a large living room with a kitchen area at one end and a curtain leading into one or two bedrooms. She invited me with a gesture to sit down on a mat then disappeared round the curtain. I did not see her again.

In a few moments Rakam slowly slid into the room, gaunt and unshaven, with a wild haunted look on his face. His eyes were blood-shot and he had obviously been crying. I rose to greet him and asked him "What's wrong lad? What in the world has happened to you? Tell me and I'll try and help you. Whatever it is we'll find something we can do to put it right. Please tell me what's wrong!" We both sat down and I waited for his response.

The story he told is not unusual, where people are poor and desperate. Ever since his father died and left his wife to run a little hill farm with only the help of Rakam and his two younger brothers, she found it virtually impossible to manage. Rakam, the eldest, had managed before his father's death to pass his school certificate and then get training as a radiography technician. It was his small salary which was largely supporting the family, but it just wasn't anywhere enough for them to get by. Rakam had decided that something additional had to be done. He was right but had chosen the wrong path.

About two months previously, he heard that if he put down a sum of money to a man he met, this would be his investment in a marijuana smuggling operation from Bhutan into India. Marijuana is grown extensively in Bhutan and smugglers enter India through little-known and remote mountain passes. The idea, he was told, was that the thousands of rupees gained from the operation would reap Rakam, as one of the investors, a substantial pay-back. Rakam's first mistake was to get involved in an illegal operation. His second and much more foolish mistake was to take a loan of money from the X-ray department at the hospital, with which he had been entrusted, intending to return it once he had got his share of the take. His third mistake was in trusting the smuggler's agent with his money.

The agent told him that the smugglers had run away with all the backers' money and there was nothing he could do about it. It was, of course a scam. The upshot was that Rakam had no money to replace in the X-ray money box, and was sure that he would be arrested as a thief. Terrified, he had run off into the hills and home. It was indeed a mess.

I told him that it was a pity he hadn't discussed his financial problems with someone at the hospital who surely would have advised him against getting mixed up in an illegal operation. He felt that he couldn't get advice from the missionaries as he and his family were not Christians, but Buddhists. He did admit that he had been very, foolish and expected he would be finished at the hospital and would likely go to gaol.

As we sat on the floor of the little house it was already dark and I wracked my brain for some kind of solution. Finally I said, "Rakam you must come back to Kalimpong immediately with me and admit to taking the X-ray money and hope that we can find some way for you to repay it. I am willing to speak on your behalf if you will promise to make good what you stole, out of your salary for as many months as it takes. There is no other way that you can possibly hope to avoid arrest. We must leave now! If we run we can catch the last garry (taxi) from Teesta Bridge! Now let's go!"

As he sat hesitating, I looked straight into his troubled face, reached out for his arm and repeated, "We must go!". He finally nodded, said he must say goodbye to his mother, which he did briefly behind the curtain where she had been listening and we ran out into the darkness.

To reach the Teesta Bridge we had to run straight down the steep mountain side, dodging trees, stumbling over rocks, sliding and slipping our descent in a headlong scramble. It must have taken us about twenty minutes or more to finally reach the road at Teesta Bridge and were relieved to find that the last garry was due in a few minutes. If we had missed it, it would have meant a very steep climb of several miles climbing over 2,000 feet.

The garry arrived and we bundled in and eventually arrived in Kalimpong. I took Rakam immediately to Dr. Duncan's bungalow, although it was by then about 9.30 pm. I explained the situation and that I would try to arrange for Rakam to repay what he had taken in monthly payments. Fortunately for Rakam, Janet agreed with my proposal and that nothing would be said to the police provided he repaid all that he had stolen. We agreed that the details would be drawn up in the morning and then I told Rakam to go to his house and get some sleep. After checking in on my patients, I walked slowly down to Guild Mission house and my bed. It had been a tiring day and I prayed that everything we had agreed would work out.

Rakam was as good as his word and in due course he repaid all he had taken. It was an object lesson to him as to how Christian colleagues were willing to support and trust each other. It was also a great surprise to him. Unfortunately later, when

Dr. Craig returned from his extended sick leave, and after I had left on furlough, he was shocked and angry that we had been so kind as to give Rakam a second chance and immediately took steps to terminate Rakam's position as Radiography and lab Technician!

I did not hear of his having been fired until years later, but I am happy to say that in the time after we had reinstated him he did two very significant things. First he wrote a play about a Buddhist boy who had done something wrong against Christians, but who had been forgiven by them, as Jesus forgives us if we admit our mistakes. The play was put on in the Christian College and was very well received. I did not see it myself. Some time after I had left, Rakam went to the local minister Pastor Peter Targain and said that he wanted to accept Jesus as his Saviour and Lord. Eventually he became a Christian. After he left the Charteris Memorial Hospital, Rakam got a better paying job in Gangtok, the capital of Sikkim and eventually set up a private X-ray and laboratory services department of his own. Many years later, I learned that he had been happily married with children and grandchildren and had been the senior elder in the local Christian Church.

Shortly before I was to return to Scotland, the Rani arrived in her car with a tall distinguished-looking Bhutanese gentleman, whom she introduced as one of her sons. He was the Foreign Minister for Bhutan, Jigme Dorji. Briefly he wished to discuss with me his invitation for me to go to Bhutan and be the first foreign medical doctor in that country. My job was to set up the first hospital in Bhutan, to include emergency, surgical, medical, obstetric and gynecology departments, with adjoining chronic care and infectious disease wards. I could remain a missionary of the Church of Scotland, but would not be allowed to engage in any proselytism. My belief and practice was to witness to the power of the love of Jesus by healing the sick and by so doing to draw people to Him. This offer was both a wonderful surprise and an unexpected challenge. I knew that I must respond immediately and decided to respond to Jigme in positive terms, provided the Mission agreed. I did not discuss with him the possibility of working directly for the government of Bhutan.

Sadly, Dr. Albert Craig the senior doctor in the Charteris Memorial Hospital who had returned from his sick leave became aware of this offer to me and immediately contacted Mission Headquarters in Edinburgh by telegram, indicating that I should not be given permission to accept the assignment. It was known that he himself wanted to undertake the work. Thus, what would have been a unique opportunity was taken from me. Dr. Craig himself apparently informed the Rani directly that I would not be allowed to accept the offer.

As it transpired, Dr. Craig did go to Bhutan but made no effort to develop the hospital as proposed by the Foreign Minister. After a brief tour, he returned to Kalimpong and soon suffered a recurrence of his illness. Some months later the Bhutanese government invited an American mission to send in the first full-time Christian missionary to carry out the work which I had been asked to undertake.

Years later, I heard that shortly after Dr. Craig returned to Scotland he accepted a charge as a minister of a church, he having some years earlier received a two years study leave to complete a degree in Divinity. Dr. Duncan was left on her own. Later the Indian government took over the hospital. Dr. Duncan resigned from the hospital and went to do village work in the hills. Shortly after she had a sudden heart attack and died. Thus ended the medical mission work of the Church of Scotland in Kalimpong and Bhutan.

Eventually, it came time for me to leave. One quiet day I went up to the hospital and said my goodbyes to Dr. Duncan, Matron Karthak and the nurses and a few others like Rakam Singh, and then Pratap and Jaitee down at Guild Mission house. I got into a taxi (garry) and the last I saw of Kalimpong was at a bend in the road going down the ghat to the Plains, as the saying goes, 'never to return'. I can still clearly remember my last look back up the hill at the town of Kalimpong, before the garry turned a bend and speeded down the twisting hair-pin bends towards the Plains and the town of Siliguri and its little airport where I boarded an ancient DC9 finding a place to sit among sacks of cargo.

N. India: Matron Ongmeet Karthak, presenting new nursing graduates, Charteris Memorial Hospital, Kalimpong, 1961.

N. India: Matron (4th from the L.) and Sister Simick (6th from the L.) with some of the nursing graduates, 1961.

N. India: Nursing graduates in Nepali dress, Charteris Memorial Hospital, 1961.

N. India: First ever Bhutanese nurse trainees, Charteris Memorial Hospital, 1960.

N. India: Bhutanese leper patient after her operation for Acute Appendicitis, 1959.

N. India: MacFarlane Memorial Church, Kalimpong, 1959.

N. India: MacFarlane Memorial church, Paster and Mrs. Peter Targain (Center), and the Elders, 1960.

N. India: Leprosarium, Kalimpong. The church is the rectangular building with red roof at the top. To the left of the church is the white tower which could be seen from Tibet, 1959.

N. India: Rani Dorji, Queen Mother of Bhutan, at the Leprosarium, 1960.

N. India: Bhutanese leper patient, weaving, 1960.

N. India: Nepali chronic leper patient with her Christmas dinner, 1960.

N. India: Nepali and Bhutanese leper patients. Patient with bear attack (2nd from R), 1960.

N. India: Tibetan, Khamba leper patients, 1960.

N. India: Paster Noptering Malamoo, with Kalimpong on the horizon in the background, 1961.

N. India: Setting out on a District village tour. Dr. Bill Robertson standing behind Nepali guide and pony used to carry supplies, 1961.

N. India: Bamboo bridge in the hills with Pastor Noptering Malamoo, 1961.

N. India: Village church group with babies for Baptism by Pastor Malamoo. A medical clinic followed the Baptisms, 1961.

N. India: Khamba tribesman with chopi, in the hills near Tibet, 1960.

N. India: High-caste Nepali Hindu lady, 1961.

N. India: Tibetan gentleman refugee, 1960.

N. India: Charteris Memorial Hospital surgical wing,
Operating room on the second floor, 1960.

N. India: Dalai Lama 1960.

N. India: Kanchenjunga in the evening, 1960.

N. India. Dr. Bill Robertson writing operation notes in the Charteris Operating Room, 1960.

Chapter 6

CHANGE OF DIRECTION

In the long days on my return voyage to Scotland I had time to reflect on my missionary life. My arrival in India was shortly after it regained its independence after one hundred and fifty years of British rule and before that to several hundred years of Mogul rule. The entire country was in a state of change. It was also after Mahatma Gandhi was assassinated and when Mr. Jawaharlal Nehru was Prime Minister. It was Mr. Nehru who pointed out that Christianity was nearly two thousand years old in India, so I was following in the well worn footsteps of others. It was an era of relative peace in Asia, just before China took over Tibet and briefly threatened the invasion of India. It was also a period of post Second World War internationalism which began the great humanitarian wave of help to the needy countries of the Third World. While missionaries were tolerated in India, I still had to report to the police when travelling over twenty miles. Nevertheless, for Christians, it was a period of inspired renewal of missionary zeal when the young World Council of Churches was establishing the vision of a Universal Church, and I in my own small way shared that vision and enthusiasm. I felt called to provide medical services to those who otherwise would not have such care. While my time in India was brief, the care I was able to provide to thousands of sick Indians was meaningful, and had a direct bearing on their lives. In later years I would be in health education and administration, somewhat removed from direct patient care.

The missionary world was changing rapidly. After my arrival in India, by about 1957, I recognized this change. In correspondence with my sponsoring parish, St. David's Memorial church in Kirkintilloch I made the following comments, "….the world in which the missionary finds himself in India today has changed out of all recognition compared with even fifty years ago. It is still changing fast. Some say missionaries as we knew them, will be part of history in a generation. Certainly the word 'missionary' is going out. Its successor is 'fellow-worker.'" In my time in India I witnessed the continuing shift as former missionary positions were taken over by educated Indians, which is what I supported. Yet, as I travelled back to Scotland, I knew the role of the missionary would still take time to dissolve, and there were other Third World countries needing their services in health and education.

The reasons why an individual chooses to become a missionary differ. For me, I had family members who worked in various parts of the British Empire including an aunt who had been a missionary in Africa for thirty-five years. My family on both sides had strong church connections and as a Christian I was aware of the great needs of the poor and sick of the Third World, and believed in the power of prayer and the need to send money and material things to help those less fortunate. In addition, I absorbed an international point of view through my schooling and the Boy Scouts. So, although I grew up in the small town of Kirkintilloch outside Glasgow, I had a world view through my various relatives and contacts. In addition, following the Second World War, like many others, I was impressed by a great sense of renewed World Brotherhood. As a young man who had missed the war, I felt the need to go and do something myself. But background and ideals are not, in the end, enough to sustain the missionary life. There has to be the certainty of a 'Call', a call 'to go forth'. That call came to me in my final year of medical school.

People who go as missionaries tend to feel like volunteers for a potentially dangerous assignment because there are many dangers from disease as well as violence in the places missionaries are sent to. In my time in India I contracted several illnesses which would leave me with a lifetime of health issues. In addition to disease and possible violence, one faces an array of different languages, climates, food and cultures. While some aspects of these may be anticipated, the realities are infinitely more intense and even spectacular than one could ever imagine.

Statistics show that missionary life can be difficult for families. Missionaries wives often had problems with the climate and food and were not happy with the quality of education available for their children. For some, the stress often resulted in illness and a return to their own country. As such, Frances's attitude towards the mission field was not entirely unusual, it was made more difficult by her unwillingness to discuss her feelings and the unexpectedness of her departure.

My medical experiences in India had two distinct patterns; in South India I worked with medical colleagues in a relatively modern hospital while in North India I was pretty much on my own providing surgical services in a poorly resourced facility. At the peak of my medical abilities, I was returning to Scotland with a great deal of uncertainty as to whether I would be returning to India or any other mission field. Change in the mission world meant that there were fewer medical positions now that countries were training their own health professionals. While mission work is not easy, it was an infinitely rewarding and rich experience. My original calling to the Mission Field had been for life and I continued to hope that this would happen. With all of its difficulties I enjoyed my missionary work, particularly my time in North India. I had changed a great deal in the years abroad and had very mixed feelings as I sailed towards my homeland.

I could write a detailed account of my trip back home, but it was just like other travel journeys and not specially memorable. One thing I remember, as I write, was the shock of seeing, for the first time in over six years, the sight of a large group of white people, in fact the deadly white unhealthy-looking faces of the Liverpool dock workers.

It is difficult to express my feelings as I made my way back to Scotland, via rail, and sea and rail, finally arriving several weeks later at the little mission furlough house in Colinton, a suburb of Edinburgh, where Frances greeted me at the gate, then took me into the little house to meet my daughters. That was the first time I had contact with Frances in nearly two years, although I had written regularly. As expected, Christine and Marjory, didn't know me. Barbara, now four, was shy at first. In time I got to know the children and we eventually established a routine. For the next year, I would be on Church of Scotland Deputation duty throughout Scotland, so, once settled, my first stop was to check in.

In Edinburgh, I reported to Rev. Ian Paterson, Director of the Overseas Mission Department of the Church of Scotland at 112 George Street to discuss my status vis-a-vis Kalimpong. Ian was a pleasant fellow who was obviously unhappy about how things had turned out for me first in South India then in North India.

In the South, the fact that my original position had been taken over by the Church of South India without informing him had hurt him and was the direct cause of the confusion into which I had been catapulted. It was only due to the initiative of Dr. Julius Savarirayan in inviting me to Ranipet, and my willingness to go and work in an American mission hospital, that enabled me to do the kind of medical missionary work for which I had been assigned. But that was temporary as I was supposed to be working for the Church of Scotland. Eventually Ian had opportunistically used Dr. Craig's illness and my willingness to move with my family to the other end of India, to resolve the foul-up of my posting and get me back into the Church of Scotland mission at a hospital somewhere in India.

I had mastered the various hurdles by becoming a medical missionary, completing the Theological training at St.Colm's College in Edinburgh and later at the United Theological Seminary in Bangalore, learning Tamil and working at the Scudder Memorial hospital. In addition, I had been silent on the run-a-round which Rev. Shaw, the Mission and the Church of South India hierarchy had given me, about which I would have been justified in resigning on the spot. But with no permanent position in South India I had little choice but accept the temporary assignment to Kalimpong.

In North India, my services were badly needed. The Church of North India wanted me to stay and petitioned Edinburgh and the Church of South India to make my appointment permanent. I prayed as the years passed everything would sort itself out for the long term. However, when Dr. Craig came back from four years of sick leave, I learned that he had contacted Mission Headquarters to state that I was supernumerary in Kalimpong. So, when I discussed my future in Kalimpong with Ian, he informed me that I could not be sent back there. Instead all he had to offer me was a six month temporary position in a leprosy colony in Nigeria. That would have meant moving my family to another country, and facing a new climate, culture and language with no permanent job offer. Basically, I could not ask this of Frances and the girls, they had been through enough. Yet, one other faint possibility existed.

The American Presbyterian Mission in South India having heard of the mix-up in my posting, offered me a permanent position in one of their hospitals. Since I was fluent in Tamil and Nepali, plus a working knowledge in Hindi and Tibetan, I was fully qualified and experienced to work in India as a medical missionary. For obvious reasons I seriously considered this offer, although it would mean cutting my ties with the St. David's Memorial Church in Kirkintilloch, who had been paying my salary. For better or worse, Frances categorically refused to return to India and would not have considered Nigeria. So sadly, I had to refuse the offer.

Thus, as I sat in Ian Paterson's office, I knew I was at a major cross-roads in my life and not a happy one. In addition to the six years of Medical studies I had spent seven more years becoming expert in my chosen profession as a medical missionary, which I was now contemplating throwing away. What of my original missionary calling over nine years before? It took much prayer and silent thought to come to terms with what was an unpalatable impasse. Frances remained silent.

The Church had said its piece. In the meantime we had a mission house in which to live while I completed the Deputation Work all over Scotland. The Deputation work involved speaking to many Church of Scotland congregations about the Church's medical mission work in India. While I enjoyed helping church members understand and appreciate what missionary work entailed and how much medical missions did to heal the sick and relieve the suffering in the Third World, I was struggling with the realization that I would not be returning to the work to which I had been called.

As the months passed I had to begin planning what I could do when the Mission stopped paying me my modest salary. I was well aware what I was facing. In the United Kingdom doctors must start at the bottom of the ladder in hospitals, as I had done back in 1954, and gradually work their way up. By 1962, although I had accumulated considerable experience in hospital medical work I knew that having gone to India I had 'deserted the ship' in the opinion of the United Kingdom doctors who existed in the tight and competitive National Health Service (NHS) world of that time. While my best hope of immediate work might be in some surgical unit, especially an orthopedic unit, I would have to start again at the bottom.

I first found a part-time job as a Demonstrator in Anatomy at Edinburgh University, but more permanent work was vital to sustain my family. So one cold January day, I walked down the street from the University and entered the Edinburgh Royal Infirmary looking for any possible job. On spec, I walked into the Orthopedic Department and asked the secretary if the Professor was in and if he would meet me. By God's grace he was in his office and agreed to see me.

Professor J.I.P.P.James was a famous surgeon and the world's expert on Scoliosis spinal surgery. He was also the famed and courageous surgeon who had been parachuted into the mountains of Yugoslavia during WWII to treat the partisans fighting the Nazis. After operating on the sick, at great risk, he was returned to Britain, only to repeat the dangerous process again and again. A remarkable man! If I had known all this about him as I entered his office, I might have been rather intimidated. But I was oblivious to his fame and simply said I was looking for work. He asked me what I had been doing. When I told him he seemed impressed and after a brief moment said that 'yes' he could offer me a position as a Senior House Surgeon at the Princess Margaret Rose Orthopedic Hospital in the suburbs of Edinburgh, beginning in October 1962. My Mission salary was going to cease at the beginning of April and when I told him this he very helpfully suggested that I should contact Professor MacWhirter, the famed

Radiotherapist, who might well be needing someone in April, until the orthopedic position was available. He added that he would phone MacWhirter himself, with whom he was well acquainted and put in a word for me. This was more than I could have hoped for and in minutes I had obtained confirmation of the orthopedic job in October and was on my way out to the Western General Hospital, by bus, where the Radiotherapy Unit was located. Briefly Professor MacWhirter saw me and offered me the Senior House Officer position in his unit, starting in April. It was almost too good to be true and certainly God was helping me in my dilemma. Now at least I was going to be able to provide for my family, if only at a rather basic level.

As I wended my way back by bus to the mission house in Colinton, I realized that my life and career were already undergoing major change. From being a key doctor in the Charteris Memorial Hospital in Kalimpong with major clinical responsibilities, I was soon going to drop back down to a lowly Senior House Officer position at almost the bottom of the clinical medicine ladder. All my efforts of the previous hard work in India would count for nothing. It was a very hard pill to swallow.

Having arranged my immediate future it was now beyond any doubt that my next action would have to be to resign from the Mission to which I had originally dedicated my life. I would learn at this point, and not for the first time, that large bureaucratic organizations like the Church of Scotland Overseas Mission Department, seldom express more than a slight sigh of disappointment when a dedicated worker resigns. In this case there was no official farewell from the mission. Probably because I had expressed the hope that I would be able to return to mission work later. Maybe the fact that they had failed in their part of the bargain and perhaps had begun to realize that the end of medical missionary era in India was imminent. This was confirmed many years later when I learned that all overseas Western missionaries of all kinds had been withdrawn from the churches and hospitals in India. If I had managed to remain in India my departure would have simply been delayed until I was in my fifties instead my thirties. Maybe in the last analysis I was lucky.

In addition, I also had to write to the Minister and Kirk Session of St. David's Memorial church in Kirkintilloch, officially resigning as their missionary. It was for me all very sad, but when circumstances change one has to realistically take a new direction, like it or not. As the old saying goes, "Needs must when the devil drives". To survive, one must adapt.

In the weeks before my mission appointment officially terminated and the job with Professor MacWhirter began, as I sat in the Anatomy Department teaching medical students the minutiae of the human body, my mind was also tackling the dual challenge of what was to be the new goal of my life and what to do about the immediate practical realities. I had to find a house for us to live in and a car. A doctor must be mobile and the jobs I had been promised required me to have my own transport. With little money I was facing another dilemma.

When a young man with a wife and three children needs money he has to go to a bank. Because I was a medical doctor the bank was interested in offering a loan, knowing that over the years I would most probably earn enough to pay the loan back with all the interest. On the strength of this Frances and I went looking for a small but adequate house in Edinburgh, near schools and not too far away from the hospitals in which I was going to work. The house market in Britain in those days was a rat race of individuals intent on selling their house to the highest bidder. There were no rules and rip-offs were common. Several such people gave us the run around, but finally I found someone who stated a reasonable price and the deal was done. We would be living in Corstorphine in the west of Edinburgh. Barbara being five began school immediately, while the twins followed two years later. Next was a car.

I needed a reliable car as I had to travel across Edinburgh to attend emergencies and a second-hand jalopy would not be permitted. The cheapest new car on the market in 1962 was a Mini Van at a cost of 300 pounds (about $600 Canadian). It doesn't sound like much but I could only just manage it. That little minivan was our family car for the next three years. So there we were, the five of us newly settled in Corstorphine and all entering the next stage of our lives.

My plan then, was to embark on orthopedic work and hoping to study for my Fellowship in Surgery (F.R.C.S), leading to a life as a British orthopedic surgeon. Frances seemed happy not to be in India, but as to what she thought about or hoped to do at that new stage of her life she gave no hint or comment, but continued with her reading and industrious knitting of needed clothes for the girls. The one addition to her daily round was that she had to do the shopping for groceries, the cooking and the cleaning, as she no longer had servants to carry out these chores.

Most days I was up early and off to the hospital before the children were hardly out of bed and did not return until supper time, if then, as I had to stay in the hospital two nights a week on call. After supper, when the girls went to bed I often told them stories about the adventures of Candy Mouse or sang little bedtime songs to them accompanied by my guitar. I can still remember the words I composed for these and can remember how they would lie peacefully listening and soon fell asleep. After this, I would go into the front room and study for the FRCS Primary Examinations until bedtime around eleven thirty. The bedtime ritual with the girls included the following.

> Barbara's Bedtime Song
>
> Sleepy, sleepy Barbara
> Now its time for bed
> Time to go to dreamland
> And be snug in bed.
>
> Sleepy, sleepy Barbara
> Time to say a prayer
> Time to thank Lord Jesus
> For His love and care.
>
> We give thanks Lord Jesus
> For all happiness
> We are little children
> And Thy name we bless.
> Sleepy, sleepy Barbara
> Jesus safe will keep
> Through the night till morning
> While she lies asleep.

(*Sung to a little tune which I "composed", but since I can't write music properly, you'd have to hear it*) ; *Next* is Christine and Marjory's Bedtime Song.

Christine and Marjory Are Going To Bed

Two little girls with very sleepy heads.
That dreamland chu'chu' train is calling
And soon you'll both asleep be falling.

Christine and Marjory are saying a prayer
"Thank you Lord Jesus for all your love and care.
Forgive us for the times we've not been good
And help us do just what we always should".

Christine and Marjory are fast asleep
O'er their little beds Jesus watch will keep.
He loves them both so tenderly
And they'll be safe the whole night through.

(Sung to another little tune I composed)

Most nights the girls were fast asleep before I finished singing all the verses.

My time was divided between five areas of activities; hospital work, family, gardening, being an Elder in St. John's Presbyterian Church, Corstorphine and studying for the Primary FRCS examinations. The days passed quickly, too quickly. Late nights studying or on night duty at the hospital meant little sleep, but I was accustomed to that in India. The sacrifices were accepted as they were all in the hope of becoming an orthopedic surgeon. Professor James encouragement was enhanced with the offer that when I passed the FRCS he would ensure that I would be appointed to one of the limited specialist positions approved on a national basis in the United Kingdom. He told me of this assured appointment in confidence and I was fully aware of the very special help which he had arranged for me. Again it seemed another miracle on the way to the recovery of my medical career.

Two memories remain with me from my time at Princes Margaret Royal hospital. One was at Christmas when I dressed up along with a Canadian doctor as a nursing sister and we had a great time entertaining the children in the chronic orthopedic wards at their Christmas Party. Another different occasion was during one of Professor JIIP James's intimidating grand ward rounds when a doctor from South Africa studying for his FRCS in Orthopedics took his turn, as we all had to, in describing each patients condition, with its differential diagnosis. The poor fellow was so terrified of Professor James' exacting style that he went slightly crazy and began to talk complete nonsense, a sign of immense stress. We had to lead him away gibbering to his room from which he needed three weeks to recover. He did recover and went on to pass his FRCS.

I struggled on through 1962, 1963 and 1964, attending some expensive cram courses to help me get up- to- date with the advances in biochemistry and physiology which had taken place since my undergraduate medical studies of 1952. The Primary FRCS exams in those days were reckoned to be some of the most difficult of all postgraduate exams in any subject and routinely only about 20% of examinees passed. Most candidates had to re-sit at least two times before passing and after that there was, of course, the clinical surgical Finals to surmount. I had every confidence that I would be able to pass the Finals, if only I could pass the Primary. In this I was one of thousands of aspiring surgeons. My problem was that I had to work full time, and I did not have the time to spend several years concentrating on these exams. However I did sit the Primary and almost passed and was sure that I would attain it on the second time around.

But one day as I was working away in the hospital enjoying the clinical orthopedic work in the wards, clinics and operating rooms, I got a call from Mr. Lawson Dick, Professor James' older professorial colleague, asking me to accompany him to his home for a chat. This was ominous. Calling me 'Bill' was another signal. In those days calling a member of junior staff by their first name was usually unheard of and, in addition, I had not had all that much contact with Lawson Dick.

I followed his Rolls-Royce in my little minivan to his home. He was a world-famous orthopedic surgeon who had pretty well written the most respected textbook on Orthopedics, during and after WWII. Arriving at his spacious mansion somewhere in the most upscale suburb of Edinburgh, Morningside, he ushered me into his living room and asked me what I would have to drink. This was at about 2pm and as I momentarily hesitated, he interjected, 'double Scotch' and proceeded to pour me and himself very large drinks. He motioned me to sit and when we were both comfortably seated he took a generous gulp at his whisky while urging me to drink up, which I did. By this time, my mind was madly searching for the most likely reason for this unusual meeting. I knew that it was about something either very good or very bad. Not being aware of anything bad, I at first felt a dawning hope that it was going to be about something good. However, Lawson

Dick, even after another large quaff of his drink, did not look a happy camper, so I quickly realized that he had bad tidings.

He began by asking me in a very friendly way about my family. "You are married aren't you Bill ?". "Yes" I replied. "And you have three little daughters, don't you, Bill ?". "Yes" I replied, wondering where this was leading. "It must be hard for you on your small salary and with your studies. It will be years before you can hope to have a worthwhile salary, as a surgeon". I nodded silently. Having got that off his chest, poor old Lawson Dick, obviously embarrassed for some reason, then launched into what I knew was the nub of our conversation. "Bill you will recall that Professor James promised you that when you passed your FRCS examinations, that he would see that you were given one of the seventy new orthopedic specialty positions in the United Kingdom, which had been approved by Prime Minister Harold Wilson". I said quietly "Yes". "Well", he continued, looking fixedly at the rich pile of the carpet, "That miserable socialist bastard Wilson has reneged on his promise and so, very unfortunately, there will be no assured specialists position for you even when you pass the FRCS". Adding almost in the same breath, "I'm most terribly sorry old chap".

Now I understood why he had pressed me to a double Scotch. I took a large gulp of my drink. Naturally I must have looked disappointed. After a silent pause he asked "What will you do Bill ?". I said that I would have to think about that.

In my mind I realized that this was the end of my dream of becoming a fully qualified surgeon in Britain.

Seeming to know my thoughts he continued, "Bill, if you were to continue your studies and get the FRCS you would be in your late-thirties at least. Since all the existing positions are currently spoken for, it would be a fruitless task and the quality of life for you and your family would not improve. Maybe it is time to think of alternatives?".

I nodded and he continued. "I have an old classmate, a very fine doctor, who is seriously thinking of retiring from his practice in the near future. He is looking for a likely partner and successor for his very fine general practice in a beautiful west-London suburb and I have today recommended that you would be the best candidate he could find. He has been in general practice for many years and is highly respected in his community and a man whom I am sure that you would get along with most excellently. Would you be interested in pursuing this opportunity ?"

I looked as happy as I could and thanked him profusely for arranging this fine opportunity for me and confirmed that I would indeed be interested. It was extremely kind of Lawson Dick to have spoken for me in such glowing terms and

I would follow up on his very kind initiative. Not very many others would have offered such substantial help to a young doctor in distress and I was certainly in distress.

He reached for a note on a side table, saying "This is my friend's address and telephone number in London, do call him as soon as possible". He rose and ushered me to the front door. We shook hands and he wished me good luck. I took my leave. As I drove home I decided to immediately contact Dr.Cameron in London, as the best possible strategy following a rather bad day.

Frances was non-reactive to the news but, I felt that if it worked out it would be good for the girls, as they would likely be able to go to a posh private school and end up as well educated English ladies with numerous opportunities.

That evening I called Dr. Cameron. He was most affable and invited me to visit he and his wife at their home as soon as possible. We arranged that I would travel down by train later in the week.

After arranging two days leave I caught the London train the next day, dressed in my best suit, my only one, and that evening found myself in Dr.Cameron's comfortable living room, sipping tea with he and his wife.

He said that he would arrange for me to meet the local Mayor and some of the key people in the town, at a local select pub, in the best tradition of English custom. While he was out of the room telephoning I noticed a framed photograph of a young man on their mantle-piece and asked Mrs. Cameron if that was her son. She became quite animated telling me in a somewhat nostalgic tone that he was a young doctor too and had gone to Canada. I noted her look as her husband returned and said that all was arranged. We just had time to go along to meet the mayor and several of his councilors.

The pub was a very well upholstered establishment and everybody to whom I was introduced eyed me with great but polite intensity. I was under scrutiny and Dr.Cameron would be taking note. After a pleasant chat we returned to his home. As we travelled I reviewed the situation. Certainly it would be a very fine opportunity to become established in General Medical Practice in such a fine community. It would put the family on a sound financial footing. I decided that if offered I would accept.

The next morning before I left, Dr.Cameron pretty well confirmed that he would be offering me the partnership in his practice. He said that he would be in touch within the week. This was indeed a very positive outcome and I was looking forward to his letter to confirm the position.

I became concerned when a week passed, and definitely worried when three weeks passed without a letter. Then I received a very polite but brief letter from Dr. Cameron, saying that he was sorry but something else had come up. He wished me good luck, in seeking a position. ". So that was that. My own assessment was that Mrs. Cameron had immediately phoned her son in Canada saying that this would be his last chance. If he wanted his father's practice he'd better get back home at once. The son likely did arrive and took the position. For me, it was a great disappointment.

Weeks and months passed. In addition to my surgical work, I had given up studying for my FRCS in orthopedics. I was still learning much about this clinical service. During this period, I also reorganized the typing pool arrangements which we all used and which were essential to the accurate follow-up of patients, especially in orthopedics. When the job at the Princess Margaret Orthopedic Hospital came to an end, Professor James got me a job looking after the convalescent orthopedic patients from the Princess Margaret, at the Edenhall hospital in Musselburgh. It was a quieter job but the system needed tightening up as the nursing staff had little idea what the various surgeons wanted for the convalescence of their post-op patients. Complications were common. I organized a detailed yet simple system so that everybody knew what they were to do and it worked very well.

Most of the convalescent patients were elderly, recovering from hip and femur fracture surgery and most were too disabled to get home. In the female wards, I remember all the patients were around seventy-nine and eighty years old. I would have the opportunity to revisit this ward five years later. Little had changed except the patients were five years older. The charge nurse stated that due to the excellent nursing care they had all received, they were still going strong. She invited me to do a little ward round and much to my surprise as I passed each bed almost all of them said "Good morning Dr. Robertson". Tough old survivors in their mid-eighties.

When that job finished I got the job as Registrar of the Central Paraplegic Unit for Scotland, which had been established in the grounds of Edenhall. It was a promotion and provided a little more money. It was also a very important position, as the number of paraplegic patients was increasing. Scotland had decided to concentrate their care in one central unit, to provide a uniformly high standard of care. It was a busy job. I enjoyed learning all about the very special medical and physiotherapeutic treatments required for these unfortunate patients. It also involved me doing some surgery again, which I liked. This was a two year appointment to terminate sometime in late 1965. I had some good colleagues including several younger doctors who did night on-call duty while they were studying for higher post-grad exams, like I had been doing while still working full-time.

Time passed and I still had no clear idea of what I was going to do with my career or what to do about it. It was a time of great confusion and stress.

At the week-ends I cleaned up the little garden around our home in Corstorphine, planted a hedge and made vegetable and flower beds. It was a good distraction and I loved a garden, however small.

Barbara was doing well at school and the twins had begun school. All three seemed to like school, which was good.

We went for a few runs in the minivan, one to Dunbar. It was for me a happy time going places with my family. During those years I remember my three daughters as healthy little girls, full of vim and vigor, laughing and giggling. For me those were the best years as their father. Frances always made sure they were neatly turned out in nice little coats with sweaters which she skillfully knitted and sewed. Knitting, sewing and reading were always her main activities and that's how I prefer to remember her.

By 1965, I still had no clear idea of my future. Having made such a strong commitment to being a missionary a decade before, it was a difficult time. My prayers seeking guidance were daily and fervent. Finally, there was a break.

One Sunday after attending the church at Corstorphine, in which I was an Elder, as I stood up to leave, a tall blond broad-shouldered young man approached me with outstretched hand, saying "Hullo Bill, long time no see".

At first I did not recognize him and he, realizing that, said, "You won't remember me, as I was two years behind you at Glen's and was one of the smaller boys that hero-worshipped you as a Prefect, Rugby star and School Athletic Champion." Wow, I thought, no one had said that before. Then I recalled him as a tough younger rugby forward who was an up and coming player, whom we Prefects used to say would be in the 1st fifteen after we left school and indeed he was. Anyway, he continued, "Where have you been? We thought you had died and gone to Hell". Soon we were getting each other up to date and as we parted he invited Frances and I to visit him and his wife and promised to contact me soon.

About a week later, one evening he phoned and invited Frances and I to dinner the following week. I accepted making some excuse for Frances as she refused to participate in such occasions.

So the following mid-week I arrived at my friend's house The three of us had a pleasant supper and talked about school days at Glen's and something of my years in India and his time in Scotland. He had found a government job in Edinburgh at St. Andrew's House, the central national administrative headquarters of all Scotland's government services, except foreign affairs and the armed forces. He had been working at the initial level of medical staff in the Health Department and was involved in the planning and implementation of new programs and enjoyed the challenges. After he had discovered something of my situation, including the obvious fact that I was still at the bottom of the medical ladder even after all my experience, he suggested with helpful pragmatism, that he was sure that I could get a position in hospital administration in Scotland and promised to let me know if he heard of any possible openings. What a kind, helpful thing for him to promise me.

A few days later he phoned to inform me that a Dr. Scoular, the Area Medical Superintendent for the North and South Ayrshire Hospital Boards was looking for a Deputy. I called Dr. Scoular and he invited me to meet him in his office in Ballochmyle Hospital two days later, which I did. We got on very well and after a morning discussing my experience he offered me the position of Deputy Area Medical Superintendent for Ayrshire, covering a population of over five hundred thousand. I accepted and we signed a contract. That evening I was able to report to Frances that we would be going to Ayr and that I would have a salary over twice what I had in Edenhall. Finally! However, while I was struggling with my career, life was also changing for my parents.

IN retrospect I realize that Dad was concerned about what his son was going to do with his life and family after he had had to retire from medical missionary work. I had confirmed to him sometime in 1963/64 that I would not be returning to the Mission Field and that I was searching for some way to recover the momentum of my damaged career.

He had some knowledge of my efforts to gain an FRCS and of my subsequent forced decision to alter that plan following the Prime Minister's cancellation of the additional Orthopedic specialist positions. He would also have known of my unfruitful visit to London and would have understood that I could not continue as the Resident Physician at the Central Paraplegic Unit at Edenhall Hospital, Musselburgh, as it was a dead end job. Then after my visit to Dr. Scoular in Ayrshire he saw that I had finally obtained a position which would allow me to look after my family in a more permanent sense.

At that point, some time in early 1965, well before our move to Ayr, Dad, with great kindness and foresight, as I have mentioned above, settled a part of his estate in equal parts on his two children, Marjory in Australia and myself in Scotland. This he did in order to provide me with enough funds to pay for the move, put a ten percent down-payment on a mortgage for a new house, buy some extra furniture and a new car, plus some funds to enable me to develop a garden on the property. With Dad's money we were able to start planning for a more secure life as the girls were getting older.

When I left for India in 1955, Dad had graying hair and was still quite robust as a man of sixty-six years, but when he and Mum came to visit us in Kalimpong in 1959 at the time of the twins birth, his hair had turned completely white and he looked frail and old at seventy. He never complained. He was not a man that invited personal comments about his health or life in general.

In 1965 my mother and father moved from Rosebery, Kirkintilloch, to live a few streets away from us in Corstorphine. One day when he and I were alone for a few minutes he did a most unprecedented thing. He opened his jacket and asked me to feel his upper abdomen (in the region of his stomach and liver). Normally Dad never touched me, so, surprised but without comment, I did so. I found that his whole upper abdomen under the skin was as if one was touching a mass of rough concrete. Medically I knew immediately that I was palpating a huge mass of cancerous tissue which must have been developing over a number of years. I said briefly, "That's not too good Dad. I recommend that you see a specialist as soon as possible". I knew a very fine surgeon in the city to whom I could speedily refer him. Dad agreed and he made no further comment. That, I knew was the way he wanted it.

The surgeon agreed to see Dad in a few days and then phoned me to confirm that Dad had a very advanced cancer, probably originating in his pancreas, but that it would not be possible to confirm the diagnosis until post-mortem. He estimated that Dad must have been suffering the cancer with stoical courage for some years and, at best, he had only a few weeks left.

That was, I recall in early March. Dad had begun to vomit continuously and rapidly lost weight. He did not want to be admitted to hospital, so I advised Mum what she should do to help him during the day and every evening for three weeks I went to see him, wash him and try and make him comfortable. By the end of the three weeks he was in a pitiful state, had lost much weight, such that I could lift him with one hand under him as I cleaned him and remade his bed.

Mum was quite unable to handle the situation further. At that point I arranged for Dad to be moved to a quiet Nursing Home nearby where he would have the bed-side nursing care which he needed. During one of my daily visits, just after my lunch-time, he sat up in bed and said that "Tomorrow I am going to sell King Street". King Street was the last Robertson and Co. Ltd. store and I had been hoping that Dad would have sold it long before, but he had kept it as something to do. I had understood his feeling but was glad he had at last made a decision.

Finishing this statement, he looked very tired and I said "Why don't you lie down for a bit Dad, while I go and talk to the nurse". He agreed and sank back onto his pillows. I went out of the room to discuss with the nurse my father's condition. We both knew that it was only a matter of time. She gave me a cup of tea and we talked briefly. I then returned to Dad's room and found that he had quietly passed away.

He had obviously known about the serious nature of his illness for years, but had said nothing. In moving to Edinburgh, he most nobly had done everything possible to help Mum to be near us so that we could help her when he died. He also ensured in his Will that mother would not be able to change its provisions after he died. This proved to be a very wise precaution as Mum did not know how to handle money and would have certainly spent it all long before she followed him to her rest, fourteen years later.

I arranged Dad's funeral in the family cemetery in Shettleston where his parents and grandparents had been buried. I thought that was all that would be needed, however I had forgotten about King Street.

The lawyers who looked after the legal matters of the business were Forsyth & Son in Glasgow. Mr. Forsyth senior, a friend of Dad's at law school, had long passed away. His son, John Forsyth, was now in charge. He got his secretary to phone and inform me that I would have to come and see to the sale of the business as my father had made no arrangements in that regard. I had no knowledge of the business, as Dad had kept things to himself, which had suited me for over twenty years. I knew that Dad had always disliked the Socialist tax policies which had been in place since the end of WWII. I was soon to understand that he had no wish to see what the tax people would do to his estate, or rather the business, the proceeds of which were suppose to be divided between himself, his sisters Lydia and Jessie and their descendants, if any.

It was all pretty complicated. I knew none of the details as I travelled to John Forsyth's office in Glasgow, one spring day, expecting to sign a number of documents which awaited me. When I arrived at the old office and entered its foyer

I was faced with a long high desk or rather a wall at least four feet high, behind which a prim little lady demanded who I was and what was my business. After I explained she became a little more pleasant and said," I will see if Mr. Forsyth will see you" and disappeared through a large black door.

Time passed and after at least ten minutes she returned and very firmly declared that Mr. Forsyth could not see me today. Now I already had to make special arrangements, to travel from Edinburgh and was in no mood to be refused in this most unprofessional way. I told the lady that I had to see Mr. Forsyth immediately, but she again repeated that that was not possible. This was just not good enough and at that point, to her shock and surprise, I vaulted over the barrier, brushed her aside and in a moment was in Forsyth's inner office.

The sight which presented itself was at once pitiful and deplorable. There, sitting behind his large desk sat Forsyth, hunched over in what was immediately obvious, as a drunken or drugged stupor. I told him very firmly that I had come to finalize the arrangements for W.B. Robertson Co. Ltd., and that I would not leave his office until such action had been attended to. He raised his bleary eyes and without comment pointed to the floor of his office which was filled with piles of documents covering most of the available space. There must have been at least twenty such piles, each I realized, representing a current client's uncompleted case.

I quickly found the Robertson pile and pointing at it I demanded what he was going to do. In reply he half raised both hands in a helpless gesture and then dropped his head into his hands and appeared to be weeping.

The situation was a potential disaster and could well put my mother's financial security at risk. I shouted to him that something had to be done and that I needed to know who else I could contact better able to take action on his behalf. He muttered a name and when I urged him he at length repeated it more audibly.

I quickly left the room and demanded from the secretary who this man was and how I could contact him. She by now realized that there was no need to pretend any longer and more cooperatively looked up a file and gave me the name and telephone number of the man. I immediately called him and after explaining my problem he admitted that his friend and fellow lawyer had unfortunately become a chronic alcoholic and was unable to conduct his business. He attempted to put me off, but soon realized that I was hell-bent on getting satisfaction and at last promised to attend to my business which he admitted was routine, and would send me the necessary documents at the earliest possible date. I then re-emphasized my determination to have this matter finalized to my satisfaction and for the security of my mother, and he promised to address it immediately.

There was nothing more I could do. I had to trust this stranger whom I had never seen and hope for the best. I then vaulted back over the barrier and was soon out of the offices of Forsyth & Co., and glad to be back in the fresh air of the street, leaving behind the little secretary in a state of shock.

As I have said before, sometimes in life the people to whom one is most indebted are of brief acquaintance and are never seen or heard of again. Such was the case with Forsyth's friend. True to his word he did finalize the will and estate of my father and forwarded all the necessary papers and money to my mother's account as I had requested.

However it was at that point that I understood my father's reluctance to sell the business to see what the tax authorities would do to him. Without going into the sad details I came face to face with the unhappy fact that for some reason my father had not been complying with the excessive taxation demands of the Socialist government. Because of this delinquency of payment, the government had fined the estate, cutting a huge slice out of it. It was still going to be enough to support mother and my two aunts at a modest level, but fell far short of what my father surely felt was just, he having served and sacrificed for his country for over fourteen years. No doubt if Dad had not been an honest man he could have found a way to avoid the unjust thievery of the Socialists' grasp. Many others have done so.

Thus and so my father was gone to his eternal rest. I was approaching thirty-six years of age and although I did not fully realize it at the time was about to enter the mainly non-clinical years of my career in which I would become more dependent on my earlier abilities in Public Health and Medical Jurisprudence, rather than on my more recently proven skills and experience in Clinical Medicine. In a way Dad would have better understood this new part of my career, as it was more in line with his own experience and abilities. But it wasn't to be. My father died just as his son could have begun to share his interests.

Soon after we settled in Ayr, and my father's death, we looked for a suitable house for my mother in Ayr, so that she could be nearer our family. We found a small bungalow near the beach where she would spend the remaining fourteen years of her life. I say quite happily for as I had come to know since I was a teenager, my mother was never and could never be entirely happy. There was a shadow over her, the reason being revealed to me years after her death.

The first thing I did with mother was to arrange that she had a trio of a good lawyer, accountant and banker in Ayr. My mother had spent all her married life under the tight financial control of my father. He gave her a weekly allowance and forced her to beg for any extras. I had noticed this in my childhood and thought my father was a rather mean, selfish individual. But, as an adult, I came to understand it was not the case.

Anyway, after surveying what resources mother had in Dad's Will, I suggested that she had sufficient funds to take a three month trip to Australia to see my sister Marjory and her family in Sydney, Australia. She would travel out by air and return by ship across the Pacific, all of which I knew Mum would just love. And so it was arranged and mother took the trip, met Marjory and her family and thoroughly enjoyed her voyage home on the luxurious liner the Southern Star. It was during this sea voyage she had at least one proposal of marriage. Mother was at seventy still a very attractive lady. She told me that she declined the offers as she felt it would not be right. Without doubt she was correct in that decision, for as I came to know, she was one of those very attractive women who was not interested in men, but nevertheless seemed to attract them irresistibly.

In moving to Ayr I had to give three months notice to the South-East Board of Hospitals, then started the process of looking for somewhere to live. At first I thought that it was going to be very difficult as we would only have the money from the sale of our little house in Corstorphine, most of which was, of course, wrapped up in a mortgage. As an ex-missionary I had virtually no money except my salary from the hospital which barely covered our living expenses, so I was sure it was going to be a difficult process.

It was at this point that my father's generous gift came to good use.

The house in Ayr was newly built and stood on the corner of Sunningdale Ave. It was a nice modern building with enough space to develop a garden, with a little driveway up to a small garage. As we took occupancy I remember hoping that it would mark a new and happier chapter in our lives, especially between Frances and me. Unfortunately that was not to be.

For most of 1966/67 I was away studying for my Diploma in Social Medicine at Edinburgh University. That proved to be very important, because without it I would never have been offered an Associate Professorship at Dalhousie Medical in Halifax, Nova Scotia, Canada or my succeeding jobs from the sixties to the eighties.

This course involved one year of academic study at the Usher Institute, Edinburgh University School of Medicine and a further year of health services research. This diploma was a completely new academic preparation for medical administrators working in the British National Health Service (NHS). In Edinburgh, it replaced the former one year Diploma in Public Health (DPH) which had been the requirement for medical doctors working in the field of Public Health. In its new two year format the Diploma in Social Medicine included, in addition to the academic requirements for the Diploma in Public Health, a range of courses (i.e. economics, accounting, hospital services, personnel and construction etc.) to prepare medical administrators for executive positions over hospital services. The research component and thesis consisted of a review of a key aspect of health service delivery. I successfully passed all course requirements.

My professional life was improving, which also ameliorated our standard of living. From 1965 to the end of 1968, while Dr. Scouler concentrated on the construction of two new hospitals, I, as the Deputy Area Medical Superintendent for North and South Ayrshire, had the daily responsibility of handling the administrative matters of twenty-two acute care hospitals plus chronic health facilities for a population of over half a million people. The duties included the staffing of resident medical doctors, nurses, physiotherapists, occupational therapists, and other ancillary health workers and their working facilities. The only group I did not have direct responsibility for were the medical specialists. Monthly, I had to report to two health Boards. I was enjoying my job and was able to make a number of much needed improvements in the Ayrshire Hospitals and their overall administration. But things were not very happy on the home front.

Nothing I did seemed to make Frances happy. There was also a nasty episode of finding dozens of unpaid bills one day in a kitchen drawer. The incident came to a head when I received a lawyer's letter indicating that if all these bills were not paid immediately I would have to go to Court which could have landed me in gaol. Maybe that is what she wanted, I never knew, she refused to talk about it. After that I had to take complete control of our finances. Gone were the days of mutual trust and the advanced approach to sharing which I had followed. All that had to be discarded for the security of our family and home.

Realizing Frances was so unhappy, I made arrangements for her to get her driver's license, and her own car. Then I suggested she might like to study at the

Ayrshire College of Education. She seemed interested but as far as I knew never did anything about it. I next suggested that she might like Scottish Country Dancing, which she joined and thoroughly enjoyed meeting new people. Finally I arranged through my friend Tom Limond, who was the Chief Administrator for the Ayrshire County Council, for Frances to be offered a part-time teaching job at a local school. She accepted the job. I never knew how much she was paid or what happened to the money. For a few years she was on a path which seemed to please her. At this point in time, we also faced the added responsibility of caring for one of her family members.

Mrs. Grace Anderson, or as we came to know her, Gran Grace, was Frances' paternal grandmother, having married an Anderson whose family had been farmers in Dumfriesshire, where Norse Vikings had settled around the 7th or 8th centuries. She herself was a MacGregor, whose father had been the famous Editor of the Glasgow Herald and had written several histories. His father or grandfather had been a famous sea captain of trans-Atlantic sailing ships. Gran Grace had thus an illustrious family background. Her own life had been sad.

Her husband died in the 1921 world influenza epidemic, leaving her a distraught widow with one child, Frances father, at the age of about forty. She returned to her job as an accountant of some kind in the Post Office, but she was not happy and developed arthritis which eventually forced her to resign.

Meantime one of her three sisters had emigrated to Calgary, Alberta, Canada. When this sister's husband died Gran Grace went to live with her in Montreal expecting her sister to look after her. In time Gran Grace had become almost a basket case and would do little if any work even around the house. Time passed. They were in Montreal where Frances was a child. When Frances's mother became sick after her father tragically died of Cancer of the Lung in his late thirties, they cared for Frances.

Some time later, Gran Grace and her sister returned to Scotland to take advantage of the United Kingdom's National Health Service. They settled in Glasgow, where we visited a couple of times. Unfortunately, the sister died of Cancer of the Breast and left Gran Grace alone. The remaining two sisters, who lived comfortably in Glasgow, refused to take her in which meant that she would have to go to a government home for the elderly, the thought of which terrified her. Upon hearing of this I felt that as the husband of her only grand-daughter, I should offer her refuge in our home which she accepted.

She was not an easy lady to live with. Although she declared that she could not walk and I had to carry her to and fro from her bed to an easy chair in the living room every day, as time passed I discovered that she was much more mobile, and in fact, got up to all kinds of mischief when we were out during the day. We did our best for her but without much thanks.

One evening when I was alone at home with Gran Grace, while sitting in the living room she suddenly rose from her chair with a shriek and collapsed down onto the carpet in a heap. When I went to her aid I noticed immediately that she had suffered a fracture of the femur and that the bony ends were almost piercing the skin. It was a tragedy which she herself had created, by years of total inactivity which had caused her to have advanced osteoporosis. Briefly without going into details I carried her back to her bed and arranged her leg with appropriate support and called the chief orthopedic surgeon who was well known to me. He kindly came in a few minutes and soon Gran Grace was on her way to Ayr County Hospital for treatment where she stayed for about six months after which she was transferred to a convalescent bed at Ballochmyle Hospital. She remained unhappy, and eventually informed us that she would not return to stay with us as she felt that she would not receive the care and attention she needed. I was able to arrange, with some difficulty, for her transfer to the Broomhill and Lanfine Home, Kirkintilloch, near one of her sisters. Several years later in her 88th year she passed away peacefully. This had been a stressful period for the family.

During these years, apart from my work and being an Elder in a local Ayr Presbyterian church, I found time to sing in the tenor section of the Ayr Choral Union, which was a well-known choir of about ninety singers, specializing in religious chorales and cantata. On a few occasions I enjoyed going fly-fishing with Tom Limond in some of Ayrshire's excellent trout streams and lochs. As a family, apart from going to church together, we spent a holiday at the Isle of Arran across the Firth of Clyde. I remember going round the island and visiting the rings of ancient standing stones. We also went swimming at Brodick beach, when I took an hour to climb Goat Fell the highest mountain on Arran. Every effort was made to create family outings.

I worked very hard in Ayrshire. The hospitals had many problems due to old buildings, shortage of junior staff and a rather poorly organized health services system. I worked hard to help sort out numerous administrative problems, as nothing succeeds like hard work. My working relationship with Guy Scoular was good and I could have stayed there, but I would not have had a promotion for years as my senior colleague had over fifteen years to his retirement. Finances remained an issue as I was still trying to catch up after my time in India. Accordingly, I looked for other positions during the period 1967/68, in Glasgow and Birmingham, but before I was pressed to make a decision on either of these positions in the summer of 1968, I received a letter from a Canadian doctor, Dr. Aden Irwin whom I had met in Edinburgh during my post-graduate studies. His letter indicated that he had recommended me for a position in the Department of Preventive Medicine at Dalhousie University in Halifax, Nova Scotia. I wrote back with a positive response of interest.

Shortly thereafter I received the offer of the position of Associate Professor of Public Health and Preventative Medicine in the Faculty of Medicine at the university. This was quite an offer and one which few immigrants get. The offer included a paid visit to Halifax to survey the job, local housing, schools and other amenities.

So, one Thursday I took two days leave and flew from Prestwick to Halifax, met the Professor and Head of the Department, his colleagues, had a tour of the university and the city, housing and saw the local schools and other facilities on the Friday and Saturday, then returned home.

Even after some discussion about this offer, I was not entirely sure what Frances thought about returning to her native land of Canada after nearly twenty years. What she was not divulging was the fact that she had met a man at Scottish country dancing and hoped he would marry her. His refusal to have anything to do with three children closed this avenue for her. This maneuvering delayed her arrival in Canada by six months. I would not know of this until years later. When she finally arrived with the girls she was even more unhappy.

I accepted the offer as it would give my family many opportunities which I did not have open to me in the United Kingdom. My family would be better off and, I hoped, would have more possibilities in North America. Thus, I arrived in Canada as a landed immigrant on January 2, 1969. When Frances and the girls arrived six months later, we found a nice house in Clayton Park, near schools and not far from Mount Saint Vincent University. Our Canadian lives had just began. Adventures in this new setting would constitute another book.

Thus, in a span of just over a decade, I had been in three parts of the world; India, a return to my own country, Scotland, and now Canada. While I planned to go to India, I did not anticipate a move to Canada. In those years in the fifties and sixties, I struggled to adapt to many challenges personally and as a medical doctor. Circumstances kept shifting my plans. My original 'calling' to be a missionary had to be tabled with regret, my efforts at becoming an orthopedic surgeon was stymied by political decision makers, and my willingness to accept the invitation to another country was always with the hope that this move would improve life for my family. The ups and downs of each change had been difficult and was exacerbated by my ongoing marital problems. There was always the great joy in seeing my children grow into fine young women. While, I was always willing to adapt and was fully aware that this new land would present both positives and negatives, I could not have envisioned the complexities which lay ahead.

NOTES & REFERENCES

Ch 1: A Frontline Emergency
1. The figure of 1.2 million Tibetans is the estimated death toll for the two decades immediately following the uprising in 1957. It represents approximately one-fifth of the region's population, and may not account for those who died in prison or during the destruction of over 6,000 monasteries, temples, and cultural buildings. Website: www.tibet.com . (Taken from the book of Gregg Braden (2004). The God code. Hay House Inc. London. P252)

Ch 2: Roots of Service
1. HRH Prince Michael of Albany (1998). The forgotten monarchy of Scotland. Element Books, Boston. p70.

2. Ibid p.12, and 63.

3. Reid, J. Robertson (1933). A short history of the clan Robertson. The Observer Press, Stirling. P17.

Manufactured By: RR Donnelley
Momence, IL USA
June , 2010